Making Time in Stanley Kubrick's
Barry Lyndon

Making Time in Stanley Kubrick's *Barry Lyndon*

Art, History, and Empire

Maria Pramaggiore

Bloomsbury Academic
An imprint of Bloomsbury Publishing Plc

B L O O M S B U R Y
NEW YORK · LONDON · NEW DELHI · SYDNEY

Bloomsbury Academic
An imprint of Bloomsbury Publishing Inc

1385 Broadway
New York
NY 10018
USA

50 Bedford Square
London
WC1B 3DP
UK

www.bloomsbury.com

BLOOMSBURY and the Diana logo are trademarks of Bloomsbury Publishing Inc.

First published 2015
Reprinted 2015

© Maria Pramaggiore, 2015

No responsibility for loss caused to any individual or organization acting on or
refraining from action as a result of the material in this publication
can be accepted by Bloomsbury or the author.

Library of Congress Cataloging-in-Publication Data
Pramaggiore, Maria, 1960-
Making time in Stanley Kubrick's Barry Lyndon : art, history and empire / Maria
Pramaggiore.
pages cm
Includes bibliographical references and index.
ISBN 978-1-4411-6775-0 (hardback : alk. paper) – ISBN 978-1-4411-9807-5 (pbk. : alk.
paper) 1. Barry Lyndon (Motion picture) 2. Ireland–In motion pictures. 3. Historical
films–History and criticism. 4. Thackeray, William Makepeace, 1811–1863. Barry Lyndon.
5. Thackeray, William Makepeace, 1811–1863–Film adaptations. I. Title.
PN1997.B268P84 2015
791.43'72–dc23
2014029597

ISBN: HB: 978-1-4411-6775-0
PB: 978-1-4411-9807-5
ePub: 978-1-4411-2554-5
ePDF: 978-1-4411-4741-7

Typeset by Newgen Knowledge Works (P) Ltd., Chennai, India
Printed and bound in the United States of America

Contents

Acknowledgments

I consider myself extremely fortunate to have so many friends and colleagues who patiently tolerated my obsession with all things *Barry Lyndon*, which, at times, has included incessant references to Kubrick's work and the oversharing of salacious details surrounding Ryan O'Neal's career.

First, I thank the archivists and librarians who helped me to see the materials related to Kubrick's film. Leith Adams made my 2006 visit to the Warner Brothers archive both enjoyable and productive. Between 2009 and 2013, I was able to visit the Stanley Kubrick Archive at the London College of Communication on numerous occasions. My colleagues there became friends and I thank them profusely for their kindness. Foremost among them are Richard Daniels and Wendy Russell, who inspired me with their love of the archive and gently corrected my errors and misconceptions. Monica Lilley and Joanna Norledge were also part of that wonderful support team. I thank Marihelen Stringham, Cindy Levine, Darby Orcutt, and the staff of the Interlibrary loan office at DH Hill library at North Carolina State University, who always supported my research with professionalism and good humor.

Some of the friends who have offered ideas, guidance, friendship, and sustenance of all kinds along the way include Gwenda Young, Jim Morrison, Diane Negra, Joe Gomez, Tom Gunning, Toby Miller, Steve Elworth, Ora Gelley, Inga Pollmann, Bob Kolker, Eibhear Walshe, Lance Pettit, Gregg Flaxman, Markos Hadjioannou, Deb Wyrick, Shilyh Warren, Jean Walton, Mary Capello, Bella Honess Roe, Bob Burgoyne, Dana Bartelt, and Amelie Hastie.

I offer special thanks to Tony Harrison, the world's best department head, for his support and friendship.

While I have drawn more than I will ever know from these friends and colleagues, all errors, oversights, and omissions remain my own.

I presented work related to this book at conferences and invited talks, and I gratefully acknowledge the individuals who gave me opportunities to share my work: Ruth Barton, who organized the Screening Irish America Conference at University College Dublin (2007), Jim Morrison, who organized the panel on the long take at the New Orleans SCMS Conference (2011), and Diane Negra, who gathered the panel on transnational Irishness at SCMS in Boston (2012). Gwenda Young invited me to present my work at the University College Cork Seminar (2009); Bella Honess Roe invited me to present work at the University of Surrey (2011); and Inga Pollmann asked me to speak at the Triangle Film Salon (2012). I thank those whom I met over the course of the project and who kindly included early versions of this material in their books: Tatjana Ljulic and Richard Daniels, and Constantin Parvulescu and Robert Rosenstone.

I gratefully acknowledge the Fulbright fellowship that brought me to Cork in 2007 for a semester that provided the impetus for the project. The College of Humanities and Social Sciences and the English Department at NC State University supported several trips to the Stanley Kubrick Archive in London.

I thank President Philip Nolan and my colleagues in Media Studies at the National University of Ireland Maynooth—Stephanie Rains, Gavan Titley, Jeneen Naji, Kylie Jarrett, Anne O'Brien, Denis Condon, and Anne Byrne—who graciously supported my leave in the fall of 2013 so that I could finish the manuscript and welcomed me to Maynooth with the utmost courtesy and collegiality.

Four anonymous readers were instrumental in helping me to shape my argument. Ryan Craver provided indispensable assistance in locating images.

Katie Gallof at Bloomsbury has been unflagging in her support, from start to finish. She gave me the gift of time, friendship, and autonomy: true luxuries for academic writers. Mary Al-Sayed ensured that the production process was painless.

Good friends who constantly reminded me that the world does not revolve around *Barry Lyndon* include Beth Hardin, Deb Wyrick, Ellen Garrett, Kim Loudermilk, Annie Merrill, Sharon Joffe, Dorianne Laux, Melissa Rossi, Francesca Talenti, Andrea Gomez, Susan Miller-Cochran, Val Coogan, Anne O'Malley, Elaine Orr, Shanti Ferguson, Amanda Roop, Jenn Gerteisen Marks, Leslie Blackwell, Celeste Pearson, Lakshmi Om, Padma Om, Ganesh Om, and Satya Om. I thank Chandra Om, who always inspires by example.

A film like *Barry Lyndon,* which deals with generational loss, cannot fail to bring that subject to consciousness. I regret that I wasn't able to discuss this film with my father, Alfred, who knew more about movies than I ever will. My mother, Jeanne Lacy Pramaggiore, prized her Irish roots and would have offered me a great deal to think about if I had had the opportunity to hear her thoughts. My sister Anne never fails to embrace my work and to support my sometimes unorthodox choices. My nephew Jack, with his preternatural wisdom and enormous heart, offers me hope for the future.

Tom Wallis, who has an astonishing ability to remain grounded no matter what I throw at him—from endless looping of the "Sarabande" to bringing home one more rescued dog to transatlantic relocation—stands at the center of every frame.

Introduction

Ireland mustn't be such a bad place so, if the Yanks want to come to Ireland to do their filming.

Johnnypateenmike, *The Cripple of Inishmaan*

In an interview aired on May 2, 2013 on National Public Radio's "Morning Edition" program, David Chase, the creator of the popular HBO television series *The Sopranos* (1999–2007), shared his list of "must-see" movies with host Steve Inskeep. During their discussion, Inskeep mentions that Chase has included several famous film directors on his list, but has not always recommended their best-known films. A case in point is Stanley Kubrick's *Barry Lyndon* (1975). Chase agrees with Inskeep, then expresses his admiration for the film's Victorian complexity and explains his particular fondness for its protagonist: "the guy is a rapscallion, and a rake, and a kind of a scumbag" (Chase and Inskeep). Remarking upon the importance of duels in *Barry Lyndon*, Chase continues: "what's great about it is that, with all this violence, there's this overlay of the most civilized conduct, you know, with the handkerchief inside the sleeve" (Chase and Inskeep).[1] At this point in the interview, Inskeep proposes a comparison: Kubrick's *Barry Lyndon* and Chase's *The Sopranos* both depict an "elaborate code of honor that is laid on top of a basically violent existence" (Chase and Inskeep). After confessing that he has never thought about his work in this way, Chase endorses Inskeep's comparison, admitting that what he loves most about the Soprano family milieu is that "there were rules; there was a mafia code that you

---

[1] This motif has been duly noted by film scholars Marvin D'Lugo, in "*Barry Lyndon*: Kubrick on the Rules of the Game" and James Naremore, in *On Kubrick*.

had to go by. But of course, the code is ridiculous: it's a code among sociopaths" (Chase and Inskeep).

Having spent several years thinking about Stanley Kubrick's *Barry Lyndon*, I listened to this exchange with great interest. The discussion brought into relief some of the political and aesthetic questions that initially drew me to the film. One central question that the film raises for me is: what does the world look like when an entire society, indeed a burgeoning global empire rather than a troubling, self-destructive gangster subculture, is governed by a "code among sociopaths"?

While many films, novels, and television programs made before and after *Barry Lyndon* envision this scenario as an apocalyptic breakdown of social order, Kubrick's unique contribution to the cinematic discourse on humanism— not only in *Barry Lyndon*, but also in *Lolita* (1962), *Dr. Strangelove or: How I Learned to Stop Worrying and Love the Bomb* (1964), and *Eyes Wide Shut* (1999)—may be his elaboration of a potentially shocking concept: that culture may, in some circumstances, be synonymous with sociopathic violence. In a well-known interview with Michel Ciment, Kubrick made a pointed observation on this subject: "Hitler loved good music and many top Nazis were cultured and sophisticated men, but it didn't do them, or anyone else, much good" (163). Here Stanley Kubrick echoes the thinking of Walter Benjamin, who wrote in his unfinished *Arcades Project*, "Barbarism lurks in the very concept of culture—as the concept of a fund of values which is considered independent not, indeed, of the production process in which these values originated, but of the one in which they survive" (467–8).

Kubrick's intellectually challenging and emotionally rich films, created within the historical context of modernist cultural aspirations and against the backdrop of the industrialized slaughter of two world wars, the Holocaust, and numerous genocides, suggest that history is nothing but trauma—James Joyce's nightmare— and that social life continues to be governed by violence and domination. That violence is not masked by, but rather enacted through, the codes, gestures, and trappings of civility. Scholars have questioned whether Kubrick's films should be described as nihilistic (Shaw 221). To me, the more salient question is how to account for the power of Kubrick's work, given his self-professed doubts about the capacity of aesthetic experiences—which, if not inherently complicit, can be recruited to serve political ends—to intervene in what Nietzsche called the human will to power.

Barry Lyndon, like so many of Kubrick's films, is concerned with violence and social hierarchy. Unlike most other films of Kubrick's, the film mounts a critique of domination primarily through the language of aesthetics, addressing a variety of issues that are central to visual, and not merely cinematic, representation. The film's subject matter and production history speak to the transnational character of twentieth-century cinema. The narrative is based upon a mid-Victorian serial by Calcutta-born William Makepeace Thackeray, who revised that work, turning it into a fictional memoir and publishing it in novel form in 1856. More than a century later, in the early 1970s, Stanley Kubrick, an expatriate American director living in the United Kingdom, began shooting the film on location in Ireland. The story documents the adventures and misadventures of Redmond Barry, an insouciant Irishman who barely survives his stint as a reluctant foot soldier in King George II's army during the Seven Years' War (1754–63), a global imperial conflict instigated by European territorial expansion in the Americas. After the war, Barry finds his fortune, while failing to secure his patrimony, by marrying into the British aristocracy.

This project initially grew out of my interest in the politics of visuality and, more specifically, in the way Irishness has been figured in global image culture. It has been nurtured by my love of British and Irish literature and history, as Thackeray sets his tale in the eighteenth century, engaging on a formal level with writers such as Swift, Fielding, and Edgeworth.

The study of screen Irishness in all of its forms is necessarily a transnational and transmedial project. It encompasses the history of the early twentieth century, when Canadian Sidney Olcott and Kerry-born American James Mark Sullivan returned to their "native" Ireland to establish Kalem films and The Film Company of Ireland, respectively. It also touches on the careers and work of numerous Hollywood writers, actors, and directors from the silent era to the present whose understandings of Irish identity have informed their films and performances. Irish cinema studies—a field pioneered by Luke Gibbons, Kevin Rockett, John Hill, Martin McLoone, Ruth Barton, Diane Negra, Lance Pettit, and Brian McIlroy—not only addresses the construction of Irish identities across international screen cultures, but also examines Irish filmmaking as a project informed by ideologies and practices of national and cultural identity.

While I was working on a book about the films of Neil Jordan, the Irish director whose career grew out of his fiction writing in the 1970s, I became intrigued by that decade for several reasons. First, it was a time in which Ireland figured prominently in the imaginations and on the television screens in the

United States, where I was growing up, because of the Troubles in Northern Ireland. Furthermore, as I learned while conducting research on Jordan, Irish film took off during that decade: a new wave of "indigenous" Irish cinema (McLoone 131) flourished in the works of Bob Quinn and Joe Comerford, whose Irish language films *Poitín* (1978) and *Traveller* (1981), along with Comerford's *Down the Corner* (1977) and Thaddeus O'Sullivan's *On a Paving Stone Mounted* (1978), are considered precursors to the independent cinema that emerged in the 1980s, 1990s, and 2000s in the work of Cathal Black, Pat Murphy, Gerry Stembridge, Orla Walsh, Paddy Breathneach, John Carney, and Lenny Abrahamson, among others. Irish cinema scholars have considered the often politically and aesthetically challenging films of the 1970s and early 1980s within the context of Third Cinema (McLoone 123) and avant garde traditions (Barton 87). Colin McArthur has made the case for the desirability of a "poor Celtic cinema": a local, low-budget filmmaking practice related to Italian neorealism and the *nouvelle vague* that would link disparate Celtic cultural zones across Europe (112).

Prior to the 1970s—and, some might argue, even since then—the dominant images of Ireland and of Irish identities were purveyed by filmmakers from the United States or the United Kingdom in what many scholars of Irish cinema consider an exercise in cinematic neocolonialism (Pettit 28–45), with filmmakers such as Robert Flaherty (*Man of Aran* 1934), John Ford (*The Quiet Man* 1954), and David Lean (*Ryan's Daughter* 1970) appropriating the Irish landscape both imaginatively and economically, and, in the bargain, reiterating colonialist tropes of Irish backwardness, lack of industry, and supernaturalism.

What specifically interested me about Ireland in the 1970s was the relationship between international productions and local culture, and the assumption that, during this decade, foreign productions thwarted the Irish film industry rather than helped it develop. My interest was informed by the "spatial turn" in the humanities (Warf and Arias 1) as well as the growing focus on material culture within film scholarship, which has spurred an interest in the archive as well as in the geographical and social spaces of film production and cinema industries.

My interest was piqued equally by the fraught dynamics of national and cultural identity in Ireland in the 1970s and by the political economy of location shooting. In 2007, I was fortunate to spend a semester teaching at University College Cork, and I began to develop a better sense of the lingering material impact of American film productions on the Irish cultural and physical landscape. I visited *The Quiet Man* museum in Cong in County Mayo[2] and listened to my friends' stories about *Divine Rapture*, a 1995 film production that shut down after 2 weeks of shooting in the picturesque coastal town of Ballycotton in Cork. The screenplay for *Divine Rapture*, written by an American and based on an article published in *The Los Angeles Times*, revolves around the character of Mary Fitzpatrick, an Irish housewife who returns to life after the parish priest splashes her with holy water while delivering her eulogy. She is promptly dubbed a saint.

The case of *Divine Rapture*—recounted in Pavel Barter's documentary, *Ballybrando* (2009)—bears further examination because it speaks to the disruptive effects of location filmmaking, with its ephemeral infusion of capital and its longer-term impact on landscape and community. Developed by producer Barry Navidi with backing from CineFin, a company with a history of financial improprieties, the film was to star Marlon Brando as the priest; he persuaded his friend Johnny Depp to join John Hurt and Debra Winger in the cast. After production began, the funding never materialized, however, resulting in a string of unpaid bills, bounced checks, and a limousine literally abandoned in the middle of the street. The locals dubbed the experience "Divine Rupture" (Sweeney). Brando had secured $1 million of his $4 million fee up front (Barter, "Brando") and made a hasty departure, which prompted a headline in the *Independent* citing the actor's best-known role: the production was pronounced the "Godfather of all let-downs" (Murdoch). A sign of the tension surrounding the production was the publication in British tabloids of unflattering pictures of the corpulent Brando in his hotel room wearing only his underwear.

In addition to underscoring Hollywood fraud and excess, *Divine Rapture* highlighted the waning influence of the Catholic Church in Ireland in the 1990s. When the Bishop of Cloyne, John McGee, banned the production from filming in the Catholic churches in his diocese (Murdoch) and spoke out against the film from the pulpit, his fulminations prompted another snappy headline: "Bishop Defies Godfather" (*The Scotsman*). *Divine Rapture* also offers insight into the surreal ambiance of the boom and bust Celtic Tiger economy, a disastrous example of the consequences of a small economy's dependence on external capital.

---

[2] *The Quiet Man*'s impact on the Irish landscape remains an ongoing saga in its own right, independent of the continuing scholarly interest in the film. Factions of preservationists in Ireland and in the United States have attempted to restore the ruined cottage featured in the film to its former glory. The two most prominent are the *White O'Morn Foundation* and *Save the Quiet Man Cottage*.

Remarkably, in 2012, Barry Navidi resurrected *Divine Rapture*—a rebirth not unlike that of its protagonist Mary Fitzpatrick—renamed it *Holy Mackerel,* and announced Geoffrey Rush as a possibility for the priest role (Jagernauth). In late 2013, ImDb Pro listed the film as in development and Barter's *Ballybrando* was re-aired on Irish television, featuring Navidi's sentimental return to Ballycotton to show footage from the original shoot to the residents.

My perspective on transnational productions such as *Divine Rapture* and *Barry Lyndon* is necessarily informed by my status as an American observer, and it is subject to the dynamic interplay between US and Irish cultural production. Perhaps, no one captures this tension better than another observer of Irish culture—British playwright and filmmaker Martin McDonagh—who gleefully satirizes stereotypes of Irishness in American cinema in his 1996 play, *The Cripple of Inishmaan.* The play is set on the Aran Islands during the making of Robert Flaherty's documentary film, *Man of Aran,* in 1934, where the locals openly mock the romanticized version of Irishness that Flaherty "documents," including a shark hunt in waters where sharks have not been seen for decades. Treated as a second-class citizen, the play's title character Billy Claven decamps to Hollywood to become a movie star. After a screen test for a role as a doomed Irish immigrant, the role he is clearly playing in "real life," Billy loses out to an American actor and returns home to die. Like Mary Fitzpatrick in *Divine Rapture,* he is given more than one death scene to play.

In this and in other plays and films by McDonagh, including the black comedy *Seven Psychopaths* (2012), the entanglement of Irish and American identities and ideologies becomes a source of radical satire that cannot be easily resolved through assertions of cultural or national authenticity. Still, these images are marked by relations of power, and, in particular, the persistent global dominance of American film and popular culture. Which returns me to the subject of *Barry Lyndon,* a film about British colonial power whose textual dynamics and production history, in part, reflect the power of the American and British film industries within which Stanley Kubrick worked.

*   *   *   *   *

What we have valued in film are our confrontations with time and time's passing.

D. N. Rodowick, *The Virtual Life of Film*

Having taught a course on postwar American cinema anchored by the figures of Robert Altman and Stanley Kubrick, I began to look more closely at their Irish productions of the 1970s. Altman's *Images* (1971) and Kubrick's *Barry Lyndon* (1975) are two very different, very beautiful, and very idiosyncratic films. My interest in gender and sexuality initially drew me to Altman's *Images*, whose protagonist is a woman writer experiencing a sexually charged psychotic break while she is sequestered at a country house to write a children's book. The setting is a bleak, eerie landscape that is nearly unrecognizable as the Wicklow mountains south of Dublin. Although shot in Ireland, *Images* unfolds in an explicitly otherworldly place, the mythical land in which the writer sets the action of her children's tales. Indeed, Altman's first draft of the script refers to a somewhat generic space: "Rugged coastal country [. . .] it could be Big Sur, the Vancouver area, or even Maine" (22). Altman succeeds in conveying this deterritorialization by shooting some truly uncanny landscapes in the film, including the waterfall at Powerscourt, a location that epitomizes the Romantic sublime. There is one tangible caveat to the film's spatial indeterminacy: there are automobiles in the film with steering wheels on the right side of the vehicles.

In the final analysis, I found myself drawn to *Barry Lyndon* because it is a film that, unlike Altman's, seems to be trying to say something about Irishness, although this aspect of the film has not received as much attention as it might have. Mark Crispin Miller's essays from the 1970s, "Kubrick's Anti-Reading of *The Luck of Barry Lyndon*" and "*Barry Lyndon* Reconsidered," remain the strongest commentary on the film's Irish associations.

I was also intrigued by the fact that, amidst the growing number of scholarly books on Kubrick, many written or reissued after his death in 1999, *Barry Lyndon* remained a less-studied film than the others. My work on this book began about 2 years before the British Film Institute selected the film to run in repertory at the Kubrick season (2009) and also prior to its reappraisal by American critics and filmmakers such as Richard Schickel (one of the first to review the film at its 1975 debut) and Roger Ebert. As my UK colleagues have pointed out, *Barry Lyndon's* obscurity was far more pronounced in the United States than in Britain or Europe. Yet, in 2014, on the eve of the fortieth anniversary of its release, the only book devoted to *Barry Lyndon* remains Philippe Pilard's Italian monograph.

It may be possible that I deferred my rendezvous with *Barry Lyndon* and toyed with *Images* for some of the same reasons that even diehard Kubrick fans have allowed the film to slumber in the annals of film history. At 3 hours and 4 minutes (plus intermission), *Barry Lyndon* might seem to be a daunting prospect, particularly in the post-YouTube era of instant audiovisual gratification. More important, with an average shot length (ASL) of about 13 seconds, the film's pace is slow: it is noticeably slower than its immediate contemporaries, films such as *Dog Day Afternoon* (5 seconds), *One Flew Over the Cuckoo's Nest* (5.5 seconds), *Jaws* (6.5 seconds), and *Chinatown* (just under 9 seconds). For the record, *Barry Lyndon* is not Kubrick's "slowest" film: *Lolita*'s ASL exceeds 17 seconds and *Eyes Wide Shut*'s ASL is 15 seconds (all figures courtesy of the Cinemetrics database). Also, it should go without saying that slowness in cinema should not be considered synonymous with a lack of compelling material; I discuss the film's relationship to the phenomenon of "slow cinema" in Chapter 1.

The first time I saw *Barry Lyndon*, I was a member of one target demographic for the film. Before tweeners existed, there were teenyboppers. We were fans of Ryan O'Neal, fresh from his successes as preppie heartthrob Oliver Barrett IV in *Love Story* (1970) and nerd hottie paleo-musicologist Howard Bannister in *What's Up Doc* (1972). We saw *Barry Lyndon* because of Ryan O'Neal. My only recollections of that experience are first, a sense of cognitive dissonance arising from seeing contemporary jet setter stars like O'Neal and Marisa Berenson dolled up in period costumes and, second, a confusion regarding just what the lead character's name actually was, a failing which I attribute to an American unfamiliarity with the rules of the British aristocracy. Despite my embrace of feminism, it was hard to understand why Redmond Barry, after his marriage, changed his name to Barry Lyndon. I believe that I was part of one anticipated demographic for the film because of Kubrick's own comments about casting the lead role; he grants his daughters Katharina, Vivian, and Anya a large say in the process. Although Robert Redford, Clint Eastwood, and O'Neal were all considered for the role because of their box office clout, Kubrick's daughters, and particularly Vivian, who would become friends with Tatum O'Neal during the shoot, preferred O'Neal.

My second, adult encounter with the film left me in a fugue state that lasted for several days. I didn't feel transported *back* in time to the eighteenth century, a claim that some of the film's contemporary reviews forwarded. How would I know whether or not I had experienced time as it was felt in the eighteenth century? Instead, my post-*Barry Lyndon* experience felt like I had relinquished all participation in time's forward march; I was marching to the tune of a different drummer. The experience may have "set off a trip wire," to quote Gregory Flaxman, paraphrasing Gilles Deleuze in *The Brain is the Screen*, resulting in a "synaptic frenzy through the faculties" (13). This Kantian "vibration" and Deleuzean sensation creates a situation where "something in the world forces us to think" (Deleuze quoted in Flaxman 13).

The film certainly made me think: rather than closing down possibility through its apparently overdetermined narrative of one character's rise and fall, *Barry Lyndon* "proliferate[s] disjunctions between the visible and the articulable, thereby catalyzing a kind of thought that diverges from strict determination" (Flaxman 26). In other words, Kubrick's film raises the specter of the failure of representation, which affords us the possibility of looking beyond its structures.

Deleuze's concern here is rethinking thought in Western philosophy; the ambitions of my project are not nearly as lofty. I became interested in the way *Barry Lyndon* produces temporality, and I began to think of the way emotions and critical judgments are intertwined in that process as the creation of *aesthetic time*. In contrast to Fredric Jameson's assertions in *Signatures of the Visible*, I am suggesting that the visual is not "essentially pornographic" having its end in "mindless, rapt fascination" (1), but can, under certain circumstances, afford viewers the possibility of both feeling and thinking, a chance to, perhaps, correct the Western tendency to subordinate emotions—which, like our aesthetic capacities, have come to be denigrated as superfluous, feminized, and inessential—to instrumental reason (Ahmed 3). I have specifically chosen the term aesthetic time to signal my desire to reclaim aesthetics not as an idealist escape but as a thoughtful and engaged social practice. The opportunity to feel and to think occurs, I am arguing, when the time, and the timing, are right.

So a project undertaken because of my assumption that *Barry Lyndon* might be productively examined within the context of Irishness expanded to encompass what has become, for me, its most compelling aspect: the film's enactment of and discourse regarding temporality. Many scholars and cultural critics, including Fredric Jameson, Jean Baudrillard, and Gilles Deleuze, have focused on the spatial aspects of *Barry Lyndon*, emphasizing and, in some cases, rejecting its visual beauty, its "achieved perfection" (Jameson "Historicism" 92), without, I think, fully grappling with the way the film's rendering of space is dependent upon time, and thus becomes space-time. This concept from physics, which acknowledges the interconnectedness of the spatial and the temporal, corresponds to Mikhail Bakhtin's narratological notion of the chronotope and is a relationship that Maya Deren theorizes in her discussion of cinematography. Writing about the demise of film, not as a time-based form, but as a photochemical medium, David Rodowick suggests that what "most powerfully affects us in film is an ethics of time" (73). Drawing upon all of these ideas, this book became, in part, an examination of the ethics of time in *Barry Lyndon*.

My exploration begins from the premise that privileging the film's relationship to time provides access to its discourse on narrative, history, and aesthetic experience from new vantage points. In *Barry Lyndon*, Kubrick orchestrates various modes of temporality and, in particular, the time signatures of sequence, cycle, and stasis (or interval). In heightening the importance of temporal relations, I argue, the film offers viewers a way of thinking through the emotions provoked by aesthetic experience, rather than treating thought as an intellectual act divorced from affect. While this line of argument comes close to invoking Kantian notions of the sublime—a concept that has been thoroughly reexamined in postmodern theory—my ultimate aim is not to identify a single appropriate philosophical rubric for understanding Kubrick's film. Instead, I want to make the claim that aesthetic time, which is not the exclusive province of cinema and, indeed, is an experience I discuss in relation to Thackeray's writing in Chapter 2, is critically dependent upon the way literature and film evoke temporality.

In arguing for the film's emotional power, I diverge in emphasis from Kubrick scholar Robert Kolker who emphasizes the way the film withholds satisfaction and thwarts expectations. He writes, "the viewer is not permitted complete satisfaction of aesthetic or emotional desire" (167). I join the ranks of commentators who speak to *Barry Lyndon*'s emotional reach, including James Naremore, who directs his reader's attention to Kubrick as an "artist who was dealing in emotions" (24). I am interested in the way emotion and thought find a place in the rhythms of this film.

Another keen observer of Kubrick's work who emphasizes the emotional aspects of *Barry Lyndon* is director Martin Scorsese. In a 2001 interview with Charlie Rose, Scorsese states, "I'm not sure if I can say that I have a favorite Kubrick picture, but somehow I keep coming back to *Barry Lyndon*. I think that's because it's such a profoundly emotional experience" (Charlie Rose). Scorsese's response circles back to where I began, with David Chase and *The Sopranos*. In the hypermasculine screen worlds of Chase and Scorsese—and

Kubrick—violence and emotions are rarely divorced from but, rather, are embedded within, gestures of civility.

*   *   *   *   *

A radio is not a louder voice, an airplane is not a faster car, and the motion picture (an invention of the same period of history) should not be thought of as a faster painting or a more real play.

Maya Deren, "Cinematography, the Creative Use of Reality"

Stanley Kubrick's *Barry Lyndon* asks what are, for me, searching and profound questions about the politics of organized brutality and about cinema, a medium that presents a world to us not merely through the indexicality of the photographic image and the fidelity of the sonic register, but also through a space-time of its own making. Theories on film time, from the work of Maya Deren and Andre Bazin to that of Philip Rosen, Mary Ann Doane, and Gilles Deleuze, as well as the ideas of philosophers and historians, guide my thinking about the way that *Barry Lyndon* creates and comments on multiple temporalities, including serial time, cyclical time, stasis, and rhythm.

In Kubrick's film, each of these temporal modes corresponds to a set of formal and ideological problems. A close examination of serial form, for example, demands that we revisit succession both as it relates to structures of temporal order and sequence and also as it relates to filial inheritance or patrimony. Whereas serial form possesses an intrinsic relationship to film representation, which is based on sequences of images, cyclical time is not uniquely cinematic. In fact, temporal cycles are associated with pre-capitalist agricultural societies and, in the work of Fredric Jameson, with the empty repetition of postmodern pastiche. In my analysis of *Barry Lyndon*, historical cycles inform both the production history and narrative design of the film and also reflect certain cultural assumptions about Irish history and identity. The treatment of stasis—or, more properly, the interval—in *Barry Lyndon* revisits the concept of simultaneity, an important trope within modern art that is associated with cinema's cross cutting and with the spatial juxtaposition of collage. Kubrick's cultivation of stillness in *Barry Lyndon* inevitably directs the viewer's attention to the formal relationships between and among paintings, photographs, and moving images, yet it also speaks to the political underpinnings of the periodization (or sequencing) of art history.

In Chapter 1, I look at *Barry Lyndon* in the context of Kubrick's enduring interest in temporality, examining issues of time in film and in film studies. Chapters 2 and 3 focus on the interconnected questions of adaptation and succession. Here I am not primarily concerned with Kubrick's appropriation of a literary text, a process thoroughly addressed in the voluminous scholarly literature on cinematic adaptation and on Kubrick as well. I am more interested in the way that William Makepeace Thackeray's and Stanley Kubrick's versions of *Barry Lyndon* share a fascination with the politics of narrating history and express this fascination through techniques that foreground expectations surrounding sequential time as well as the conventional relation between words and images. D. N. Rodowick speaks to the importance of sequence for cinema when he writes, "the quality of succession is at the heart of the mechanical nature of cinema. It catches us up in a peculiar temporality, a passing present of uniform instants over which we have little control" (65). It is equally clear to me that Kubrick's interest also lies in the human and organic aspects of succession, which adds to the emotional valence of his work.

Chapter 4 turns to the temporality of repetition and cycle, the voyage and the return, or the odyssey and the homecoming. Here *Barry Lyndon*'s Irishness—in terms of its national, transnational, and colonial/postcolonial frames of reference—becomes especially relevant. Chapter 5 considers what is often called the visual surface of the film by exploring the film's use of paintings. Examining the temporality of rhythm and the interval (the rest) enables an investigation into the dialectical relationship between portrait and landscape painting and between painting and film. *Barry Lyndon* makes evident the way that visual and sonic rhythms can undermine the strict differentiation between stillness and movement, the very basis for cinematic representation. Chapter 6 takes up the matter of *Barry Lyndon*'s timing, and potential untimeliness, as a film of the 1970s.

Barry Lyndon remains a somewhat less-studied work of Kubrick's, and yet there is no dearth of commentary on the film or on the director's work. I am grateful to have had so many voices to inspire my thinking along the way. This book is not an attempt to provide a definitive look at Kubrick, or even at *Barry Lyndon*, a film worthy of many essay collections and monographs. Instead, what occupies and preoccupies these pages is a fascination with the film's invitation to engage with multiple temporalities and its creation of aesthetic time—a time in which to both think and feel something about the idea of succession, the limitations of cause and effect logic, and the relation of narrative to history. This is the case not only because this film merits an in-depth analysis on the subject of time, but also because *Barry Lyndon* has something important to say about image making, culture, and power, a nexus as relevant in 2015, when we find ourselves fully ensconced within the digital era, as it ever has been, and about which cinema studies has, and ought to continue to have, a good deal to say.

1

Barry Lyndon and Aesthetic Time

Eternity itself rests in unity, and this image we call time.

Plato, *Timaeus*

A new relationship to time was the most significant change, and perhaps the defining development, of the French Revolution.

Lynn Hunt, *Measuring Time, Making History*

When it emphasizes the time in which things take place, their duration, cinema almost allows us to perceive time.

Jacques Aumont, *The Image*

Upon its US premiere in December of 1975, critics and audiences alike greeted *Barry Lyndon* with somewhat less fanfare than director Stanley Kubrick had hoped for. Although the film eventually met with modest success in Britain and in Europe, it was, according to Kubrick himself, speaking about his films in 1987, "the only one that did poorly from the studio's point of view" (Cahill). Adapted from William Makepeace Thackeray's mid-Victorian novel, *The Memoirs of Barry Lyndon, Esq.* (1856), the film pairs Ryan O'Neal, a box office darling at the time, and supermodel Marisa Berenson in a fictional tale of an Irish adventurer abroad in Europe in the eighteenth century. At the midpoint of the decade, when Kubrick's film was released, moviegoers seemed more enamored of films that stridently announced their allegiance to the 1970s, including *Dog Day Afternoon, One Flew Over the Cuckoo's Nest, Jaws*, and *Nashville*, four titles that were, along with *Barry Lyndon*, contenders for the best picture Oscar for 1975. Whereas in the previous year, cineastes had been willing to entertain the nostalgic and cynical charm of Roman Polanski's *Chinatown* (1974), in this newly post-Watergate, but not yet post-Vietnam, era, they seemed unable to make sense of Kubrick's mannerist morality play, despite its scathing critique of the global military upheaval known as the Seven Years' War (1754–63). That pan-European conflagration over empire and dominion prefigured the world wars of the twentieth century. Kubrick's American audience members—who, if they knew about the war, had learned about it in school, parochially, as the "French and Indian war"—were, apparently, unable or unwilling to make connections between that conflict and the quagmire in Viet Nam.

One media source clearly relished the numerous opportunities that *Barry Lyndon* afforded for critique. Whereas Pauline Kael groused about the "relentless procession of impeccable, museum-piece compositions" (49), the self-styled low-brow magazine named *Mad* consecrated Kubrick's epic as a quintessential film of the 1970s in one of Stan Hart and Mort Drucker's brilliant and anarchic parodies, a spoof entitled *Borey Lyndon*. As Figure 1.1 makes evident, the movie mavens of *Mad* indicted the film for its dearth of dialogue and its barely moving images. In their view, *Barry Lyndon* did not qualify as a film at all.

Figure 1.1 MAD spoof questions the status of "Borey Lyndon" as a moving picture. From MAD #185 copyright E.C. Publications, Inc.

Nominated for two BAFTAs and seven Academy Awards, the film won four Oscars for art direction, cinematography, costume design and music, becoming Kubrick's most decorated film. Amidst the field of iconoclastic nominees that year, *Barry Lyndon* lost the Best Picture Oscar to Milos Forman's *One Flew Over the Cuckoo's Nest*, which garnered a total of nine nominations and won five awards. This evidence suggests that the industry recognized and respected the sumptuous spectacle that Kubrick had orchestrated. Oddly enough, however, a critical consensus centered on this highly stylized film's claim to documentary realism. Prevalent in press accounts was mention of Kubrick and cinematographer John Alcott's technological acrobatics, which involved retrofitting a camera with a 0.7f Zeiss lens originally created for NASA; the lens was used to film some scenes using only candlelight. This rarefied technological achievement, along with Kubrick's attention to the details of setting and costumes, was understood by some as serving the goal of "re-creating" the textures and temporalities of a century that no living person had witnessed. *TIME* magazine critics Martha Duffy and Richard Schickel were not alone when they described the film as a "documentary of eighteenth century manners and morals" (163).

André Bazin, whose observations regarding the relationship between photographic images and reality remain salient well into the digital age, famously made a distinction between directors who put their faith in reality versus those who put their faith in the image ("Evolution" 24). The visual regime of *Barry Lyndon* makes it abundantly clear that Stanley Kubrick put his faith in the reality *of* the image. At the same time, his modernist skepticism whittled away at Bazin's binary construct from both sides. The film's most apparent conceit is that social relations and aesthetics are mutually determinative, an idea expressed in part through the film's emphasis on the relationship between eighteenth-century British painting and colonial empire.

For many readers, the name Stanley Kubrick conjures up visions of imagined American futures rather than the somewhat inaccessible past of eighteenth-century Ireland, England, and Europe. His best-known films, including *Dr. Strangelove or: How I Learned to Stop Worrying and Love the Bomb* (1964), *2001: A Space Odyssey* (1968), and *A Clockwork Orange* (1971), have shaped more than one generation's ideas about human progress in the twenty-first century, as anticipated from a vantage point at the middle of the twentieth. No matter how outlandish the technological innovations, linguistic inventions, and fashion sense of Kubrick's near-future dystopias, his mordant certainty that folly underlies the human will to power remains their animating principle.

In Kubrick's universe, the past and the future are never very far apart: the unforeseen but inevitable consequences of human action unfold through time as they suddenly, or eventually, attain the status of historical events. Witnessing the mingling of past and future in films such as *Dr. Strangelove* and *A Clockwork Orange* may enable some viewers to experience Heidegger's *ekstase* (ecstasy)— the feeling of standing outside oneself in time. The uncanny precariousness of that state precludes any sense of comfort with the here and now, however. In fact, the unease associated with the multiple modes of temporality at work in Kubrick's films gives us cause to question the organization of past, present, and future as successive moments in time.

Despite the strong association between Kubrick and speculative fiction that his iconic works have established, the majority of his films draw upon the quotidian, everyday, milieus of late twentieth-century America. The narratives of *Killer's Kiss* (1955), *The Killing* (1956), *Lolita* (1962), *The Shining* (1980), *Full Metal Jacket* (1987), and *Eyes Wide Shut* (1999) play out in a present-tense world of America's urban streets, tourist highways, racetracks, military bases, and moldering grand hotels. Kubrick's final film, adapted from Arthur Schnitzler's *Traumnovelle*, relocates a 1926 story from Vienna to New York's upper west side in the 1990s, exploring what at the time was called the yuppie lifestyle. The director's views on the possibility of progress in the span of a single century can be inferred from the fact that the narrative was not revised to mark the temporal shift between the 1920s and the 1990s. Kubrick reportedly felt that relationships between men and women had changed little during that period (Raphael 26–7).

Whether or not Kubrick's films are firmly situated in the twentieth century, they all question the assumption that humankind as a species has made progress over time. This occurs most strikingly and directly, perhaps, through an engagement with technologies that augur the end of chronological time in *Dr. Strangelove* and *2001*. Stanley Kubrick's interest in science, both empirical and speculative, is well known. In keeping with the physicists' concept of T-symmetry—which claims that, at the microscopic level, the laws of physics are invariant under the condition of time reversal—Kubrick's work often, and sometimes scandalously, implies that the direction of "time's arrow" might be merely academic and that the difference between moving backward and forward is not always so easy to ascertain.

As texts that trouble human time, Kubrick's films participate in a rethinking of temporality that D. N. Rodowick associates not only with philosopher Gilles

Deleuze's time-image, but also with a larger postwar project spanning biology and physics. Rodowick writes, "the relation between time and thought is imagined differently in the postwar period, as represented in the signs produced by the time-image no less than by changes in the image of thought in biological sciences and in the image of time introduced by probability physics" (13).

Kubrick's *Barry Lyndon* makes time by engaging with ideas about the passage of time. From even before its initial release, the film was subjected to a discourse concerned with problems of time: its production period was seen as excessive, its running time prodigious, and its generic pedigree as a costume drama outdated. Not surprisingly, perhaps, the film has been marked by this emphasis, although detailed analyses of the film tend to focus on its spatial attributes and its formal beauty.

In some ways, the film has been cast as a victim of its time. *Barry Lyndon* has been seen as disadvantaged by the decade of its release—the 1970s—and also by its running time of 184 minutes. Not a bawdy picaresque in the vein of *Tom Jones* (Richardson 1963), a film to which it is often compared, *Barry Lyndon* is a stately drama released at the midpoint of a decade whose cinema has become celebrated primarily for gritty realism, rapid editing, and showy camera techniques. In point of fact, a number of films of remarkable length were made during the 1970s, including *Ryan's Daughter* (Lean 1970) at 195 minutes; *The Godfather* (Coppola 1972) and *The Godfather*, Part II (Coppola 1974) at 175 and 200 minutes, respectively; *Scenes From a Marriage* (Bergman 1973) at 167 minutes; *Nashville* (Altman 1975) at 159 min; *1900* (Bertolucci 1976) at 345 minutes; and *Berlin Alexanderplatz* (Fassbinder 1980) at 931 minutes.

A number of these directors have been retroactively designated the progenitors of "slow cinema," a development within the international cinema of the 1990s and 2000s that Jonathan Romney associates with the work of Béla Tarr, Aleksandr Sokurov, Hou Hsiao-hsien, Pedro Costa, Apichatpong Weerasethakul, and Albert Serra ("Are you sitting"). In his 2003 address to the 46th San Francisco International Film Festival, Michel Ciment constructs a historical trajectory for this "cinema of slowness, of contemplation," and specifically mentions *Barry Lyndon* as part of a group of "antidote films" that rejected the rapid pace of Hollywood films made in the 1960s ("The State"). Ciment asserts Kubrick's *bona fides* as both a technologist and a contemplative artist, as if the two temperaments were incompatible, and as if an interest in technology presupposes a desire for speed: "Kubrick, himself a master of technology, has produced antidote films such as *2001: A Space Odyssey*, *Barry Lyndon*, and *Eyes Wide Shut*, with their provocative slowness" ("The State"). Slow films exhibit an "intrepid and rigorous formal invention" ("Are you sitting") in Jonathan Romney's view and "downplay event in favor of mood, evocativeness and an intensified sense of temporality" ("In Search" 43). In these films, in contrast to a contemporary American cinema that has "lost interest in awe and mystery," Romney finds, "the spiritual is at least a potential force" ("In Search" 43). These claims do not merely apply to contemporary cinema; they also appropriately describe *Barry Lyndon.*

Despite Ciment's remarks about *Barry Lyndon,* Kubrick's film rarely surfaced amidst the lively polemic that developed within cinema studies around the pleasures of the protracted pace. After *Sight and Sound,* editor Nick James indicated that he appreciated "the best films of this kind," but considered slow films to be "passive-aggressive, in that they demand great swathes of our precious time to achieve quite fleeting and slender aesthetic and political effects" (5), blogger Harry Tuttle lambasted James in *Unspoken Cinema* ("Slow films"). Tuttle's broadside, in turn, elicited a response from Steven Shaviro, who compared the contemplative cinema of the 2000s to that of the 1970s and found it lacking. Shaviro considered the twenty-first century crop of slow films "nostalgic and regressive" because they "give older cinematic styles [. . .] a new zombiefied life in death" ("Slow cinema versus fast films").

At the time of its release, and in the years since, Kubrick's *Barry Lyndon* has been subjected to similar criticisms. In both commercial and scholarly terms, the film never fully recovered from doubts expressed by the public, the critics, and the academic philosophers. The mixed critical and popular response to the film was not unusual for Kubrick's work, as Thomas Elsaesser has eloquently noted, writing that Kubrick's films generally "me[et] with indifference and incomprehension, and, only later, with hindsight, [reveal] their place in a given generic history" (140). Whereas Judith Crist praised *Barry Lyndon's* beauty in *The Saturday Review* (61) and *TIME's* Duffy and Schickel called it an "art-film spectacle" (160), *The New Yorker's* Pauline Kael resisted the film's static compositions and apparent commitment to historicism, seemingly annoyed by the film's "refusal to entertain us, or even to involve us" (52). Her views were echoed humorously in the *MAD* parody discussed earlier, which itself suggested that the film was an emblem of high culture seriousness and thus, implicitly, nostalgic, regressive, and deserving of mockery. Through my examination of modes of temporality in *Barry Lyndon,* I hope to reconsider some of the charges leveled against the film, and particularly, that it is boring and hermetic, in light of recent characterizations of slow cinema as a contemplative form. In its slowness, and its attentiveness to diverse temporal modes more generally, the film affords viewers opportunities for verbal and visual as well as for emotional and intellectual engagement.

Moving from the low culture of *MAD* and popular film criticism to high theory, I turn to Fredric Jameson and Jean Baudrillard, who weighed in with critiques that foreground *Barry Lyndon*'s formal beauty and yet also implicitly consider the film's relationship to (its own) time. Jameson writes about *Barry Lyndon* only in the context of Kubrick's subsequent film, *The Shining*, thus framing his discussion within a relationship of sequence and succession, and treats the former work as an exemplar of the historical crisis within postmodernism. He suspects that *Barry Lyndon*'s "very perfection as a pastiche intensifies our nagging doubts as to the gratuitous nature of the whole enterprise" ("Historicism" 92). In making reference to pastiche, the textual juxtaposition of historical references unencumbered by critical judgment, Jameson relegates the film to the status of an empty imitation, a technically proficient copy. Baudrillard also complains about *Barry Lyndon*'s cold perfection: without "a single error," he writes, the film simulates rather than evokes (45). Its "very perfection is disquieting" (45). As it does for Jameson, *Barry Lyndon*, for Baudrillard, stands for an entire generation of cultural production: it represents "an era of films that in themselves no longer have meaning strictly speaking" (46). Reexamining *Barry Lyndon* through an analysis of its modes of temporality calls attention to the way that the perceptions of the film's "perfection," its surface beauty, and its obsolescence are historical artifacts themselves. I would argue that Kubrick's film generates meaning precisely through parody—with an irony that exposes the politics underlying practices of visual culture within modernity.

Not surprisingly, given the challenges it posed to American cinema-goers of the 1970s, Kubrick's magnum opus "failed in the laboratory of commerce" as Thomas Doherty delicately puts it (B10). "Demanding and uncommercial" in the eyes of Robert Kolker (6), *Barry Lyndon* proved to be Kubrick's least lucrative cinematic endeavor, grossing only $20 million in the United States against a production budget of $11 million; in comparison, *Cuckoo's Nest* took in $112 million with a budget of just over $4 million (IMDb.com).

Over the course of three decades, which included a rerelease in 1977, *Barry Lyndon* was rarely screened in the United States and descended into obscurity. In *Stanley Kubrick Companion*, James Howard observes "*Barry Lyndon* rivals *A Clockwork Orange* as the least visible of the director's works" (143). This is actually saying a great deal, as Kubrick asked Warner Brothers to withdraw

A Clockwork Orange from circulation in the United Kingdom in the early 1970s after controversies arose involving supposed copycat crimes. In *The Complete Kubrick*, David Hughes underscores the extent of the critical and popular neglect of *Barry Lyndon*:

> *Barry Lyndon* was misunderstood upon its initial release, as almost all of Kubrick's more considered creations were: yet the scarcity with which the film is seen today means that opinion has not been revised as dramatically as it has on many of Kubrick's other films. It is almost as though, a quarter of a century later, the jury were still out. (195)

Moreover, *Barry Lyndon* was given short shrift amidst the books and memorabilia that proliferated after Kubrick's death in 1999. In a review essay, Tony Pipolo considers ten such books, yet fails to mention *Barry Lyndon* at all, an omission that is remarkable when you consider that Pipolo devotes space to two films Kubrick never made, including the Napoleon project and *AI* (Spielberg 2001). Adding insult to injury, Jon Ronson opens his captivating Channel 4 (UK) documentary, *Stanley Kubrick's Boxes* (2008) with a chronological montage that jumps from *A Clockwork Orange* to *The Shining* and then breezily moves on to *Full Metal Jacket* without ever acknowledging *Barry Lyndon*. Even Warner Brothers may have contributed to the obscurity of *Barry Lyndon* by failing to include it in the Kubrick DVD box set the studio released in 2007.

Around 2008, *Barry Lyndon* began to experience something of a resurrection. The British Film Institute presented a Kubrick season in 2009 and selected *Barry Lyndon* to run in repertory, where it played to packed houses. In that same year, Roger Ebert placed the film on his list of great movies, considering it one of the "master's best" ("*Barry*"). In 2010, 35 years after reviewing *Barry Lyndon* upon its theatrical release, Richard Schickel framed his remarks about the film by discussing its place in time and history. "In its cover story," he writes, "*TIME*, almost alone, predicted history would judge the film a masterpiece. Thirty years later history is beginning to agree" ("All-TIME"). Recognized by some as the director's "neglected masterpiece" (Robey), the film enjoyed a blu-ray release in 2011.[1]

---

[1] It may be sheer coincidence, but a seductive one nevertheless, that Harvard's Houghton Library mounted a bicentenary exhibit on the tale's original author, William Makepeace Thackeray, in the summer of 2011.

Surely, *Barry Lyndon* has emerged from obscurity in part because of Kubrick's sustained prominence as a major postwar director with a relatively small body of work. I suspect the timing of the film's reemergence is not accidental, however. Slow cinema, arising from a broader set of slow movements in food, art, and fashion that developed in the late 1980s, has clearly played a role in its reemergence. Mainstream films and art films have expanded their temporal dimensions in the 2000s and 2010s, including work such as Martin Scorsese's 2-hour and 59-minute long *The Wolf of Wall Street* (2013) and Lars Von Trier's two-part *Nymphomaniac* (2013), whose international release exceeded 4 hours in length. In fact, *The New York Times* reported that the top ten grossing films of 2012 were 20 minutes longer than those in 1992 (Hynes).

Moreover, the discourse surrounding the "death of cinema," which attempts to theorize the radical changes visited upon film art in the digital age, is another context for a reconsideration of *Barry Lyndon*. David Bordwell dismisses the angst around digitality as a mere "journalistic trope" ("Observations"). But this trope has nevertheless gained traction and generated widespread interest in the potential affective, aesthetic, and economic losses associated with the demise of the motion picture camera—a device that ARRI, Panavision, and Aaton announced they would no longer produce after 2011—and film—also being phased out, as Fuji announced the cessation of motion picture film manufacturing in 2013. In this context, Kubrick's *Barry Lyndon*, whose aesthetic and technological achievements (including the adaptation of the Zeiss lens) sometimes became synonymous with the film itself, returns to the forefront, not only as a work considered "the most visually beautiful film ever made" (Miller 827) but also as one that addresses social technologies of vision in a way that remains relevant and rich in the digital age.

In this book, I hope to redirect some of the discussion about *Barry Lyndon* away from an emphasis on its spatial and surface attributes and toward a lesser-examined element of the film: its discourse on time, as manifested through a self-conscious approach to narrativity and a scrupulous attention to the temporalities associated with written texts, paintings, and cinematography. My central concern is the film's ability to forward a theory of time and history through the articulation of diverse and competing aesthetic temporalities.

Mary Ann Doane draws upon the periodization scheme that situates the modern turn at the dawn of the twentieth century when she writes, "cinema is a crucial participant in an ongoing rethinking of temporality in modernity"

(20). *Barry Lyndon's* characterization of modern time, by contrast, suggests that the temporal register of the modern began to develop around the time of the French Revolution, as historian Lynn Hunt's epigraph suggests. After the temporal "reboot" represented by the French Revolutionary Calendar and its proclamation of the Year One, a host of issues concerned with beginnings, endings, the old and the new, and the perception of the flow of time were rethought in a variety of aesthetic forms, perhaps most famously in the experiments of literary modernism and visual arts movements such as Italian Futurism and surrealism. "Modernity, though the term itself was not yet well-established, was the by-product of [a] conflict between proponents and opponents of the revolutionary rupture in time," writes Hunt (72). This perceived traumatic disconnection from the past may have produced a modern form of melancholy, but it also gave history writing a more prominent role than it had previously enjoyed. As Hunt notes, "modernity and history writing thus became complicit" (74).

In *Barry Lyndon*, Kubrick commits firmly to the sequentiality of narrative and cinematic form—and to exposing their idiosyncratic assumptions—as he considers the sweep of modern time. He probes the manifestation of time in serial literature, in figural painting, and in the photography and cinematography that are the currency of twentieth-century aesthetics. Whereas Kubrick's *2001* prognosticated the "Dawn" of humankind in relation to images of apes, *Barry Lyndon* announces the dawn of the modern in a closing scene in which the date "1789"—a year that some of France's revolutionaries considered to be Year One of Liberty[2]—is beautifully scrawled on a check transferring capital from Lady Honoria Lyndon to her estranged husband Redmond Barry. Like Lady Lyndon's check (an eighteenth-century technology) and her penmanship, many elements of the film—its intertitles, its intermission, and its voice over narration—seem old fashioned by the standards of the 1970s. Yet, because these elements represent different versions of the announcement, they implicate the film in the culture of the new. Their forward-looking orientation marks them as emblems of the modern.

Stanley Kubrick's films typically adopt a long view on history (*Spartacus, 2001, The Shining*) and they are generally interested in both the larger rhythms and the minute measures of time (*Killer's Kiss, The Killing, Dr. Strangelove, A Clockwork*

---

[2] A debate regarding whether the year of the revolution (1789) or that of the establishment of the republic (1792) should be considered Year One was decided in favor of the latter.

Orange). His interests harmonize with the historiographical concept of *la longue duree* developed within the Annales School of social science during the mid-twentieth century, which emphasizes long-term trends and social history as opposed to the greatest hits versions offered by official accounts. In Kubrick's work, *la longue duree* inevitably engages with the ideas of the eighteenth century. That era's neoclassical sensibility, which weds historicism and aesthetics, appears again and again in Kubrick's films, from the paintings that adorn the walls of the general's chateau in *Paths of Glory* to the death chamber of astronaut Dave Bowman in *2001*. Critic Eva-Maria Magel emphasizes the centrality of this period to Kubrick's work: "[a]n era of breaking with old ways, and of a new beginning pointing forward to the modern age, the eighteenth century had always had a peculiar appeal for Kubrick" (24). Frank Rich sees Kubrick's interest as a genealogical one, based on the era's associations with science and rationality. For Rich, the eighteenth century is "the point when the orderly underpinnings of this doomsday modern world were formalized—during the Age of Reason" (19).

It was during the eighteenth century that the secular study of "History" emerged. This process was closely linked to the ideas about progress put forth in Nicolas de Condorcet's posthumously published *Sketch for a Historical Picture of the Progress of the Human Mind* (1795), which argued in part that the past represents a trajectory of human improvement. Historian Reinhart Koselleck writes about the new view of history in *Futures Past: On the Semantics of Historical Time*: "Since the French Revolution, history has become a subject furnished with divine epithets of omnipotence, universal justice, and sanctity" (33). Exploring the world with a newly historical consciousness in the eighteenth century, in turn, affected the notion of time itself and thus, "the tendency to look at things historically led to a correspondingly vast extension of the world in time" (Whitrow 152). It is during the eighteenth century that the "modern time schema" (Hunt 128) developed. This schema endows time with the attributes of universality, homogeneity, depth, and a future orientation (Hunt 25), and, according to Lynn Hunt, were foundational to the practice of history, a practice that interests Thackeray and Kubrick greatly as they render the story of Redmond Barry/Barry Lyndon.

The *Barry Lyndon* narrative possesses its own history, one that traverses centuries, nations, and aesthetic modes. The project originates with a nineteenth-century serial whose action is based on both historical and fictional sources from the previous century. The serial, the fictional memoir that it gave rise to, and Kubrick's film all grapple with the conjunction of word and image, and the interplay of aesthetics and British imperial history. Thackeray's inquiry into fictional and historical narratives provides Kubrick with a means of addressing the relationships among narrative form, history, and cinematic time, a nexus of interest that recurs throughout the director's films.

This last assertion situates this book within an auteurist approach, which also bears some burdens of temporality, as it is often considered an outmoded scholarly paradigm. Yet, a wealth of extant scholarly and critical writing has explicitly and implicitly deemed this framework appropriate and useful when considering Kubrick's work. Kubrick's career spanned an era in which authorship was debated in cinema and literary studies and beyond; more generally, the model of patriarchal authority that obtained prior to the World War II was challenged by the civil rights, antiwar, feminist, and gay liberation social movements of the 1950s, 1960s, and 1970s. In that period, the *Cahiers du Cinema* collective, and particularly Astruc, Truffaut, and Godard, "invented Film Studies" (Ray 27) in part by defining the concept of the film author through *la politique des auteurs*. Roland Barthes proclaimed the death of the Author and Michel Foucault analyzed the author-function as a "privileged moment of individualization" that, he argued, a text refers to as an external and preexisting entity (225). In the 1970s and 1980s, another version of auteurism emerged, as Hollywood filmmakers were transformed into celebrities with attendant star personas, offering a "brand name vision whose aesthetic meanings and values [were already] determined" (Corrigan 40).

Although the commercialization of authorship has been attributed to the postmodern condition (Notaro 87), the financial exploitation of the author figure is not unique to the twentieth century. The mid-Victorian era in which William Makepeace Thackeray wrote, a period during which a mass reading public developed, witnessed the rise of literary agents and celebrity authors such as Charles Dickens. Thackeray himself embarked on 6-month speaking tour of the United States in 1852, lecturing on eighteenth-century writers; he became such a favorite with American audiences that he returned in 1855.

Judging from the numerous books published on Kubrick's life and work, the critical consensus has coalesced around the case for Kubrick as an auteur; James Gilbert's essay in Robert Kolker's collection on *2001* is entitled "Auteur with a Capital A" (29). Given his penchant for adaptations and the ability to exercise control over many aspects of his productions (from art design to budget to publicity), Kubrick can be understood both as the working auteur theorized by Truffaut and *Cahiers du Cinema*, imposing a perspective on literary material adapted for the screen, and also as a luminary associated with the celebrification of post-studio directors. A distinctive, although not necessarily accurate, star persona arose during the 1970s, creating a "brand name vision."

The celebrity discourse that has come to envelop Kubrick and his legacy speaks to the seeming inevitability of, or at least the difficulty of completely avoiding, the star-director model that emerged after the breakup of the Hollywood studio system. Writing on Kubrick's authorship, Thomas Elsaesser considers the "effort required in the latter half of the twentieth century to control one's image, if one wished to remain (in and for the film industry) that totemic individualist *par excellence*" (137). It is arguable, however, whether or not Kubrick wished to become or remain a "totemic individualist." He certainly strove to maintain control over the creative, fiscal, and marketing aspects of his work—that is, to control not his image, but his images—at a time of industry decentralization that, ironically, minimized the power of the newly visible class of star directors. He sought to avoid making the same film twice—a radical proposition in an increasingly risk averse industry that came to depend upon the branding of actors and directors to sell films.

If Kubrick can be said to have fulfilled both aspects of the film auteur, it was not because he aspired to become a brand name. A Kubrick brand was certainly generated in the late 1960s and early 1970s by the burgeoning post-studio publicity industry and its ineluctable dialectic of hagiography and defilement. Kubrick chose to avoid rather than to participate in that mythification, particularly after a preponderance of early negative responses to *2001* in the American press and especially after the controversies surrounding the copycat crimes linked to *A Clockwork Orange* (Krämer xii). A Kubrick mystique emerged, comprised of speculation that his physical distance from Hollywood was indicative of a profound antisociality. In reality, the decision to remain in the United Kingdom was made in large part because his children began school in Britain during the production of *Lolita*, partly because he enjoyed access to the filmmaking facilities in London, and, possibly, because he found Hollywood to be rife with an atmosphere of "destructive competitiveness" (Cahill). After the moral panic surrounding *A Clockwork Orange*, rumors arose regarding his reclusiveness, his obsessiveness, and his misanthropic perfectionism as a director. The charges of perfectionism gained credence after the release of his daughter Vivian's BBC documentary, *The Making of the Shining* (1980), which depicted an impatient Kubrick admonishing the actress Shelly Duvall, who had repeatedly missed her cue. Kubrick's brother-in-law Jan Harlan, who produced *A Clockwork Orange* and

Kubrick's subsequent films, gave an interview at Cannes in 2011, commenting on Kubrick's oversight with regard to the press. His "big mistake," Harlan said, "is that he never talked back to the press. Nonsense was written, but his attitude was 'Don't talk to them or you'll never get rid of them.' He could have avoided all that by being a bit more accessible, but he just hated it" (Rose).

The discourse of Kubrick as eccentric hermit savant, together with that of Robert Altman as his merry prankster foil, preserved, at least psychologically, the possibility of an art cinema within American film culture in the late 1970s and 1980s. In that period, the Hollywood Renaissance "film generation" directors (Cook 35), including George Lucas, Steven Spielberg, and Francis Ford Coppola, moved into big-budget blockbusters. Kubrick's status as crackpot expatriate ratified the sense of a growing dichotomy between art cinema and mainstream films in an era in which financial success rather than creative risk-taking once again became the *sine qua non* of Hollywood success. James Naremore writes, "Kubrick's films were nearly always made and received in the aura of art" (9). This may be true; in point of fact, however, his career was built upon a foundation of medium-sized productions that were moderately profitable. *Dr. Strangelove* was made for less than $2 million and grossed just under $10 million. Even *2001*—an admittedly ambitious undertaking that went over-budget and ultimately cost $10 million—took in $68 million at the box office. Its better than 6:1 ratio compares favorably to other popular films released in 1968, including *Funny Girl* (4:1) and *Planet of the Apes* (5:1).

Thus the case for Kubrick as an independent European-style art cinema auteur is tenuous at best. As Robert Sklar observes, Kubrick's reputation for being a maverick obscures the ways in which his career represented not a retreat from the American film industry, but, rather, a prototype for post-studio film production. "He and his films," Sklar writes, "have played a much more central role than has heretofore been recognized in the transformation of industry practices in the era since the breakup of studio monopolies" (115). Those practices include guerrilla filmmaking on *Killer's Kiss*, the roadshow release format for *Spartacus*, the distribution of *Lolita* before obtaining the approval of the Production Code Administration, the creation of his own production companies, and the negotiation of finance and distribution deals with major studios (after *A Clockwork Orange*, this became Warner Brothers exclusively). Speaking to the way aesthetics and industry concerns were intertwined for Kubrick, Michael Herr observes that the director made "art films with blockbuster pretensions" ("Kubrick"). Jan Harlan put it another way: Kubrick "wanted to make films that mattered" (Charlie Rose). In this book, I implicitly make the argument that *Barry Lyndon* is a film that matters; however, my goal is not to argue for the recognition of *Barry Lyndon* as Kubrick's masterpiece or, to borrow from the sensibility of the film itself, his legitimate heir. Rather, I examine the film in the context of its times; that is, in the context of temporalities of its own making and in the context of film and history at the end of the twentieth century.

Kubrick's time

Time is a strange thing. When you have a little of it and you want it to last, it scatters away in all directions and you never know where it's gone.

Walter Cartier, *Day of the Fight*

A number of scholars and critics have characterized Kubrick's *oeuvre* broadly in terms of a distinctive, twentieth-century sense of alienation. In *On Kubrick*, James Naremore situates Kubrick's work within the modernist tradition of the grotesque (28), whereas Robert Kolker places his films amidst a postwar "cinema of loneliness" (152). Jerold Adams frames Kubrick's sensibility within existentialism in *The Philosophy of Stanley Kubrick*. The modes of alienation that these critics identify are, for me, inseparable from the way Kubrick chooses to address questions of temporality and to explore the ways that humans construct and measure historical time.

Philip Rosen's observation about the way temporality functions within both past- and future-oriented films helps to explain the way Kubrick's films navigate past, present, and future but do not rest easily in any single space-time configuration. Kubrick's films—most obviously, *2001*—constantly displace previously established timeframes that might produce comfort. Rosen implies a larger project at work in films that relinquish their attachments to the idea of the present: "At a formal, compositional level," Rosen writes, "there need be little to differentiate future settings of science fiction from the past settings of a historical fiction [. . .] both propose a narrational or epistemological stance that transcends its own 'real' temporal location in the present" (80). Most of Kubrick's films—even those ostensibly set in the present day—enact a version of Rosen's temporal transcendence. The coldness and emotional distance that Robert Kolker, Jean Baudrillard, and others identify within Kubrick's films arise, in part, from the way his films conceive of and manifest the passage of time, within particular spatial configurations. Kubrick marshals a sense of history's protracted and inexorable cyclicality in ways that minimize the significance of characters, motivations, and actions. Narrative elements involving backstory, plot events, and cause and effect—along with the potential for spectator identification—are attenuated, no longer obeying the injunctions of time. Ambition, greed, and lust shrivel into petty absurdities under Kubrick's withering gaze, which takes its rhythmic cues from the epochal, not the ephemeral.

Thematically, Kubrick's films situate individuals within social, technological, and cosmic systems that govern historical change with little regard for the fate of humankind. *2001* may be the quintessential example of a film with a temporal sensibility that encompasses millennia. Yet it also throws us off track by drawing our attention to the phenomenological, embodied, and microcosmic experience of human time; as in the scene in which we hear astronaut Frank Poole's breathing. Paying attention to the breath, according to the teachings of mindfulness mediation, permits us to live in the present moment. Here, the abrupt cessation of Poole's breathing brings chronological time to a halt, obliterating both the moment and the continuum of past–present–future; it signals Poole's imminent, silent demise, which is no less violent for being unheard. The whiplash these moments induce, as we move from the scale of seconds to that of aeons, is one reason *2001* could be advertised in 1968 as "The Ultimate Trip," after it became clear that the film's target audience was young, adventurous, and not averse to chemical experimentation.

Kubrick's trip(s) also trip us up, however: it's not always comforting to move through the various temporal orders of magnitude that his work offers us. Annette Michaelson describes *2001* as a film that models the momentum of space travel by manifesting the "apparent absence of speed which one experiences only in the fastest of elevators, or jet planes" (62). Martin Scorsese notes that the film "stopped how you normally experience time" (Charlie Rose). James Naremore locates the film within a post-Einstein, quantum physics universe in which time and space are interdependent: "What makes [*2001*] unique is the way it slows time in relation to the vastness of space [. . .] no other big-budget science fiction film has even been paced so slowly" (143–4).

2001 draws attention to temporality in obvious and abstract ways, from its title to its own lack of dialogue—more than 80 minutes of the film are dialogue free—to its frequent attenuation of physical movement. I would like to suggest, however, that each of Kubrick's films, from *Day of the Fight* (1951) to *Eyes Wide Shut*, foregrounds various, competing, and sometimes even incommensurable modes of temporality as a theme as well as a formal element. One possible reason for the director's consistent engagement with temporalities may be that they embody our desire to control existential chaos; they represent an attempt to impose order in a fundamental way. As historian Penelope Cornfield writes in *Time and the Shape of History*: "we operate routinely within a time-infused cosmos [...] temporality is simultaneously all-important and completely beyond our control" (6).

In Kubrick's films, the way that time's passage is remembered, recorded, and envisioned assumes a position of critical importance to narrative structure, editing, and visual design. The disruption of the linear timeline appears early in Kubrick's work, making its debut within his still photography, as I discuss in Chapter 2. That particular challenge remained a consistent theme and formal concern. Michael Herr describes Kubrick's love of "long takes and long scenes [...] every one of his films mak[es] its powerful assertion that pace is story as surely as character is destiny" ("Kubrick"). The way time passes matters a great deal in every Kubrick film.

On one level, that of story structure, Kubrick liberally sprinkles beginnings and endings throughout his narratives. These include Humbert Humbert's new semester at Beardsley College in *Lolita*, the remarkable Colorado winter in *The Shining*, and the annual holiday gala that Bill and Alice Harford attend at the opening of *Eyes Wide Shut*. Beginnings and endings can also be contained within the same narrative event, as with the nuclear explosion that ends *Dr. Strangelove* but inaugurates the titular character's wishful-thinking afterworld in mineshafts populated by supermodels and government wonks. The gunshot that fells Redmond Barry's father in the duel that opens *Barry Lyndon* is a beginning and an ending. These moments of compression manifest Kubrick's interest in the relation between narrative and time by insistently marking time as event while also suggesting its ineffability. They also underscore the notion that stories and histories are shaped and sorted, organized and made to be timely. These elements recur throughout Kubrick's body of work, in films that, as I will argue in relation to *Barry Lyndon* specifically, foreground sequence and order, simultaneity, cyclicality, repetition, and stasis.

The vertiginous precision of the countdown serves as organizing structure and dramatic impetus for Kubrick's earliest film, *Day of the Fight*, a short boxing documentary based on a photo essay Kubrick had published in *Look* magazine in 1949. In it, New Yorker Walter Cartier, a 24-year-old middleweight whose identical twin Vincent serves as his manager, spends the day preparing for his brutal physical encounter. The tension of anticipation is reflected in narrator Douglas Edwards's script, which repeatedly makes reference to how much time is left before the fight: "For Walter, the bad part is the waiting for the thing to happen." The "pressure of the last waiting" comes roughly at the film's midpoint and, after all the waiting, the film concludes abruptly, as Cartier knocks out opponent Bobby James.

Another early documentary short, *Flying Padre* (1951), considers temporal organization somewhat more obliquely than the first film. Its central premise involves the difficulties that face contemporary missionary Fred Stadtmueller, who must pilot a Piper Cub (named *The Spirit of St. Joseph*) in order to minister to his far flung flock, which is distributed over a 400-square mile parish in New Mexico. Stadtmueller's high tech solution to this time management dilemma dramatizes the modern fragmentation of time and reorganization of space, wherein the priest's physical presence can be distributed across space and time through the technology of air transportation, just as celluloid bodies can be transported across imaginary geographies through film editing.

Kubrick returns to the countdown in both *Killer's Kiss* and *The Killing*, where he weds clockwork precision to sleazy *film noir* criminality. In the former, a boxer and a dance hall girl find themselves caught up in a romance that affords the possibility of their escape from New York. The film is narrated by Davey, the boxer, 3 days after the events have taken place. Cross cutting between boxing and dance hall scenes, with dance music accompanying both activities, produces offbeat temporal choreographies.

In *The Killing*, a film whose temporal idiosyncrasies were so troubling that the studio demanded a recut (LoBrutto 123), split seconds make the difference between fortunes and folly at the racetrack, where an elaborate heist conspiracy is underway, orchestrated by Johnny Clay (Sterling Hayden). Each conspirator is endowed not only with a backstory but also with an individual time signature. Stephen Mamber has argued that the film conveys simultaneity through repetition, which functions as the film's organizing principle (2). The use of repetition confounds the film's obsessively announced chronological structure and also introduces temporal delay. In one example of this principle, the police officer involved in the heist ignores a plea for help from a woman on the street. Over images of him driving away, the non-diegetic narrator intones: "He had timed the trip to the track on half a dozen different occasions [. . .] He knew the entire success of the plan depended on his accuracy in arriving at the track at the correct moment; a minute or two early was allowable, but ten seconds late would be fatal." The layering of image and verbal text—and the fact that the voice over describes the action at the same time the character performs it—creates information overload similar to that of "on the nose" dialogue; it also introduces temporal delay. The action and its ostensible explanation occur simultaneously, and this combination fails to function as a cause–effect connection should. These careful orchestrations of image and text, which at first appear to be devices for clarification, can in fact confound chronology. These techniques become important in *Barry Lyndon*, as I explore in Chapters 2 and 3.

Using a temporally overdetermined narrator whose "obsessive marking of the hour and minute of all events in the robbery timetable, almost suggests a mechanical, nonhuman agency at work" (Guest), Kubrick undermines the authority, and indeed, the *raison d'etre*, of the storytelling apparatus. The simultaneous, rational explanations offered in *The Killing* do not wield the explanatory power that a narrator is expected to provide. Moreover, the explanation itself satisfies on only one level. We may understand the crooked police officer's boorishness, but the woman's emergency—a potentially dramatic event—remains unresolved and forgotten. The human voice, characterized by a "clockwork precision" (Guest), contributes alternatively to a sense of urgency (where time matters a great deal) and doom (where time makes no difference at all) as it forecloses the future for the men involved in the tightly plotted heist.

Kubrick also introduces a tension between chronological and circular temporalities in *The Killing*. This clash is evidenced in the use of simulated newsreel footage at the racetrack, which Guest associates with a "present-tense realism" that Kubrick "systematically undercut[s] by the stuttered and fragmentary repetition of the same imagery throughout the film" (Guest). In both *The Killing* and in *Barry Lyndon*, as I will be arguing, an obsessively and even strategically sequenced narrative finds its counterpoint in underlying structures of abstraction, repetition, and circularity.

Spartacus, a film that Kubrick distanced himself from because as a director for hire he was subject to Kirk Douglas's authority, demonstrates his interest in the temporal peculiarity of narrating historical events whose outcome is already known. The film's opening scene presents an expanded and yet also an enclosed time frame within which to consider the actions the film depicts. In the process, it offers an assertively political stance rejecting the claim that Spartacus was responsible for ending slavery. The narration introduces Spartacus as a Thracian born into slavery who "lived out his youth and young manhood dreaming the death of slavery 2,000 years before it would actually die." Invoking dreams, death, and the distance of 2,000 years, the narration demands that we conceive of time's passage not as a trajectory bound by unidirectionality (as Arthur Eddington's "arrow of time"), but one that might be conceived of as flowing in two directions. In one line of narration, we participate in Spartacus's dreams and confront the long span of time after his death before their realization.

Nabokov's *Lolita* is predicated upon both arrested development and the urgent need to exploit time. The story is founded upon Humbert Humbert's neurotic temporal suspension, a condition that leaves him sexually obsessed with prepubescent girls. The clock is always ticking, as Humbert's desire can only be aroused by a young girl passing through the particular chronological stage he designates as that of nymphet. A flashback structure organizes the novel and film, in keeping with the backward-looking narration in *Killer's Kiss*, *The Killing*, and *Spartacus*. In *Barry Lyndon*, the narration assumes a good deal more temporal complexity, as a forward-looking third person narration, emanating from a point after all the film's events have occurred, foretells actions that have not yet taken place on screen.

The momentum of an unhinged military sortie determines the temporal urgency of *Dr. Strangelove*, whose story is driven by the need to halt the progress of numerous armed bombers headed toward their targets in Russia. The broader temporal overlay in this film, however, is not measured by suspenseful minutes, but rather involves the prospect of the instantaneous end of time. Strangelove's post-apocalypse plan reconstructs the future by making it over into a subterranean sexual playground in which human existence becomes dependent upon another slightly off-kilter temporal process: the rapid creation of new generations.

2001: A Space Odyssey possesses the clearest connection of Kubrick's films with a metaphysics of time. Its title alone signifies the kinds of competing temporal structures that are also shot through *Barry Lyndon*. It declares a specific chronological date on the Gregorian Calendar, but then challenges such precise dates by invoking the odyssey, a process that encompasses the circularity of unstructured voyage and return. The film's spiraling evolutionary leaps and circular passages through space and time "compete with the Bible in presenting the beginnings and endings of human existence" (Gilbert 31–2).

In a title that also announces competing time schemas, Burgess's *A Clockwork Orange* calls forth the posthuman imagery of a juicy timepiece. Perhaps more important, Kubrick's film defamiliarizes notions of past and future visually and narratively in the dizzying fashions and figure of Alex De Large, a primitive sophisticate, a child-man who worships the music of Beethoven and consumes drugged milk. The sequencing of crime and punishment turns out to be governed not by the logic of cause–effect but, instead, by cycles of sin, redemption, and political expediency. These temporal confusions are thrown into relief against the surrealism of slow and fast motion sequences—a technology for directing viewer attention that, in *Barry Lyndon*, will be taken up by the zoom lens. These sequences depict Alex's transcendence of ordinary time during violence and sex while also calling attention to these activities as a passage of time.

The Shining is Kubrick's ghost story, a genre which explicitly depends upon nonchronological temporality. The film depicts Danny Torrence's supernatural gift not only in terms of his possession by another (Tony) but also through his apprehension of future events. His father Jack experiences dreamy divergences from the normative flow of time as established in the opening of the film, ultimately experiencing what seems to be a continuous present during his never-beginning and never-ending stint as the caretaker at the Overlook Hotel.

If *2001* prefigures *Barry Lyndon* in terms of its abstract rendering of varied temporal schemas, then *Full Metal Jacket* most closely resembles the rigidly disciplined structure of *Barry Lyndon*, with its strictly delineated two part narrative. Thematically and temporally, the two films share an emphasis on the dialectics surrounding masculine bonding and conflict, including dueling, brawling, intergenerational disputes, and formal battles. More generally, as Jack Boozer notes, Kubrick's "political-military films (*Paths of Glory*, *Dr. Strangelove*, and *Full Metal Jacket*) also draw linkages between the male libido and imperialistic hierarchies" (87). Although Boozer does not include *Barry Lyndon* in this category, I would argue for its similarity to these "political-military" films. Its intentionally limited engagement with the combat narrative and its attentiveness to the accoutrements surrounding the enterprise of war (looting, desertion, and the awarding of medals for bravery, for example) align *Barry Lyndon* with the military culture critique of *Dr. Strangelove*, whereas its suggestion of a coming of age trajectory from innocence to experience places it firmly within the sensibility of *Paths of Glory* and *Full Metal Jacket*.

Eyes Wide Shut draws its protagonist through the surreal time and space of fantasy, an expansive nighttime and imaginative realm that is linked to the privilege of his wealthy cosmopolitan existence. The scenes of the secret society orgy that Bill Harford crashes make reference to seemingly timeless sexual rituals—pagan, Greek, Bohemian, aristocratic—that rhyme with the gambling and womanizing scenes in *Barry Lyndon*. The masked ball is a recurrent trope and, reportedly, the real-life event where Kubrick met his third wife Christiane;

he shot a masked ball scene for *Barry Lyndon* that was not used. Drawing on source material from the 1920s to depict the 1990s in *Eyes Wide Shut*, Kubrick astutely pinpoints that particular decade's source of heart-stopping dread, the viral "ticking time bomb," and emerging threat to a world of sanctioned promiscuity and infidelity. Harford is literally saved by the bell—his mobile telephone—and avoids potential HIV exposure from the prostitute Domino. This scenario emerges only in retrospect when Bill returns to her apartment the next day.

In the scholarly and popular literature on Kubrick, some scholars and critics remark upon his experiments with temporality. Robert Stam observes that Kubrick exploits "cinema's capacity for mingling apparently contradictory times and temporalities" (60). Critic Anthony Lane offers a cheekier assessment, describing the formal approach of *Killer's Kiss* and *The Killing* as "alarmingly insolent towards the demands of chronology" (122). In *Barry Lyndon*, Kubrick mingles contradictory temporalities and that insolence toward chronology together as he investigates the relationships between Empire, violence, and visual culture. Enlightenment philosopher Immanual Kant situates temporality within the ambit of human consciousness; as such, the experience of time becomes a condition of possibility for human intuition, aesthetic judgment, and, ultimately, moral judgment. Kubrick's film explores the temporal possibilities afforded by aesthetic forms, including written texts, paintings, music, and cinema. The film probes the meaning of culture, not only in the biological sense, where culture refers to the maintenance of living material in an appropriate environment for growth, but also in terms of the term's social, disciplinary, and aesthetic implications. Culture's forms, we learn from Kubrick's films, including art and history, are in no way divorced from, or capable of assuaging, the brutality associated with the human—and for Kubrick, masculine—will to domination.

Several critics and scholars have remarked upon the importance of history to Kubrick's work. Robert Kolker, Thomas Allen Nelson, and David Cook view Kubrick's films as grappling with the large questions that inform human existence, including power and control, destiny versus choice. Geoffrey Cocks, James Diedrick, and Glenn Perusek place his work within the historical context of the Holocaust and draw parallels between Kubrick's films and Theodor Adorno's aesthetic theory, writing: "Kubrick believed that the calamities of the twentieth century rendered certain kinds of art difficult if not impossible; he considered but never completed a film about the Holocaust" (6). While I concur with their assessment that Kubrick was a skeptic of the Enlightenment (6), my reading of Kubrick's work presumes a broader angle of historical vision on his part, one that encompasses the "calamities" of modernity, from the Napoleonic Wars to World War II: catastrophes engineered by human beings, of which the Holocaust may be the most remarkable. Fredric Jameson and Jean Baudrillard discuss *Barry Lyndon* in terms of history, the former claiming that *Barry Lyndon* paradoxically reveals the impossibility of historical representation and the latter accusing Kubrick of making history "an operational scenario." My approach to the film is certainly informed by Jameson's approach; as I understand it, the film, like the Thackeray novel it is based upon, aspires toward both historical representation and metacommentary. Its revelation that representing history is impossible is not, for me, at odds with Kubrick's insistence upon shooting by candlelight or undertaking a rigorous program of preproduction research into the legalities of dueling.

Barry Lyndon presents history as storytelling, a practice of power and aesthetics. Yet the film is far more interested in historiography, an inquiry that subjects various practices of and beliefs about history to the vicissitudes of passing time. One context for historical storytelling in *Barry Lyndon* is the imperial conquest represented by Seven Years' War and, somewhat more implicitly, the prior British plantation of Ireland; here Kubrick's approach parallels that of the Annales school by attending to geography, material culture, and *mentalité* (world view). Whereas Annales social scientists rejected official history, Kubrick presents one version of it in the story of Redmond Barry, an unwilling conscript who rises to prominence. But Kubrick adopts this "Great Man" approach to history, which was developed by Thackeray's contemporary Thomas Carlyle, primarily to hollow it out from within.

Like *Paths of Glory*, *Full Metal Jacket*, and *Fear and Desire*, *Barry Lyndon* acknowledges war as a proper subject for official history: after all, this history has been recorded, preserved, marked, and celebrated. Kubrick uses Thackeray's self-conscious first person narration to explore both verbally and visually the actions and emotions that fall outside the purview of official accounts. He stops short of allowing that "excess" material to be associated with an individual subjectivity, which is the bread and butter not only of Carlyle's Great Man thesis of history, but also of Hollywood's approach to historical representation, as Robert Rosenstone's work has shown. Rosenstone writes that mainstream historical films "put individuals in the forefront of the historical process" (55).

Kubrick's historiographical approach is not concerned with countering an elite "objective" history touting the grandiosity of the war machine with the subjective experience of an individual. *Barry Lyndon's* examination of war as history—which does not overtly present an antiwar argument but, rather, dissects the forces of war as instruments of culture—does not depend upon sentiment, sympathy, and identification. A useful counterpoint is Clint Eastwood's *Unforgiven* (1990), where a demythologizing critique of America's Wild West indicts the way in which that era has been fabricated by journalists and historical writers. But that critique is reversed when the film's antihero exacts his justified and violent revenge. No such dynamics attend Kubrick's framing of Britain's imperial conquest. Instead of demythologizing the British Empire (as the actualization of Enlightenment thinking) by countering its institutional power through a lone, Irish antihero, Kubrick exposes the empire's foundational illogic through narratives and characters that fail to cohere or to express. The traumatic experiences of an individual character such as Redmond Barry are relevant to this project, but the film's rhetorical strategy does not consist of generating feelings elicited by the character's experiences.

Kubrick's historical method

The film begins from the premise (and promise) of the narrative representation of history; this is the case even though it is clear that *Barry Lyndon* is a costume drama based on a narrative fiction. The film's reception was premised upon a slippage between fiction and history, and this slippage has shaped the work from its origins in Thackeray's writing. In its treatment of history as narrative, Kubrick's film resonates with the work of mid-century philosophers and historians, including Paul Ricoeur and Hayden White, whose interests encompass narrative, time, and historiography. In White's case, this inquiry culminated in the seminal essay "The Question of Narrative in Historical Theory," published in 1984. White draws upon Paul Ricouer's *Time and Narrative* project, which he calls a "metaphysics. of narrativity," in which historical narrative takes temporality as its referent (28), a proposition that has salience for Kubrick's *Barry Lyndon*, where temporalities become the film's referents. For Ricouer, as White notes, "narrativity brings us back from 'within time ness,'" defined as the experience of time as something in which events take place, to "historicality," where emphasis is placed on the weight of the past (28). The tension between the experience of being in time and the experience of time as pastness animates Kubrick (and Thackeray's) narrative experimentation in *Barry Lyndon*. Chapters 2 and 3 examine the relationship of narrative form to time and history in *Barry Lyndon*. There I argue that the formal, political, and thematic question of succession constantly threatens to interrupt "within timeness" in the novel and film; this practice thwarts narrative progress. Historicality is deployed within this framework as well—also linked to sequence and succession—as the linear, foregone conclusion of historical representation, here embodied in the rise and fall narrative.

Kubrick's competing temporal modes carry both aesthetic and political implications. They set the stage for a process that elicits both cognitive processing and emotional engagement, a combination of types of attention that produces aesthetic time. This experience, which allows for the synthesis of affect and judgment, should not be confused with the aesthetics of the Romantic sublime: the encounter with the overwhelming and the formless, which produces the "unreasoning delight" of John Dennis, the "negative pain" of Edmund Burke or the subjectivity-destroying boundlessness of Kant. The ability to combine affect and judgment in the process of watching Kubrick's films is a matter of timing: it derives precisely from the way the films orchestrate various and competing temporalities and both establish and undercut narrative expectations.

Recalling Kubrick's comments regarding Hitler and his henchmen and their appreciation for culture, I suspect that the director retained some skepticism toward purely emotional experiences. I borrow from Miriam Hansen's analysis of Walter Benjamin to propose the type of aesthetic response I believe Kubrick sought to avoid:

> Benjamin observes a similar form of miscognition at work in fascist mass politics, a splitting of sensory (visual-specular) perception from cognition (of their own situation and objecthood) and from (their own) agency. In other words, fascism has perfected a method of mobilizing the masses that at once paralyzes their practical, moral, and political judgment. (99)

The aesthetic experience provoked by Kubrick's work, I want to argue, is not merely emotional, although emotions are involved, but involves intellectual engagement—or "practical, moral and political judgment" as framed by Hansen—as well. As such, the process might be considered an ethical aesthetics. Kubrick spoke to his own investment in addressing both thought and emotions, and both conscious and subconscious levels, in an interview about *2001*: "I tried to create a visual experience," he says, "one that bypasses verbalized pigeonholing and directly penetrates the subconscious with an emotional and philosophical content" (Agel 328). James Naremore underscores this dual aspect of Kubrick's films, seeking to emphasize their affective address: "[t]he intellectual dimensions of his work can't be ignored, but we need to understand at the outset that he was primarily an artist who was dealing in emotions" (24).

Gilles Deleuze presents an intriguingly oblique way of approaching the conjunction of affect and ideation that I am proposing. He literalizes Kubrick's brain as the film screen, writing: "If we look at Kubrick's work, we see the degree to which it is the brain which is *mise en scène*" (*Cinema 2* 205). If this brain analogy is taken seriously, then temporal elements, not merely spatial matters (*mise en scène*), must be considered. For Deleuze, the brain is a machine of thought that involves movement. As he notes in a 1998 interview, "a work of art is always the creation of new space times" wherein "the image itself is a collection of time relations from which the present merely flows" ("The Brain" 53).

Deleuze's space-times emerge from specific historical, aesthetic, and cultural situations. In his work on time in philosophy, Espen Hammer points out that temporality itself is historically and culturally specific:

> temporality is not, as Kant argued in his account of pure intuition, only explanatory of some of the most fundamental *a priori* features of human existence (such as the ability to experience duration, succession, and coexistence); rather it is present in all our dealing with ourselves, others, and objects, and, as historical beings with particular practices and vocabularies, we relate to time in culturally and historically specific ways. (14)

The discourse on time and history in *Barry Lyndon*, as I will demonstrate in the chapters that follow, elucidates some of those culturally and historically specific ways that we relate to and understand time. One important paradigm used to characterize the experience of time in *Barry Lyndon* has been the temporality of boredom.

Boredom, or the slow sublime

Boredom is the dream bird that hatches the egg of experience.

Walter Benjamin, *The Storytellers*

Clocks and calendars mark time, but they do not make time.

Michael Flaherty, *A Watched Pot: How We Experience Time*

In "The End of Temporality," Fredric Jameson writes, "space was supposed to replace time in the general ontological scheme of things. At the very least, time had become a non person and people stopped writing about it" (695). Clearly, this prediction has not been borne out; time, which Jameson calls the "dominant of the modern" (696) continues to enchant and perplex us. As discussed earlier, practices and discourses of slow culture have attained prominence, which is perhaps unsurprising in an era noted for its quickening pace, for the dissolution of temporal and spatial boundaries between work and leisure, and for the fragmentation of attention associated with new media forms and forums. Furthermore, a scholarly literature on boredom—an affective state frequently associated with slowness and distraction—has taken shape in tandem with these developments. In my discussion, I decouple the concept of boredom from its association with wasted time. I want to explore the accusation that Kubrick's film is boring, not by defending against it, but by pursuing the potentially productive states of mind and feeling that might be associated with the experience of boredom.

In *The Philosophy of Stanley Kubrick*, Jerold Adams lists Martin Heidegger, who was concerned with both time and boredom, among the philosophers that Kubrick read (2).[3] Heidegger, according to David Couzens Hoy, considered temporality itself to be boring: "What is profoundly boring is time [. . .] Ontological or profound boredom is emptiness, where everything withdraws" (31). Boredom, in Heidegger's view, is far from debilitating, however. Along with perplexity and wonder—two states of mind that, I contend, are available from Kubrick's films, including *Barry Lyndon*—boredom offers "one point of entry into the domain of metaphysics" (de Beistegui 67). Boredom redirects attention to thought itself and to the passage of time. In fact, boredom is the "distinct and privileged mood" that lays the ground for "a metaphysics of Dasein" (de Beistegui 66).

Cultural theorists and historians link boredom to the modern condition and, by extension, to the anomie that film scholars have identified with Kubrick's work. Historian Frank Ankersmit returns to the century of Enlightenment to locate the source of boredom, arguing that "boredom results from the suppression of emotion that eighteenth-century social life required (and against which Rousseau would revolt)" (2005, 275). In *Experience without Qualities: Boredom and Modernity*, Liz Goodstein rejects the idea that boredom is a "transhistorical plague" (34). Like Ankersmit, she considers boredom to be "rooted in the

---

[3] I have been unable to confirm this assertion using the catalogue of Kubrick's books at the Stanley Kubrick Archive.

transformations of historical life that began in the eighteenth century" (46). Importantly, Goodstein situates the rhetoric of boredom within the "the historical field of reflection on subjective experience" (35). "Unlike melancholy, acedia, or *taedium vitae*," she writes, "such malaise is anchored in a linear vision of historical time that has its origins in Enlightenment thought" (35). Boredom emerged in full force in the 1840s, Goodstein writes, as a "peculiarly modern experience of empty, meaningless time" (3). For Bestegui, reading Heidegger, "Boredom is the disposition in which the essence of time, in its purity as it were, transpires" (70), the register in which "everything becomes equal, equally indifferent" (74).

Boredom has been associated with the narrative and the reception of *Barry Lyndon*, seen as classic examples of the emptiness of time within a modern era in which wasting time becomes an obstacle to purposive action. "What is at stake in modernity" Goodstein points out, "is the historical particularity of aesthetic forms and of the modes of perception that correspond to them" (8). These aesthetic forms and modes of perception are associated with temporalities and practices of reflection (I shall have more to say about the latter in my discussion of Thackeray's novel, a faux memoir). In *Barry Lyndon*, Kubrick attempts to explore several aesthetic and perceptual modes of modernity within the visual- and time-based medium of cinema. I am not arguing that Kubrick intended to, or succeeded in, creating an authentic timescape of the eighteenth century, but, rather, that he uses the pretense of historical fiction to put the medium of cinema through its paces, quite literally. Alexander Walker writes that "*Barry Lyndon* doesn't breathe history, for history is something in airtight cabinets or varnished paintings. Rather, it exhales historical life" (246). I would modify that observation to read that the film exhales aesthetic time.

How does cinema convey the experience of time, in the conventional understanding? Film represents the passage of time, but it also creates and occupies time. As Mary Ann Doane writes, "[t]he representation of time in cinema (its 'recording') is also and simultaneously the production of temporalities for the spectator, a structuring of the spectator's time" (24). Although cinema has been linked to modern time, both in terms of its relationship to organized time (the clock, the factory whistle) and to lived time (phenomenology), there are exceptions to this alignment of cinematic time and this insistent and controlling chronology. Bliss Cua Lim characterizes fantastic cinema as one mode that forces a reconsideration of "modern time consciousness" (11) because of the existence of "multiple times that fail to coincide with the measured, uniform intervals quantified by clock and calendar" (2). These multiple times are those that Deleuze describes, following Bergson, as "coexisting durations" (53).

For Maya Deren, attempting to make the case for the film medium's importance and aesthetic uniqueness, film is primarily a time form (160). Deren's privileging of film's relation to time provides one architecture upon which to develop an analysis of Kubrick's film, one that draws from the very fact of its sequentiality:

> the structure of a film is sequential. The creative action in film, then, takes place in its time dimension; and for this reason the motion picture, though composed of spatial images, is primarily *a time form*. (160)

Although, technically and technologically, slow motion is not a feature of *Barry Lyndon*, Maya Deren's concept that slow motion is a conceptual process, not merely a mechanical technique, further sheds light on the temporal experience of Kubrick's film. More specifically, Deren's observations about the experience of slow motion as a "double-exposure of time" (160) are instructive:

> [S]low motion is not simply slowness of speed. It is, in fact, something that exists in our minds, not on the screen . . . [i]t is because we are aware of the known pulse of the identified action while we watch it occur at a slower rate of speed that we experience the double-exposure of time which we know as slow motion. (158)

The "known pulse of the identified action" possesses cultural as well as individual dimensions; the rhythms of everyday actions, or "lived duration," as Michael Flaherty writes in *A Watched Pot: How We Experience Time*, "becomes a largely tacit aspect of interpersonal coordination" (40). We know our own historically and culturally situated understanding of time; experiments in slow cinema use that frame of reference in order to defamiliarize time. Flaherty continues:

> people are only conscious of lived duration on those occasions when time is perceived to be passing at an abnormal rate (i.e., either too quickly or too slowly [. . .] Extraordinary circumstances make for abnormal temporal experiences. (41)

The crucial factor in experiencing protracted duration (Flaherty's term for time passing too slowly) is the violation of expectations (59); in such "altered states," the emotions are implicated and thus "the sense of protracted duration can be induced by deep cognitive and perceptual immersion" (Flaherty 67).

Barry Lyndon's "slowness" is partially achieved through long takes and a moderately long average shot length of 14 seconds (Cinemetrics database).

Also contributing to the experience of slowness, and to the consciousness about time's passage, are Kubrick's centered, static compositions and slow moving actors. The performers' movements are often choreographed so that they move toward and away from the camera, attenuating the dynamism within the frame. Kubrick's film does not incorporate the technique of reverse motion, yet the ineluctable movement of the narrative of rise and fall, which returns the protagonist to his origins, provides a sense of undoing that has temporal implications, particularly in relation to the dynamics of succession, the losses of fathers and sons, that inform the story line. This process echoes Deren's discussion of reverse motion, which is not a case of true reversal in her mind but, instead, an "undoing of time" (158).

The potential of Kubrick's experiments with cinematic form in *Barry Lyndon*—his orchestration of multiple temporalities, his scrupulous attention to the aesthetic objects and visual culture that subtend the violent politics of Empire—seems to me to be the possibility for a new practice of spectatorship, one that works through the specter of boredom to link the intellectual and the emotional. Writing on Jean Renoir rather than Kubrick, Gilberto Perez links a slowed pace to a sense of consciousness: "that shot held for a moment longer than necessary to make the dramatic point; that extra moment . . . would arrest the movement of plot long enough for us to gain the sense of an apprehending mind behind the camera. [. . .] His camera, with its distinctive autonomous gaze, everywhere enacts an unmistakable movement of consciousness" (148). Instead of limiting that consciousness to a position behind the camera, I propose that Kubrick's work in *Barry Lyndon* creates a time for the spectator to reflect on her own movement of consciousness.

If we return to Sergei Eisenstein, a film theorist Kubrick spoke about (see Nelson 7), the temporal implications of this process can be seen at another level of precision. In "The Psychology of Art," Eisenstein discusses the generation of emotions in art, proposing that our affective responses have primal roots (1). He extols cinema as the culmination of all arts (3), and yet defines the hallmarks of that art as a regression to childhood or primitivity—a moving backward into magic, using the example of a circus.

In the "Conspectus of Lectures on the Psychology of Art," Eisenstein further explores these ideas from a Marxist perspective and argues that the union of affective and cognitive experiences is a feature of a "golden age": the historical period prior to the formation of social class. Eisenstein discusses the way films develop "a 'prescription' of sensuous thought in elements of the structure of form"; this unity leads the viewer (back) to experiences of primitive, tribal social structures in which emotionality and cognition were not split (11). Provocatively, he ends the "Conspectus" by defining the image of human thought as "a unity of the sensuous and the conscious—the prototype of an artistic image" (25). Setting aside the link between the sensuously conscious image and a premodern and precapitalist era, I would, nevertheless, propose that such images, those that unify the sensuous and the conscious, are precisely the ones that Kubrick achieves in *Barry Lyndon*, through formal strategies that challenge viewers' understanding and experiences of temporality, as well as through thematic elements that provoke thoughts about history, narrative form, and the veracity of images. In the chapters that follow, I attend to the thoughts and the emotions provoked by *Barry Lyndon's* temporalities, foregrounding "the highly emotional content associated with the experience of time" and, in particular, the "irresistibility of its passing away" (Reichenbach 2–3).

Historian Reinhart Koselleck has developed a theory of multiple, overlapping temporalities within modernity that lends a useful structure to the analysis of *Barry Lyndon* as a film concerned with modern time. Koselleck's multiple temporalities are "temporal layers that have different origins and duration and move at different speeds" and they pose an alternative "empty time of periodization" (Jordheim 170). Rejecting the linearity of modern time consciousness, Koselleck borrows from Herder to argue "no two worldly things have the same measure of time" (Herder quoted in Koselleck 2).

Koselleck identifies three primary modes of temporal experience: the first is the irreversibility of events (the sense of before and after); the second is the repeatability of events; and the third is the contemporaneity of the noncontemporaneous (or, the coexistence of multiple times) (95). The chapters that follow examine these modes of temporal experience as they are generated by and in *Barry Lyndon*.

In Chapter 2, I examine the problem of the irreversibility of events in relation to sequence in literature and cinema. I study Kubrick's adaptation of Thackeray's work, not only in terms of the authors' shared rejection of historical realism, but also in terms of their common interest in the temporalities associated with writing and reading and in the relationship between words and images. In Chapter 3, I explore the way that Kubrick's film explores concerns about historical change and representation. The chapter examines the film's discourse on succession in terms of visual and narrative form as well as theme. Carefully executed strategies of delay and interruption and a focus on paternity and succession bring together formal and affective registers.

Chapter 4 explores cyclical time and repetition as counterpoints to the sequentiality of Thackeray's Victorian serial, which was based upon a picaresque tale. The film's production history and Irish context are examined in relation to the odyssey, a temporal structure that recurs in Kubrick's work. As Marxist sociologist Henri Lefebvre asserts, "cyclical repetition and the linear repetitive separate out under analysis, but in *reality* interfere with one another constantly" (Lefebvre 8; emphasis in original). This is certainly also true here, as I make distinctions between these temporalities for the purpose of analysis.

Chapter 5 addresses the temporal regimes of painting and music in *Barry Lyndon*, drawing upon the interval—the gap, the rest, or the pause—and the closely allied matter of rhythm. Nietzsche argued that rhythm is the most primary sensation of time and, indeed, may be the form of time itself. My primary emphasis in the chapter is Kubrick's elaboration of the aesthetics of empire, notably through the use of the British portrait and landscape paintings as the picturesque environment in which his sublime Irish hero must function. The tensions that are produced between immediacy and artifice—a version of Michael Fried's absorption and theatricality—speak not only to narrative concerns but also to Kubrick's broader investigation of temporality and aesthetic form.

Chapter 6 explores the notion of the untimely in relation to *Barry Lyndon*. I situate the film in the milieu of 1970s cinema and probe the concept of the untimely, borrowing from Friedrich Nietzsche and Fredric Jameson. The untimely can also signify something that exists outside of time, which dovetails with the traditional framework for conceiving of the masterpiece. Jonathan Gil Harris writes, "The untimely is that which is out-of-time, inhabiting a moment but also alien to it. By resisting absorption into a homogeneous present, it also brings with it the difference that portends the future even as it conjures the past" (para 12). It might be said that *Barry Lyndon* inhabited 1970s cinema but was alien to it, both in terms of its modernist abstraction and its seemingly outdated genre. Thomas Elsaesser proposes that *Barry Lyndon* was a genre experiment that arrived ahead of schedule, becoming the "opposite" of the blockbuster (217), with its temporal profile of immediacy. In addition to this perspective, I consider the film in relation to the concept of lateness—"the idea of surviving beyond what is acceptable and normal" (Said 13)—as elaborated in the work of Edward Said and Theodor Adorno.

Barry Lyndon is remembered for its visual beauty and its tone of profound sadness, because these elements together create a site of mourning, not for the attributes of the historical time period—objects, textures, environments, and social regimes—but for the lost possibilities that permit us to imagine and experience different modes of time. *Barry Lyndon* both performs and enacts the loss of the fullness of time, a concept that derives from a Biblical phrase (*Galatians* 4:4–5, ESV), signifying not merely the culmination of a process, but also a sense of fruition, of proper completion. There is a tragic sense of incompleteness to *Barry Lyndon*, which relates to its narrative of masculine loss through gentlemanly violence, war, accident, and cupidity. The aesthetic and temporal frameworks of the film conspire with this narrative trajectory, offering the illusory comfort of lost times and providing a glimpse of imminent losses associated with the absorption of cinema's temporalities into newer technologies of representation.

2

Adapting *Barry Lyndon*:
A Tale of Two Auteurs

A great narrative is a kind of miracle.

Stanley Kubrick, 1971

[Stanley Kubrick] thought that Thackeray was better than any screenwriter alive.

Ken Adam, *Ken Adam and the Art of Production Design*

Stanley Kubrick "aspired to be the novelist of American filmmakers," according to Robert Kolker (97). His films have been compared to those of Max Ophuls, the Viennese director whose mobile camerawork Kubrick admired in a 1968 interview (Gelmis 104). Scholars, collaborators, and biographers have remarked upon the way Kubrick's grand visual style recalls that of Ophuls's "rapturous, delirious camera" (Herr 149). In a departure from the frequent comparisons made between Kubrick and Ophuls in terms of cinematography, Katharine McQuiston identifies similarities in their use of music, describing *Eyes Wide Shut* as Kubrick's greatest homage to Ophuls (191).

The two directors shared a fascination with the process of story development and screenplay construction. Laura Mulvey has proposed that Max Ophuls should be understood as a "director of adaptation" (75), a phrase that is equally appropriate as a description of Kubrick's career. His early years as a photojournalist and documentary filmmaker gave way to a clear commitment to narrative feature filmmaking, as he adapted the novels of Vladimir Nabokov, Anthony Burgess, Stephen King, Arthur Schnitzler, and William Makepeace Thackeray. According to Michael Herr, who coauthored the screenplay for *Full Metal Jacket* with Kubrick, the director "was drawn to his projects as much by the writing of the source material as by anything else" (185). Although Kubrick's relationship to screenplay credit has at times aroused controversy, most prominently in the case of *Spartacus*, what is not in dispute is that he contributed to the story development of all of his films.[1] He is credited as a writer on 12 of the 16 films he directed. In a 1971 interview, Kubrick said that he would never film a story he was not "finally in love with" (Houston 115).

Jan Harlan attributes Kubrick's intense focus on writers and writing to a recognition of his own lack of expertise: "Stanley was not a great writer. He had no false pride in this area and hired writers to help him" (Grey). Ken Adam's opinion concurs with this view: he told interviewer Christopher Frayling that Kubrick was "proven wrong" for the first time on *Barry Lyndon* when he learned that he couldn't "just shoot the book" (120). "Although Stanley could write," Adam states, "he wasn't a great scriptwriter by any means" (121). Kubrick also told Diane Johnson, with whom he cowrote the screenplay for *The Shining*, that he looked for novels that were not masterpieces so that he could improve upon them: the one exception to this rule, he claimed, was *Lolita* (Steensland, Ciment 293). Yet Kubrick rewrote Nabokov's screenplay, shortening it significantly, and ultimately used about 20 percent of his script by Nabokov's own reckoning.

Kubrick saw himself as an author beyond the construction of the screenplay. To him, directing was the "continuation of the writing" of a film (Kozarski 308). The production process often rendered scripted scenes open to modification through multiple takes, with Kubrick "always in search of a mysterious 'I-don't-know-what' that presumably he would recognize" (Naremore 5). Frederic Raphael observed about writing with Kubrick that the director "always knew what he didn't want" (122). In an interview with Vicente Molina Fox published in *El Pais* in 1980, Kubrick stated "no matter how good [the screenplay] looks on paper, the minute you start on the actual set, with the actors, you're terribly aware of not taking the fullest advantage of what's possible if you actually stick to what you wrote" (Fox).

---

[1] Since screenwriter Dalton Trumbo, a member of the "unfriendly ten" jailed for refusing to testify before HUAC, had been blacklisted, producer Edward Lewis placed his own name on the *Spartacus* script (adapted from Howard Fast's 1951 novel) when it was submitted to Universal, prior to Kubrick's involvement in the project. During later discussions among Kirk Douglas, Lewis, and Kubrick, the latter reportedly offered his own name in place of Trumbo's. According to Trumbo, Lewis decided to credit Trumbo and, ultimately, the film was celebrated for ending the blacklist. In his memoir, *I am Spartacus: Making a Film, Breaking the Blacklist* (2012), Kirk Douglas claims that he alone made the decision to credit Trumbo.

In the language of information processing theory, Kubrick worked in a serial rather than in a parallel mode. Diane Johnson found Kubrick to be unique among the directors with whom she collaborated in that he worked on only one project at a time (Steensland). He edited his films in their entirety at the end of the production process, which afforded the possibility of further modifications to the narrative, as he explained to Joseph Gelmis: "particularly when you're dealing with dialogue scenes, you have to look them over again and select portions of different takes and make the best use of them. The greatest amount of time in editing is this process of studying the takes and making notes and struggling to decide which segments you want to use [. . .] writing, shooting, and editing are what you have to do to make a film" (99). If Kubrick considered a great narrative a kind of miracle, his magic was hard won through a protracted process during which new ideas and possibilities, and opportunities for decisions, would invariably arise. Kubrick called movies "a series of creative and technical decisions" and the film director a "kind of idea and taste machine" (Gelmis 102). For better or for worse, his deliberately sequential process allowed for intervention at every point.

For most of his films, Kubrick adapted contemporary works of fiction: these include Lionel White's *Clean Break* (1955/*The Killing* 1956); Humphrey Cobb's *Paths of Glory* (1935/1957); Vladimir Nabokov's *Lolita* (1958/1962); Peter George's *Red Alert* (1958/*Dr. Strangelove* 1964); Arthur C. Clarke's "The Sentinel" (1951/*2001: A Space Odyssey* 1968); Anthony Burgess's *A Clockwork Orange* (1962/1971); and Stephen King's *The Shining* (1977/1980). Gustav Hasford's *Short-Timers* (1979) and Michael Herr's *Dispatches* (1977) served as source material for *Full Metal Jacket* (1987). *Eyes Wide Shut* (1999) was based on Arthur Schnitzler's *Traumnovelle* (1926), which was first published in installments in 1925. The link to Max Ophuls asserts itself again here, as Schnitzler's *Reigen* was the basis for Ophuls's *La Ronde* (1950).

This list provides evidence of Kubrick's commitment to narrative filmmaking, and it also suggests the potentially anomalous position of *Barry Lyndon* within his *oeuvre*. Adapted from William Makepeace Thackeray's 1856 novel, *The Memoirs of Barry Lyndon, Esq., Of the Kingdom of Ireland*, a first person faux memoir adapted from a serial adventure tale published in 11 installments in *Fraser's Magazine* in 1844 as *The Luck Of Barry Lyndon: A Romance of the Last Century, edited by George Savage Fitz-Boodle*, the film was the only one Kubrick made that was drawn from material written before the twentieth century. It is the second film for which he took the sole screenwriting credit; his previous film, *A Clockwork Orange*, for which he adapted Burgess's novel, was the first.

Writing *Barry Lyndon*: Texts in time

Barry Lyndon is one of three films that Kubrick set in the past. The other two deal with more properly—or at least more recognizably—historical protagonists, in contrast to the fictional Redmond Barry. They are *Spartacus*, based on Howard Fast's 1951 novel, whose historical events take place during the Third Servile War in 73–71 BCE[2] and *Paths of Glory*, which deals with an ignominious affair involving General Gerard Réveilhac's shelling of his own men in the French trenches during World War I (1914–18) and his subsequent execution of the four corporals he held responsible for the unit's failure to advance, an incident known as *L'affaire des caporaux de Souain*. The "Dawn of Man" sequence in *2001* is also set in the past, functioning as a fictional and anthropological prehistory of humankind, with a proto-human society populated by hybrid creatures Kubrick described as "man apes" (Gelmis 91).

The narrative shape of Kubrick's *Barry Lyndon* sets a naïve and newly fatherless Irish protagonist adrift against the backdrop of Europe's first industrial war. The young Redmond Barry is duped in an impetuous duel that he instigates because of his infatuation with his cousin Nora Brady. Believing himself to be running for his life, he is swindled and robbed by a highwayman and finds his only recourse is to join the army of King George II, who is allied with Prussia against France, Austria, and Russia. After numerous misadventures and the gallant rescue of a superior officer, Barry becomes a spy for the Prussians. He later escapes the military life and perfects his skills at gaming and swordplay with the help of a fellow Irishman who is masquerading as a Chevalier. Barry engineers a strategic marriage to the wealthy, landed Lady Lyndon. Attempting to secure a peerage by currying favor with George III, he sends a regiment to the American colonies. But Barry's abusive treatment of his wife and his stepson, Lord Bullingdon, and the death of his heir, the tenderly indulged Bryan, dash his hopes for a final social ascension that will pay dividends for future generations. After his resentful stepson Bullingdon challenges him to

---

[2] Kubrick preferred Arthur Koestler's 1939 novel *The Gladiators* to the Howard Fast novel because the former suggested the possibility that a variety of motives, both altruistic and self-interested, motivated the slaves' rebellion. See Natalie Zemon-Davis.

a duel—which culminates in the loss of his leg to an amputation—Barry must relinquish his claims to the Lyndon fortune, dissipated after years of overspending and mortgages. Lady Lyndon and Bullingdon endow Barry with an annuity provided he leaves England, and he disappears from the narrative in a scene that concludes with a freeze frame. This last detail is one of Kubrick's modifications, as Thackeray's novel ends with a bitter, insane Barry, cared for by his mother, writing the last pages of his memoir as a debtor in Newgate Prison.

Barry Lyndon not only deals with the mindless slaughter of the Seven Years' War and the brutal artifice that serves as the social scaffolding for the British aristocracy, it also contrasts these sanctioned forms of ritualistic violence with Redmond Barry's spontaneous and personal aggression, which erupts into seemingly unnecessary duels and immature brawling. As art historian Bille Wickre notes: "Despite his pursuit of a peerage through bribery, lavish spending and entertaining, Barry is unable to gain the status he desires because he fails repeatedly to control his emotions" (168). The subtext of the film thus addresses familiar Kubrick themes of individual freedom and social hierarchy, violence and control, and sexuality and masculinity. As I argue in Chapter 4, Barry's troubling emotionality connotes Irishness and is intimately tied to the film's dialectical treatment of empire and colony.

Like *Paths of Glory* and *Spartacus*, the *Barry Lyndon* tale explores a military milieu; unlike those two, it revolves around a character that is only very loosely based on an actual historical figure. In many ways, the project seems to define the high brow literary "tradition of quality" against which the *Cahiers du Cinemas* critics rebelled when they defined the film auteur. However, Kubrick took an approach to the cinematic adaptation of the realist novel that was strikingly different from the approach of the screenwriters whom Francois Truffaut set in opposition to the auteur in "A Certain Tendency in French Cinema" (1953–4). Truffaut argued that writers such as Jean Aurenche and Pierre Bost were "men of letters" who undervalued the cinema and relied upon "formulas, puns, and maxims" in their attempt to deliver psychological realism (226).

Kubrick's film, drawing from elements within Thackeray's source material, firmly rejects psychological realism. Thackeray's fictional memoir represents neither an historical novel nor a character study, but instead stands as a highly self-conscious exercise in verbal self-construction. The immediacy of the narrative voice and the artifice surrounding the memoir's storytelling apparatus are predicated on the temporal order of sequence and succession. But this ostensible adherence to sequence as the basis for cause and effect storytelling and self-construction is subtly undermined throughout the work and finally abandoned.

This chapter explores *Barry Lyndon's* origins in Thackeray's writing and in Kubrick's Napoleon project and examines the way that Thackeray and Kubrick both reject the assumptions of historical realism, including the attributes of the hero figure. This discussion, in turn, sets the stage for a reading of the film's dismantling of narrative sequence in Chapter 3. The analysis there reveals the way Kubrick's formal experiments articulate the aesthetic, political, and highly personal problematic of succession.

Film adaptation itself is a historical and sequential process, involving what is in contemporary parlance called versioning, which implies sequences of texts, successions of authors, and repetitions of ideas and tropes. Tom Gunning's lucid comments about film adaptation help to frame Kubrick's relationship to that process and to its temporal structure. "Adaptation," Gunning writes, "forges a relation to literature, rather than proclaiming independence from it" (42). A "literary appropriation" in Gunning's terms "[stakes] a claim or filiation to a specific work" (43). Eisenstein foregrounded the relationship of cinema to literary traditions and to realism through his citation of Dickens, and Kubrick does the same by invoking Thackeray: the relationship between film and literature is ratified and an affinity with a single literary work is announced. Gunning's use of the word "filial" proposes a generational, family resemblance and yet implies something a bit less directly patriarchal than "patrimony," which is the term Dudley Andrew uses to characterize this relationship (*Mists* 277). To examine *Barry Lyndon* as an adaptation is to ask, as Gunning does: "what does this film's appropriation of a literary text do: for the viewer, for the scholar, and perhaps most intriguingly, for filmmakers?" (44).

Leaving aside for a moment the marketing of *Barry Lyndon* as a literary adaptation, the most fundamental aspect of the filial relationship between a film and its literary source is what Gunning calls "textual transformation": the temporally marked and "frequently protracted process" that every narrative film undergoes as it moves from "verbal text to final filmic text" (43). Gunning characterizes cinema's earliest adaptations as transformations of verbal texts, revealing the way that temporality became fundamental to the adaptation process at the formal level. He writes that "peak moments" of narrative interest were extracted from literary sources because the running time for one-reelers did not allow the full appropriation of the literary work's "substantial narrative action" (44). As it happens, a similar temporal issue prevented Kubrick from adapting Thackeray's better-known work, *Vanity Fair*. He decided against that project because he anticipated difficulties in compressing the complex plot into a coherent screenplay within the appropriate running time for a narrative feature film.

The language of adaptation studies has come to rely primarily upon spatial rather than temporal metaphors, although these can be mixed together as well. In attempting to distinguish adaptation from intertextuality, for example, Dudley Andrew describes adaptation as a vertical line that is "ruled by past and future" and "anchors a film to its literary substrate" ("Economies" 27). He envisions intertextuality, by contrast, as a horizontal network in which "textual contagion counts more than interpretation" ("Economies" 27). This formula comes close to reproducing the too-neat dichotomy of the synchronic versus the diachronic. Andrew, perhaps intentionally, conflates terms related to time (past and future) and space (anchoring, horizontality), but finally privileges the spatial model of textual congress as contagion. This view is consistent with Robert Stam's notion of intertextual dialogism, wherein:

> every text forms an intersection of textual surfaces. All texts are tissues of anonymous formulae, variations on those formulae, conscious and unconscious quotations, and conflations and inversions of other texts. ("Dialogics" 64)

Andrew's and Stam's approaches emphasize spatial aspects of intertextuality—intersections and tissues—rather than temporal considerations. Thus they are not entirely helpful for marking the important difference between the adaptation of an explicitly "older" text and an "other" text.

In the case of *Barry Lyndon*, Kubrick consciously departed from his typical reliance on source material with contemporary salience and popular appeal (perhaps especially in the cases of *Lolita* and *A Clockwork Orange*). One reason Kubrick's costume drama was treated with indifference by the public—"written off as nothing more than a coffee-table movie, a day at the Prado without lunch" (Herr "Kubrick")—was partly that it, unlike nostalgia films such as *Bonnie and Clyde*, *Chinatown*, *American Graffiti*, and *The Great Gatsby*, emerged from and depicted not only a different world, but also an explicitly foreign, earlier world. Thackeray's nineteenth-century text defined eighteenth-century Ireland and Britain from the perspective of a foreign writer from an earlier century. Setting aside for a moment the defamiliarization of the film's slow pacing and voice-over narration, the era itself represented the distant past for North American audiences. The imminent US bicentennial provided one context for the story, which includes Redcoats, and Kubrick and Warner Brothers marketing staff took note of the event in correspondence regarding publicity. However, even the bicentennial project faltered when it attempted to grapple with the question of representing history. With American culture "plagued with a host of uncertainties about itself" (Clark 436) due to economic crisis, the evident fracture within the putative postwar consensus, and the political scandal of Watergate, it is unsurprising that subjects related to colonial and revolutionary era American history might be sensitive, a problematic that was made evident both in the cheerful boosterism of the musical *1776* (made into a film in 1972) and in the "grimness" and "oddness" of the "Bicentennial Minutes" that were televised from 1974 to 1976 on the CBS network (Marshall).[3]

If the American audience for *Barry Lyndon* had trouble assimilating the film within the fraught intertextuality of this pivotal historical moment, Kubrick's process of adapting Thackeray's *Barry Lyndon* clearly involved a different form of textual contagion, not least of which was its "infection" by Kubrick's Napoleon project. In what follows, I examine the development of Kubrick's *Barry Lyndon* as a process percolating through the Napoleon project, which might well have provoked the decision to adapt Thackeray's *Barry Lyndon* text. I then consider the intertextual dialogue between Thackeray and Kubrick, which revolves around a shared concern with war and heroism, but also around a keen interest on the part of both men in the temporal aspects of verbal and visual representation. I examine Kubrick and Thackeray's thematic and formal interests in formal and political questions related to realism, history, and fiction on the one hand, and heroism, narration, and character on the other.

Thackeray, Kubrick, and Napoleon

The genesis of the *Barry Lyndon* project was Stanley Kubrick's Napoleon film, a massive undertaking for which he began preproduction in 1967.[4] I am not

---

[3] The citation of Sarah Marshall's useful contribution to *The Awl*, a blog, reflects a dearth of scholarship on this important bit of US television history.

[4] Kubrick's fascination with Napoleon—like his penchant for chess—has been elevated to the status of an obsession and viewed as part of his eccentric directorial persona. But he is hardly unique in harboring a keen interest in Napoleon. In fact, the Corsican-born general continues to captivate the public in the twenty-first century: his martial exploits have engendered a board game, "Napoleon's Battles" (1989), and two video games "Waterloo: Napoleon's Last Battle" (2000) and "Napoleon: Total War" (2010).

alone in considering the transition from the Napoleon project to *Barry Lyndon* to be the first step in the process of adapting Thackeray's novel for the screen. Alexander Walker describes *Barry Lyndon* as a film "born on the rebound" (234) and production designed Ken Adam called it a "dress rehearsal" for the Napoleon film (Frayling 123). The historical frame for the narrative, set in the time period just prior to the Napoleonic wars, permitted Kubrick to repurpose at least a portion of the research he had undertaken for the Napoleon film. Kubrick told Joseph Gelmis "terrain is the decisive factor in the flow and outcome of a Napoleonic battle. We've researched all the battle sites exhaustively from paintings and sketches, and we're now in a position to approximate the terrain" (83). *Barry Lyndon*'s meticulously choreographed battle scenes, for which British military historian John Mollo consulted, make evident the investment made in the depiction of landscape and warfare.

Thackeray's engagement with Napoleon may well have captured Kubrick's attention during his research on the Napoleon film, as Kubrick reported that he read several hundred books on Napoleon (Gelmis) and Thackeray returned several times in his writing, across varied genres, to this seminal figure of modern warfare and imperial conquest. Born in Calcutta in 1811, Thackeray saw the deposed emperor in person as a prisoner on St. Helena in 1816 on his first voyage "home" to Britain to begin school. He incorporated Bonaparte's exploits as the critical backdrop to *Vanity Fair*—his best-known work and one that Kubrick considered adapting—and also depicted his antiheroine Becky Sharp as a female version of the "Corsican upstart."

Thackeray encountered the emperor on two occasions, in fact. Prior to writing *Vanity Fair*, Thackeray penned *The Second Funeral of Napoleon* (1841), an epistolary work addressed to the fictional Miss Amelia Smith. The substantial essay is an appropriate background text for *Barry Lyndon* because, like the memoir, it offers a first-person perspective, authored by a fictional persona, on remarkable historical events. In this case, the events are the removal of Napoleon's remains from St. Helena, where they had been buried in 1820, and their delivery to Paris for a state funeral on December 15, 1841. The essay introduces Thackeray's ironic writing style and articulates his views on militarism, nationalism, and masculinity. It also establishes his less than fervent commitment to realism when it comes to the development of characters and narrators.

The occasion Thackeray has chosen to write about represents a curious touchstone in narrative and historical terms: not only does it represent the uncanny repetition of a trauma that is typically experienced just once—a second burial, which may be seen as a metaphor for a second death—but it also speaks to the temporal implications of death. Death is a moment, the last in a sequence of life events, and yet the state that death ushers in endures (presumably for eternity, even without presuming any religious beliefs). It also calls up matters regarding legacy—crucially important in the case of Napoleon and his influence on world historical events. Reflecting the Victorian obsession with death, Thackeray explicates a particularly gruesome moment in which the English officials disinter the coffin and open it, confirming that the remains are Napoleon's and remarking upon how recognizable the corpse still is. Decades after his death, the passage reminds us, Napoleon remained an important and contested public figure, in whom emotions were invested.

In the first section of the essay, Thackeray sets the stage with a critique of the culture of militarism. He mocks the absurdity of Anglo-Gallic tensions and establishes the circumstances surrounding the exhumation. The fragile peace between England and France is threatened by events occurring in Egypt; this provokes the captain of the ship carrying Napoleon's remains to prepare for confrontation. The passage hilariously disdains pumped up masculinism, but, equally important, it helps us to recognize Thackeray's authorial techniques. In particular, he renders sequences with immediacy (but not without a slant) and then editorializes upon them, dramatizing and investing with emotion what might otherwise become dry historical reportage. First, he outlines the sequence:

> Here is the case. The English Government makes him [the French captain] a present of the bones of Napoleon: English workmen work for nine hours without ceasing, and dig the coffin out of the ground: the English Commissioner hands over the key of the box to the French representative, Monsieur Chabot: English horses carry the funeral car down to the sea-shore, accompanied by the English Governor, who has actually left his bed to walk in the procession and to do the French nation honor. (33)

Next, Thackeray inflates and excoriates the French captain's subsequent behavior, utilizing and ridiculing the man's own language; this takes place not as part of the sequence, but with a temporal delay that provides time and space for reflection on the part of the author and the reader. He offers his own opinions in a dramatic, dialogical form, making it clear that he is not exactly a disinterested witness to the events:

> After receiving and acknowledging these politenesses, the French captain takes his charge on board, and the first thing we afterwards hear of him is the

determination "*qu'il a su faire passer*" into all his crew, to sink rather than yield up the body of the Emperor *aux mains de l'etranger*—into the hands of the foreigner. My dear Monseigneur, is not this *par trop fort*? Suppose "the foreigner" had wanted the coffin, could he not have kept it? Why show this uncalled-for valor, this extraordinary alacrity at sinking? Sink or blow yourself up as much as you please, but your Royal Highness must see that the genteel thing would have been to wait until you were asked to do so, before you offended good-natured, honest people, who—heaven help them!—have never shown themselves at all murderously inclined towards you. (34)

Penned under the obvious pseudonym Michael Angelo Titmarsh, *The Second Funeral* possesses several hallmarks of the *Barry Lyndon* narratives to come. First, its author stands apart from the material as both a legible and unstable figure. Contemporary readers would have recognized the imprimatur of Titmarsh as one of Thackeray's many personas. But Thackeray's frequent use of an editorializing voice creates slippages between story and narrator and among various narrators, undermining presumptions of authorial authenticity related to any one voice.

Moreover, the piece opens with a passage that self-consciously questions the appropriate position for the author to take in relation to the genre of the material presented and thus foregrounds Thackeray's interest in the distinction between historical and fictional modes of representation. In terms of content, Titmarsh comments directly on the status of the heroic, a conundrum to which Thackeray and Kubrick repeatedly return in their *Barry Lyndon* texts and in other work:

Many and many is the puzzle that I have had in reading History (or the works of fiction which go by that name), to know whether I should laud up to the skies, and endeavor, to the best of my small capabilities, to imitate the remarkable character about whom I was reading, or whether I should fling aside the book and the hero of it, as things altogether base, unworthy, laughable, and get a novel, or a game of billiards, or a pipe of tobacco, or the report of the last debate in the House, or any other employment which would leave the mind in a state of easy vacuity, rather than pester it with a vain set of dates relating to actions which are in themselves not worth a fig, or with a parcel of names of people whom it can do one no earthly good to remember. (1–2)

I cite Thackeray at length here to suggest the way in which, in a long sentence with a surprisingly vigorous forward momentum, the heroic and the historical are thoroughly conflated. In the author's view, neither one is worth a fig. Titmarsh continues, placing his skepticism regarding heroic aspirations and the place of

truth in history writing front and center and moving his conceit from the verbal
into the visual register:

> As we can't be virtuous, let us be decent. Fig leaves are a very decent, becoming
> wear and have been now in fashion for four thousand years. And so my dear,
> history is written on fig leaves. (4)

On a formal level, these passages reveal the important interaction of sequence,
speed, and delay, the critical and distanced stance of the first person narrator,
and the writer's skillful employment of visual figures. Titmarsh's jaded view of
history foreshadows two epistemological concerns in *Barry Lyndon*. First, how
are sequential plotting and narrative voice implicated in historical representation?
Second, does the value of historical and fictional representation lie solely in the
reader's imitation of the implausibly heroic figures encountered there? I return
to these questions after concluding my discussion of the textual contagion of the
Napoleon project.

Kubrick's historical research for the Napoleon film casts a long shadow
across *Barry Lyndon*. His ambitious preproduction process spawned a vast
archive that has itself become an object of fascination, as documented in
Alison Castle's *Stanley Kubrick's Napoleon: The Greatest Movie Never Made*
(2009). The continuing interest in Kubrick's research in the age of archive fever
became evident in 2011 when the studio Creative Differences announced plans
to revisit this subject in a documentary entitled *Kubrick/Napoleon* examining
the director's years of research on the film. *The Observer*'s Philip French
writes, somewhat snarkily, about the high expectations surrounding the
Napoleon project, then and now, and links the hyperbole to *Barry Lyndon*—
another inheritance of the successor film. "One wonders [. . .] whether
[Kubrick's] *Napoleon* would have been 'the best film ever made'—although
his subsequent historical movie *Barry Lyndon* has grown in stature over the
years" (3). French treats *Barry Lyndon* as an historical movie rather than a
costume drama, a generic conflation stemming in part from its proximity to
the Napoleon film.

Several different accounts plausibly explain Kubrick's shelving of the Napoleon
project. One attributes his deferral to the 1970 release of Sergei Bondarchuk's
unsuccessful epic, *Waterloo*, produced by Dino de Laurentis and starring Rod
Steiger as Napoleon, which not only upstaged Kubrick but also had the temerity
to do so poorly at the box office that it jeopardized his ability to secure financing.
Roger Ebert panned *Waterloo* as neither a good nor an interesting film (Ebert)

and *The New York Times*'s Roger Greenspun disparaged "the particular dullness of Bondarchuk's attempt to translate history into cinema" which made *Waterloo* a "very bad movie" (50). Another explanation for Kubrick's deferral of the Napoleon project, this one forwarded by Alexander Walker and John Baxter, makes recourse to the broader destabilization of the US film industry in the early 1970s. In 1971, MGM announced that it was scaling back film production, and subsequent changes in leadership there affected the rainmakers that Kubrick had counted on, including Robert O'Brien (Baxter 264, Walker 234).

Kubrick may have sought to "translate history into cinema" with the Napoleon project. He cited the enduring impact of Napoleon's conquests in the Joseph Gelmis interview: "[I]n a very concrete sense, our own world is the result of Napoleon" (83). Yet Jan Harlan offers additional insight into why this particular figure was so compelling to Kubrick: "Napoleon represented for him the worldly genius that at the same time failed" (Newsletter). Speaking on a Charlie Rose television program that brought together Jan Harlan, Kubrick's widow Christiane (Harlan's sister), and Martin Scorsese to discuss Kubrick's career, Harlan characterizes Kubrick's view on the reason for Napoleon's ultimate failure: "in the end, the emotions carried him away" (Charlie Rose).

For *Barry Lyndon*, however, Kubrick selected a very particular kind of story to tell: he chose a fictional narrative that also focuses on the colossal failure of a man whose skill and intellect are ultimately undermined by his ambition. The fictional character of Redmond Barry bears some similarities to the historical figure of Napoleon in that he sets his sights on power and patrimony but overreaches; his emotional outbursts and tendency toward violence finally undercut the social position he has acquired through his skill as a soldier, swordsman, and seducer. Barry navigates the rarefied heights of the British aristocracy after the Seven Years' War, the pan-European conflict that presaged both the French Revolutionary wars (1792–1802) and the Napoleonic wars (1803–15). Barry rises and falls, descending into ignominy and exile on the brink of the French Revolution, the historical event that brought Napoleon to prominence.

Using a chronological model of history, the Redmond Barry narrative might appropriately serve as prologue to the Napoleon tale, with the Barry character standing as the emperor's plucky but less successful sire. Another perspective would argue for the reverse of this filial relation, however, proposing that the Napoleon project, and its interest in the ambitious, but ultimately doomed, pursuit of victory at all costs, gave birth to *Barry Lyndon*. The recursive, nonlinear conceptualization of succession implied by the relationship between these two projects is emblematic of the concerns with history and heroism, and sequence and succession that Thackeray and Kubrick bring to their respective *Barry Lyndon*s.

A tale of two auteurs

As I examined the linkages between William Makepeace Thackeray and Stanley Kubrick through the prism of the Napoleon project, it occurred to me that the story of *Barry Lyndon* might be rendered as a tale of two auteurs, separated by a century. I have speculated, in a somewhat unscholarly way, about whether, in the midst of the disappointment associated with not just deferring but possibly burying the Napoleon project (Napoleon's third burial?), Stanley Kubrick found solace and inspiration in the work of a writer who seemed in so many ways a kindred spirit. Here I briefly pursue the "deep-structural relationship" between Kubrick and Thackeray that James Naremore alludes to in *On Kubrick*, but leaves largely unexplored (176).

The two artists shared a remarkable physical resemblance, which is made visible in their numerous and often humorous self-portraits (see Figures 2.1 and 2.2). In these self-images, each man arms himself with a tool of the trade, protecting and deflecting the question of authorial authenticity. More important, Kubrick and Thackeray approach a number of political and aesthetic interests in a similar fashion in their work. As Naremore observes, the two embrace caricature and satire (176); furthermore, both developed reputations for leveling attacks at the military and high society and for exposing hypocrisy of all kinds. Thackeray's subject of interest in his early works was "the scoundrel–gentleman" (Anisman 2)—a term that describes many of Kubrick's characters as well, from the corrupt generals in *Paths of Glory* to Bill Harford's colleagues in *Eyes Wide Shut*. Michael Herr notes that, for Kubrick "hypocrisy was not some petty human foible, it was the corrupted essence of our predicament" (44).

There is much biographical common ground between Thackeray and Kubrick. Neither one was particularly interested or attained particular distinction in school, and both exercised their artistry from an early age: in Thackeray's case, drawing and writing, and in Kubrick's, photography, working at *Look* magazine at age 17. Both attained success and even fame and became household names in their lifetimes, yet they faced equal measures of criticism and praise throughout their careers. Thackeray's position in the literary world of his era was not unlike that of Kubrick in post-Hollywood American film culture. Charles Dickens,

Figure 2.1 Thackeray's sketched self-portrait, from *Vanity Fair* (1847–8).

whose "literary and economic forms of consecration confirm[ed] each other" (Payne 68) was to Thackeray what Coppola, Spielberg, and Lucas, with their massive 1970s blockbusters, became in relation to Kubrick. "While performing much of the best of his life's work," Anthony Trollope wrote of Thackeray, "he was not sure of his market, not certain of his readers, his publishers, or his price; nor was he certain of himself" (17). As Thackeray himself put it after completing *Barry Lyndon* in June 1845: "I can suit the magazines, but I can't hit the public" (quoted in Payne 163, n. 1).

The reception of their versions of *Barry Lyndon*, a mid-career work for both Thackeray (who died at the age of 53 in 1864) and Kubrick, was no exception. Thackeray's tale met with a disappointing response a century before Kubrick's disappointing turn with *Barry Lyndon* at the box office. Thackeray's story failed to captivate Victorian readers because of "its antihero, its sordid subject matter, and its deliberate emotional detachment" (Colby 109), the latter complaint echoing

Figure 2.2 Kubrick's photographic self-portrait, c. 1946. Courtesy of the Stanley Kubrick Archive, London College of Communication, London.

numerous observations and critiques of Kubrick's work. Thackeray dissuaded his own daughter from reading the book, but Anne Thackeray Ritchie was quoted in *The New York Times* as rendering a verdict that, while *Barry Lyndon* "is scarcely a book to like" still, "one has to admire it for its consummate power and mastery" ("Thackeray's 'Barry Lyndon'").

In terms of their approach to their artistry, Kubrick and Thackeray practiced satire to such an extent that their contemporaries accused them of cynicism. Thackeray's "The Chronicle of the Drum," a poem that accompanied *The Second Funeral of Napoleon* gives voice to sentiments clearly on display in the four films by Kubrick that deal with war and the military: *Paths of Glory, Dr. Strangelove, Barry Lyndon,* and *Full Metal Jacket*:

> Tell me what we find to admire
>
> In epaulets and scarlet coats
>
> In men, because they load and fire
>
> And know the art of cutting throats. (quoted in Prawer 136)

Anthony Trollope wrote about this aspect of Thackeray's reputation in terms of the writer's obsession with "the ill side of things":

> as a writer he has certainly taken upon himself the special task of barking at the vices and follies of the world around him [. . .] it has to be confessed that Thackeray did allow his intellect to be too thoroughly saturated with the aspect of the ill side of things. (207)

Furthermore, nineteenth-century critics accused Thackeray of "adopting too superior an attitude towards his personages, and therefore towards mankind" (Tillotson and Hawes 14). This accords with critical accounts of Kubrick that praise and blame him in equal measure for his coldness and his "cynical nihilism" (Sharrett, quoted in Sperb 142; Webster 110). Theodore Martin's gloss of Thackeray, published in 1853, could serve as a description of either Thackeray or Kubrick:

> Here was a man who looked below the surface of things, taking nothing for granted, and shrinking from no scrutiny of human motives, however painful; [. . .] he had the courage to be simple. To strip sentimentalism of its frippery, pretension of its tinsel, vanity of its masks, and humbug literary society of its disguises, appeared to be the vocation of this graphic satirist. (170)

While Thackeray and Kubrick are linked to particular national traditions and time periods—Victorian literature and postwar American cinema—each one evinced a broader international, sensibility. They lived and traveled beyond their national contexts, without rejecting or distancing themselves from them. Thackeray, born in Calcutta, visited and wrote about London, Paris, Ireland, Spain, Portugal, Greece, Egypt, the United States, and Germany. In *William Thackeray: The Critical Heritage*, Tillotson and Hawes point out that Thackeray's writing was translated into French and German and observe that the ethos of his work, "unlike that of Dickens, was from the start as much European as English" (1).

Both men raised three daughters, with one following in their footsteps. Anne Thackeray became Lady Ritchie and enjoyed a career as a writer, while Vivian Kubrick made the documentary film *The Making of the Shining* and composed music (under a pseudonym) for *Full Metal Jacket*. They were both private, but not reclusive, men who enjoyed sociality under the appropriate circumstances; as Trollope wrote of Thackeray: "he was not a man to be valuable at a dinner-table as a good talker. It was when there were but two or three together that he was happy himself and made others happy" (31). Kubrick did not participate in the Hollywood social circuit but was well known for frequent phone calls to film director friends and for his hospitality at his homes outside London (first at Borehamwood and later at Chidwickbury). In his interview with Vicente Molina Fox, Kubrick called Los Angeles "the most unreal place"—but did not feel "isolated or cut off culturally in any way" in England (Fox). Michael Herr and Vincent LoBrutto have debunked the mythology of Kubrick as a recluse, but confirm that he valued his privacy.

In contrast to Kubrick's disinterest in public appearances, Thackeray established a reputation as a public speaker and became highly regarded in the United States after two tours in the 1850s. In fact, his January 23, 1864 obituary in *Harper's* indicates the esteem with which he was held in the United States; the writer lavishes Thackeray with praise for his incisive critique of society, calling him "a Bersekir in the mask of Mephistopheles, refusing to accept amiability for fidelity, or politeness for humanity. He was called a cynic by the snobs and a snob by the cynics" ("William Thackeray" 60).

Thackeray's obituary presages the transition of the Late Victorian era into modernity; the encomium appears only a few pages removed from a portrait of the Hon. Leland Stanford, former governor of California and then president of the Central Pacific Railroad. Eight years after the publication of Thackeray's obituary and Stanford's portrait, Stanford would commission Eadweard Muybridge to produce serial photographic studies of his prize horses to settle the question of whether or not they raise all four hooves when they gallop.

It would be inappropriate to imply that the biographical parallels I have drawn between these two men played a role in Kubrick's embrace of Thackeray's *Barry Lyndon* as the successor to the Napoleon project. Whereas Ken Adam attributes Kubrick's decision to adapt Thackeray's *Barry Lyndon* to the director's deep admiration for Thackeray's writing (Frayling 120), others point to pragmatic matters surrounding this adaptation process. James Naremore notes that the novel's obscurity offered several advantages: "little known outside the academy, it was a relatively minor fiction that could be freely adapted, and was in the public domain" (170). In addition to these reasons, I believe it is also possible that Kubrick developed an interest in, and a respect for, the work of Thackeray, possibly because he recognized common themes and a similar approach to form in the writer's work.

Words, images, and reading time

Contained within the astute and often hilarious critiques that Thackeray and Kubrick produced lies a shared fascination with the formal properties of their respective art forms, and, more specifically, with the complex intellectual, emotional, and temporal process of narrative, which they both explored as a dynamic interplay between verbal and visual representation. Hence Thackeray contemporary Theodore Martin's comment, reproduced earlier, that Thackeray was a graphical satirist. To put it simply, Thackeray and Kubrick were fascinated with the way visual imagery creates tension with, rather than merely illustrating, verbal narrative elements such as structure, point of view, character development, and plotting. That tension stimulates a thought process that assimilates the two modes, and produces a temporal delay in the experience of reading or watching. This is the structure that produces the possibility of aesthetic time, of thinking and feeling.

Several exemplary works make clear this aesthetic interest. Kubrick's now-famous first published photograph (Figure 2.3), depicting a newsagent apparently reacting to the news of FDR's death, makes meaning through a juxtaposition of text and image. The portrait harks back to Soviet Montage theories of the image; in a sense, it presents a version of the Kuleshov effect because it produces meaning through collage. While the image does not acquire its meaning from a sequential relation to other images, which is the essence of the Kuleshov effect, it solicits a similar type of cognitive and emotional movement. Viewers read the man's expression through the printed text headline, moving back and forth across the space of the frame. A different headline would render the man's features open to a different interpretation. In *Stanley Kubrick at Look Magazine: Authorship and Genre in Photojournalism and Film*, Phillipe Mather emphasizes the importance of Kubrick's early photojournalism and, importantly, his work on the photo essay, to his later career as a filmmaker. I would push this observation a little further and make it far more specific: the movement-based molecular form of the image–text relation found in his photography is carried through his film work.

Figure 2.3 Kubrick's first published photograph, *Look* Magazine, June 26, 1945. Courtesy of the Stanley Kubrick Archive, London College of Communication, London.

One possible framework for describing this process—although it fails to capture this relation fully—can be traced back to Eisenstein's dialectical montage theory. I refer not to Eisenstein's discussion of the dynamism or conflict between frames, but his theories regarding volumes within the frame. In "A Dialectical Approach to Film Form," Eisenstein asks:

> what comprises the dynamic effect of a painting? The eye follows the direction of an element in the painting. It retains a visual impression, which then collides with the impression derived from following the direction of a second element. The conflict of these directions forms the dynamic effect in apprehending the whole. (50)

Eisenstein then specifically cites lines, color, size, and proportion as graphic elements that can produce conflict within a painting or film frame.

Text and image juxtapositions introduce another order of complexity to this discussion. These combinations are more akin to Eisenstein's intellectual montage, where ideas, in addition to emotions, are brought into play through the collage of sequential images. Maria Nikolajeva and Carole Scott, who are scholars of word and text interaction, have developed a terminology to describe these interactions in picture books for children. They describe counterpointing and contradictory dynamics in which "ambiguity challenges the reader to mediate between words and pictures to establish a true understanding of what is being depicted" (226). In Kubrick's ironic, layered, and yet sequential *Barry Lyndon* text, that mediation process of counterpoint and contradiction engages intellectual and affective registers and animates the pictures and the paintings in Eisenstein, while also consuming time.

A survey of other early photographs of Kubrick's, many of them published in *Look* magazine and now archived at the Museum of the City of New York, reveals numerous examples of such juxtapositions of lines, volumes, and proportions as well as textual or graphic elements, often but not always involving street signs. The most fascinating collages may be those from an early assignment, "Art by Celebrities" (1948), which documents an art show sponsored by the Urban League that included stars such as Joan Crawford, Linda Darnell, Cornell Wilde, and Margaret O'Brien. Kubrick's frontal, stagy images depict celebrities posing with paintings they have just completed. In this case, the meaning of the image is dependent primarily upon the graphic interaction between two iconic elements: the visually beautiful star and the aspirationally beautiful—if only through wishful thinking—artwork.

Examples of image and graphic juxtapositions within the same frame appear often in Kubrick's films. They pervade *Killer's Kiss* (in the stairwell and outside the club), *The Killing* (racetrack signs), *Dr. Strangelove* (signs at Burpelson military base), and *Full Metal Jacket* (Joker's Helmet as well as billboards in Saigon). Jack's gibberish book in *The Shining* condenses the verbal and visual signifiers of his insanity. The opening sequence of *Day of the Fight* (1951) presents text and image juxtapositions as well: in fact, posters announcing the Cartier-Evans fight scheduled for that evening introduce the protagonist (Figure 2.4).

In each case, the graphic and linguistic import of the text is critical to the interpretation of the image and demands that the reader take note of text and image both as part of the story world and as metacommentary. Even though the intertitles and voice over narration in *Barry Lyndon* might be considered non-diegetic linguistic elements, the ornate, flourishing text and Michael Holdern's plummy British voice blur the boundary between the story world and the frame. The most important instances of this method of dialectical observation occur in scenes involving the juxtaposition of graphic elements, notably paintings and people (reminiscent of the Celebrity Art Show); often the reverse zoom is used to enhance the "reading" process.

Reading images in this way introduces mobility and temporal delay; a deliberate strategy on Kubrick's part that originates in the readerly challenges embedded in Thackeray's source material. Thackeray was, from his earliest

Figure 2.4 Words and images foreshadow the main event in the opening moments of *Day of the Fight* (1951).

years, a sketch artist. He sketched in nearly everything he read—"as if he could not read without *seeing*" (Fisher 61). He reportedly asked Charles Dickens for a job as an illustrator early in his career. Thackeray scholar Robert Fletcher alludes to "Thackeray's narrative imagination" as being "ekphrastic by training, if not by nature" (379). In arguing that Thackeray's "novels provide a rich field in which to study the workings—both cognitive and historical—of the picture story, a textual form that has become endemic in modern and postmodern cultures" (379), Fletcher suggests that his work is relevant to the contemporary picture book and graphic novel; I would extend that body of texts to include cinema. Early in his career, when he was living in Germany, Thackeray planned to create a "multi-media book" comprising text and illustrations of German culture, "the goal of which was to supplement his verbal critique with his own drawings" (Prawer 89). This project never came to fruition, but S. S. Prawer considers Thackeray's travel literature, including the *Paris Sketchbook* and *Irish Sketchbook*, to be manifestations of this impetus to join word and image (89).

Kamilla Elliott writes at length about the visual aspect of Thackeray's work, emphasizing the way *Vanity Fair* confounds the categories of static versus dynamic art forms proposed by Lessing's eighteenth-century aesthetic theory. She emphasizes the dialectics of movement and stasis, supporting the treatment of Thackeray's writing as cinematic:

> The vignettes of Thackeray's *Vanity Fair*, for example, are combinations of movement and freezing—instances where Lessing's categorical opposition of movement and stasis merge in a single pictorial form. Interspersed between lines of moving prose, they at times seem to leap out from that movement, carrying with them both the mobility of the prose and their own mobile pictorial leap from it, freezing momentarily before diving into the prose stream again. (19)

Elliott links this writing practice—and the experience of reading that it engenders—to early cinema, because Thackeray's vignettes become "arrested mobile moments" that leap in and out of a "stream of fluid prose" (19).

Like Elliott, Robert Fletcher draws on cinematic analogies and the paradox of movement and stillness to characterize Thackeray's approach to writing. However, Fletcher moves beyond formalism to remark upon the way in which Thackeray's construction of temporal tension articulates the thematics of subjectivity and the complexity of historical thinking:

> Perhaps parodying Victorian progressivism, Thackeray reverses the direction of the jump cuts so that the juxtaposed images lead him and his reader into the past, but the conclusion to this journey is still a sense of subjectivity as fragmented, as split between two time frames. (392)

Fletcher situates Thackeray at the transition to modernity, ultimately implicating his work in the decentering of the modern subject (380).

For Fletcher, Thackeray's picture stories do more than simply convey a tone of skepticism; they produce a reading practice with a double movement "horizontally through the narrative and vertically over that same ground" that instills a "skepticism of seamless realities, whether textual or imagistic" (386).

According to Judith Fisher, Thackeray's "speaking pictures" establish alternative plot lines and present "countervoices" that challenge Thackeray's narration (Fisher 60-1). She provides an example from *Vanity Fair* in which:

> the very sincerity of Becky and Sir Pitt aligns with the falsity suggested by the pictures [they are positioned beneath]. [. . .] Again, the illustration subtly betrays Becky [. . .] act[ing] as an ironic mirror, turned outward from the story to show us alternative truths of character and event. (66-7)

Here, image and text destabilize each other. Thackeray "looks askance at his own story": the narratives produced (and unravelled) using these techniques are rife with "pictorial-verbal narrative dissonances" that disrupt the narrative flow—despite Thackeray's fluid and energetic prose—and thwart the realism that underlies his novels (Elliott 43–6).

Textual destabilization through the stop and start cognitive process of reading, looking, pausing, and revising lies at the heart of Thackeray's aesthetic in *Barry Lyndon* as well and is translated to the screen in Kubrick's film. The implications for this integration of image and text are both temporal and hermeneutical: "a skeptical process of reading and seeing evolves that compels readers to endlessly revise what they have read and seen" (Fisher 72). That process of revision slows the act of reading because reflection is embedded in the layers of textuality, image, and even caricature. This formal and political–philosophical aspect of Thackeray's work, I am arguing, may have resonated with Kubrick, leading him to adapt the Redmond Barry narrative.

In addition to this temporal and processual element, Thackeray's use of irony further contributes to a doubled effect, namely the double vision of caricature as norm and deviation, in Rudolf Arnheim's formulation. For Arnheim, caricature has the potential to undermine the authenticity of realist time and space. As Judith Fisher observes, "the narrator's assertion in *Vanity Fair* that 'the world is a looking glass and gives back to every man the reflection of his own face' denies the traditional role of the artist's mirror: to reflect empirical reality" (67).

A key point here is the caricature's connection with empirical reality. As with Kubrick's film—which, although elaborately stylized, was also lauded as a quasi-documentary—Thackeray's source material and first person narration were seen as establishing an ostensible linkage with empirical, historical reality, only to depart from it. Thackeray based his story on numerous historical sources, some of which would have been well known to his audience. The claims to realism for Kubrick's film are engendered primarily through technique rather than through historical reference (this perhaps due to Thackeray's and Kubrick's different audiences), including the highly publicized costume replicas and the candlelight filming.

Revising history

In trading his Napoleon project for *Barry Lyndon*, Kubrick exchanged a story about a world-renowned emperor and military genius for a fictional character Thackeray loosely based upon a minor historical figure: an eighteenth-century Anglo-Irish soldier named Andrew Robinson Stoney (1747–1810), who became known as Stoney Bowes after his marriage to Mary Eleanor Bowes, Countess of Strathmore and Kinghorne, an ancestor of Elizabeth II. Mary Eleanor was a playwright and botanist, and probably the richest woman in England at the time. Thackeray learned about the Stoney Bowes saga from John Bowes, Mary Eleanor Bowes's grandson. Stoney is important to *Barry Lyndon* both because he was an actual historical personage and because he represents the type of historical figure—a complete scoundrel—whom Thackeray and Kubrick could use to ratify their patently antiheroic skepticism regarding human beings and the representation of history.

In his heyday, nearly a century before Thackeray wrote the *Barry Lyndon* serial, Andrew Robinson Stoney tricked the wealthy, widowed Bowes into marrying him in an extraordinary story documented in Wendy Moore's *Wedlock: How Georgian Britain's Worst Husband Met His Match*. Stoney arranged for scurrilous accusations regarding Mary Eleanor Bowes's morals to be published anonymously in the society paper *The Morning Post* (Sunniside) and then colluded in a faked duel—a pivotal plot point in Thackeray's and Kubrick's *Barry Lyndon* texts—with the editor of the publication. In appearing to defend her honor to the very death—his imminent demise was pronounced by the famous surgeon Jesse Foote—Stoney won the widow's hand, as she agreed to marry him on his deathbed. He was carried to the altar on a stretcher. After a miraculous recovery, he subjected the Countess to years of beatings and starvation, but his attempts to acquire her fortune were unsuccessful. She escaped from him with the help of a servant and initiated divorce proceedings that became a national *cause célèbre*. At this point, Stoney Bowes purchased a newspaper, the better to slander his wife's reputation. A 1787 trial publicly revealed the lengths to which Stoney Bowes had gone—abductions and starvation were two favored techniques—and prompted London debating societies to pose the question: "whether a Lady that is married to a tyrannical husband be more likely to promote her own happiness by a spirited opposition or a patient submission to his temper and conduct?" (quoted in Foyster 84). The divorce was granted in 1789; Stoney Bowes was sentenced to prison for abducting his wife during their divorce proceedings. He died there in 1810, 10 years after the death of his former wife, who was buried in Westminster Abbey.

Two additional sources for Thackeray's fictional antihero include the tribulations of Lady Cathcart, a wealthy English woman held prisoner for years by her fortune-seeking Irish husband, Colonel Hugh Maguire, and *Castle Rackrent* (1800), Anglo-Irish writer Maria Edgeworth's novel, based in part upon the Cathcart saga. Thackeray may also have followed press accounts of the divorce of Caroline Sheridan Norton (playwright Richard Sheridan's granddaughter), whose public airing of her grievances against her abusive husband in the late 1830s was instrumental in the passage of the Married Woman's Property and Divorce Act in the 1850s.

Thackeray also borrowed from "Adventures of Mr. James Freeny," a sensational narrative about an amoral Irish highwayman, which he read during his visit to Ireland in 1842, when he began the *Irish Sketch Book*. In fact, Thackeray spends 14 pages of the *Irish Sketch Book* deconstructing the hero's unnecessarily vicious and duplicitous behavior toward his victims and co-conspirators and rejecting the romanticization of that behavior by the book's narrators. The savage irony developed in this extended passage lays the foundation for the double-voiced first person narration that Thackeray employs when he revises his 11-part serial, *The Luck of Barry Lyndon*, into *The Memoirs of Barry Lyndon* (1856). Writing again as Titmarsh, Thackeray expresses his disapproval of the esteem in which the narrators hold the troubling figure of the highwayman:

> In Freeny's life, one man may see the evil of drinking, another the harm of horse-racing, another the danger attendant on early marriage, a fourth the exceeding inconvenience as well as hazard of the heroic highwayman's life—which a certain Ainsworth, in company with a certain Cruikshank, have represented as so poetic and brilliant, so prodigal of delightful adventure, so adorned with champagne, gold lace, and brocade. (164)

The passage hints at the strategy Thackeray would ultimately employ in the *Barry Lyndon* memoir, with its unwittingly honest first person narration from the perspective of a complete scoundrel. He mockingly marvels at the hero's:

> noble naïveté [. . .] as he recounts his own adventures, and the utter unconsciousness that he is narrating anything wonderful. It is the way of all great men, who recite their great actions modestly, and as if they were matters of course; as indeed to them they are. (164)

In fact, Captain Freeny does pen his memoirs, as Thackeray's fictional Redmond Barry will do as well. This writerly undertaking arises only after Freeny fails to drum up protection money from the local squires whom he has robbed and terrorized. Thackeray sounds a note of sympathy for the man who learns that he must write for a living:

> On going out of jail, Counsellor Robbins and Lord Carrick proposed a subscription for him—in which, strangely, the gentlemen of the county would not join, and so that scheme came to nothing; and so he published his memoirs

in order to get himself a little money. Many a man has taken up the pen under similar circumstances of necessity. But what became of Captain Freeny afterwards does not appear. (179)

Here, history itself become a compromised affair in the hands of the highwayman and those who valorize his deeds. The explicit suggestion that such autobiographical stories are repeated ("Many a man") casts the field of autobiography, and perhaps writing more generally, in a jaundiced light. Yet, nothing further has been reported about Freeny, which renders his historical legacy doubtful.

Thackeray's *Barry Lyndon* draws upon these stories, histories, and fictions, its author but not necessarily its narrator recognizing the complex interplay among these genres. The memoirist unwittingly parodies the sentimental novel of Thackeray's day as well as historical epics of the Walter Scott variety, books whose heroes are anything but heroic. Thackeray's fictional memoir is a *tour de force* in linguistic doublespeak, giving lie to the idea that a first person narration guarantees veracity. In short, it is a self-aware critique of realism. To Robert Fletcher, Thackeray's approach to fiction, which "forces readers to test both the speaker's coherence as well as their own grounds for judgment," reflects a mistrust of positivism: "Thackeray seems to be writing against this background of confidence in the factual (i.e. 'real') story" (493–4). In his comments on Thackeray's overall career, Fletcher pinpoints the philosophical questions at the heart of *Barry Lyndon* as both novel and film. Thackeray's writing:

> undermine[s] the link in Western philosophy between representation and knowledge, the link reforged by Carlyle's metaphor for humanity, the "living mirror" that reflects the world. In every Thackerayan fiction, and in every fiction in general (according to Thackeray), that mirror is warped, cracked and beyond repair. (495)

The warped mirror is an especially useful and visual metaphor for cinematic representation that returns us to the adaptation process, the notion of textual contagion, and the positioning of *Barry Lyndon* within Kubrick's *oeuvre*. If we closely examine the self-disclosing narrator in Thackeray's *Barry Lyndon*, we find that his verbiage rivals the similarly naïve self-justification of central characters in many Kubrick films: he is verbally adept like Humbert Humbert in *Lolita* and a virulent narcissist like Alex De Large in *A Clockwork Orange*. Like Jack Torrence, he is a frustrated writer whose grasp on reality has become compromised in ways that become glaringly apparent.

The self-made man

The opening paragraphs of *The Memoirs of Barry Lyndon, Esq., Of the Kingdom of Ireland* repay careful reading as they demonstrate Thackeray's intricate approach—his warping of the mirror—as he allows Redmond Barry to establish and simultaneously undermine himself, in his own words. (It's worth noting that Barry's own words become imagistic at times through the use of elaborate punctuation and words in capital letters). The effort produces "one of the most brilliant and sustained of ironically naïve, first person historical narratives" (Harden 231). The book opens with Barry's distinctive voice. In the second paragraph he states:

> I presume that there is no gentleman in Europe that has not heard of the house
> of Barry of Barryogue, of the kingdom of Ireland, than which a more famous
> name is not to be found in Gwillim or D'Hozier[5]; and though, as a man of the
> world, I have learned to despise heartily the claims of some PRETENDERS to
> high birth who have no more genealogy than the lackey who cleans my boots,
> and though I laugh to utter scorn the boasting of many of my countrymen,
> who are all for descending from kings of Ireland, and talk of a domain no
> bigger than would feed a pig as if it were a principality; yet truth compels me
> to assert that my family was the noblest of the island, and, perhaps, of the
> universal world [. . .] I would assume the Irish crown over my coat of arms,
> but that there are so many silly pretenders to that distinction who bear it and
> render it common. (3)

In a circular, deflationary, and hilarious spiral, Redmond Barry establishes himself as a person of noble, perhaps even royal breeding, then proceeds to disparage any pretenders (like himself) in order to assert the truthfulness of his own claims. The reason he has not visibly marked his distinction with a crown is because the crown itself has been cheapened from being ill-used by so many pretenders. The persona he seeks to distance himself from—the pretender—is not a structuring absence but a twice-invoked presence that serves as a bookend or frame through Thackeray's repetition of the term at the beginning and the end of this opening sentence. The more vehemently Barry asserts his high born status, the more he convinces the reader that he is nothing but a pretender.

---

[5] Charles René d'Hozier (1640–1732) catalogued the French nobility, charging each family 20 livres to register their names.

The linguistic figure that comes closest to describing Barry's self-presentation regarding his royal pedigree is that of the Irish bull: similar to an oxymoron, it is a ludicrously incongruous statement that "contradicts itself amusingly" (Brown 1906, v). Although the etymology of the term bull to denote a nonsense statement lies in the seventeenth century, possibly originating with the French *boul*, by the nineteenth century, the term "Irish" had been appended retroactively.

In his preface to his 1893 edition of *Bulls and Blunders*, Marshall Brown writes that the bull is a "peculiarity that belongs almost exclusively to Ireland, is always connected to thought, and originates in the imaginative power of its people" (iii). He attributes this peculiarity to the "superabundance of ideas which crowd one another so fast in an Irishman's brain that they get jammed together" (v).[6]

Setting aside the implications of these ethnically coded assumptions for the moment,[7] the temporal characteristics of this overabundance and simultaneity of thought, this sublime linguistic confusion, must be translated to a sequential form of literary presentation. Thackeray's careful rewriting of his own work—the memoir is the revision of the original serial—renders the thought process itself ridiculous: the writing represents no temporary lapse. This literary version of the bull produces a consistent style of high-blown flourishes that puncture the pretensions of the character who uses them as well as undermines the process of representation itself. Whereas Mark Crispin Miller writes that Kubrick's *Barry Lyndon* "deals with the inadequacy of language" ("Kubrick's Anti-Reading"), I would suggest that Thackeray's language, although utilized unwittingly, is all too adequate. A careful reading strategy—one that recognizes the need to dispense with sequentiality and can move forward and backward across Barry's sentences—exposes the way that language is a powerful and potentially duplicitous mode of self-construction and historical representation. This encourages, if not forces, the reader to engage with Redmond Barry primarily at the level of language and invention. We do not so much see into Barry as we see through him, to linguistic complexity rather than historical veracity. In his film, Kubrick takes Thackeray's

---

[6] Brown puts Thackeray himself on record as being the victim of the Irish bull during his trip to Ireland in 1842. Brown reports that, when Thackeray inquired about the meaning of the letters GPO, he was told they stood for "God Preserve O'Connell" rather than General Post Office (89).

[7] The problematic tenor of the assertions may have been recognized by the author himself, as no references to the peculiar Irishness of the bull appear in Brown's 1906 revision. His books were published in Chicago and Boston: two cities with large Irish and Irish-American populations. This may explain both Brown's initial emphasis on the bull as an Irish construction and his subsequent removal of a characterization that might be understood as tendentious.

representational skepticism beyond language to question whether the visual image can properly serve as an index of reality.

Arguably an early proponent of deconstruction, Thackeray emphasizes the way that narratives depend upon other narratives, and language upon itself. According to Fletcher:

> feeling that historical and fictional discourses refer to their objects in the same way—[Thackeray] tried in [*Barry Lyndon*] to show that fictions are detected and understood through other fictions. In fact, this practice of formulating alternative hypotheses and other readings—thus changing the rules of the game—is the most beneficial thing fiction can provide. (505)

An early passage in which Redmond Barry describes his mother hints at the double voiced quality of Thackeray's narrative voice. Subtle linguistic cues regarding the source of verbal utterances and their self-reflexive nature present more than one hypothesis regarding Mrs. Barry's character, alerting the reader to the fact that the "rules of the game"[8] with respect to traditions of interpretation may have shifted. Barry writes:

> my mother had great gifts in every way, and believed herself to be one of the most beautiful, accomplished, and meritorious persons in the world. Often and often has she talked to me and the neighbors regarding her own humility and piety, pointing them out in such a way that I would defy the most obstinate to disbelieve her. (11)

Later, Barry similarly undermines his own intentions but, oddly enough, shores up his credibility as a narrator when he describes the financial arrangements of his marriage of convenience to the wealthy Lady Lyndon. The reader understands precisely how Barry has ruined the estate, although he himself purports to be making a case in his own defense. He remonstrates:

> I never raised a shilling upon Lady Lyndon's property but I spent it like a man of honor [. . .] Independent of Lyndon mortgages and encumbrances, I owe myself at least one hundred twenty thousand pounds, which I spent while in occupancy of my wife's estate; so that I may justly say that the property is indebted to me. (28)

---

[8] Marvin D'Lugo emphasizes the gaming in the text in "*Barry Lyndon*: Kubrick and the Rules of the Game." *Explorations in National Cinemas*, Vol. 1, ed. Marc Glasser, Ken Moscowitz, and Hart Wegner Pleasantville, NY: Docent Publications, 1977: 37–44.

The ludicrous comedy of this passage has a deadly serious underpinning, as economic arrangements dominate Thackeray's and Kubrick's narrative of the social climber Redmond Barry. Barry is determined both to acquire a peerage and to secure the Lyndon estate for his son Bryan, the latter a goal he attempts to achieve by encouraging his stepson Bullingdon, first in the line of succession, to take a regiment to the war in the American colonies.

As these passages suggest, *The Memoirs of Barry Lyndon* is a highly ironic, coded, and astonishingly complex first person chronicle of the fictional Redmond Barry's ascent from landless Irishman to British aristocrat and his equally rapid descent to debtors' prison at Newgate. Just as Titmarsh distances his reader from the opening of *The Second Funeral of Napoleon* by considering what his authorial stance on the subject should be, a distanced commentator was present in the initial, serialized version of the tale, which appeared in 1844 under the name of another of Thackeray's fictional editorial voices, George Savage Fitz-Boodle. By converting the third person "edited" work to a first person, faux memoir, Thackeray turns the experience of reading into "an examination of the distance between event and explanation," according to Fletcher (498). That examination of distance relates to the composition and use of narrative form itself and leads to the reader's mistrust of the narrator and his structures of explanation.

Perhaps to capture this unique voice, Kubrick originally intended to use a first person voice-over narration for the film, which he recorded with Ryan O'Neal. He decided late in the production process—in the fall of 1975—to record a third person narration that was voiced by British actor Michael Holdern. This decision becomes critical to the viewer's understanding of the film's antiheroic central figure and to its temporal structure. Eliminating the first person narration lends potential dignity to the Redmond Barry character because his inflated sense of self-worth and astonishing rationalizations of monstrous behavior have been eliminated, along with access to his psychological interiority. Moreover, this shift eliminates the double-voiced quality—the linguistic layering of Thackeray's character—introducing a less-complicated linearity to the narrative at the verbal level of the dialogue. Kubrick will transpose the back and forth, unreliable reading process of Thackeray's novel, with its temporal interruptions and delays, into the visual and sonic registers.

In the fictional memoir, Barry's delusional status is magnified through first person narration, which transparently exposes the author's self-deception and misapprehension of the world around him. Mark Crispin Miller rightly observes that Kubrick simplifies Thackeray's plot—possibly to address the temporal complexity that caused him to reject *Vanity Fair* as a source text—and reasons that, "by deleting Thackeray's most involved episodes, Kubrick places the film's emphasis on the protagonist's inner life; we attend to Barry's feelings and responses, not his actions" ("Kubrick's Anti-Reading"). Kubrick reads against the grain of the picaresque, yet I disagree with the notion that the protagonist's inner life is foregrounded. Instead, I would propose that, like Thackeray's novel, the film renders actions not evidence of character, but, instead, prisms through which Barry's acts of self-construction—accomplished through verbal flourishes in the novel—are refracted.

Thackeray's serialized exploits of an historical figure from the previous century are often described as picaresque, a form based on an engaging, likable protagonist that flourished in the eighteenth century and is associated with the works of Thackeray's supposed model, Henry Fielding (Cunliffe and Watt 12). Fielding's *The Life and Death of Jonathan Wild* (1743), based on a seventeenth-century gang leader, thief, and thief taker, and *The History of Tom Jones, a Foundling* (1749) are frequently cited as inspirations for *Barry Lyndon*. Thackeray did indeed write about *Tom Jones* in *English Humorists of the Eighteenth Century*, describing it as an "exquisite" work, but, not surprisingly, objecting to Fielding's treatment of the protagonist. Thackeray asks:

> If it is right to have a hero whom we may admire, let us at least take care that he is admirable [. . .] a hero with a flawed reputation; a hero spunging for a guinea; a hero who can't pay his landlady, and is obliged to let his honour out to hire, is absurd and his claim to heroic rank untenable. I protest against Mr. Thomas Jones holding such rank at all. I protest even against his being considered a more than ordinary young fellow, ruddy-cheeked, broad-shouldered, and fond of wine and pleasure. ("Criticisms and Interpretations")

By focusing on the insubstantial and even repellant quasi-historical figure of Stoney Bowes/Redmond Barry—part Zelig or Forrest Gump, and part sadistic desperado—Thackeray and Kubrick challenge the Great Man thesis, associated with Victorian essayist and sometime Thackeray friend Thomas Carlyle. In this thesis, Carlyle presents an account of human history that defines progress through the success, and the succession, of noble individuals. In *On Heroes, Hero-Worship, and the Heroic in History*, which was based on a series of lectures delivered in 1840, Carlyle writes: "Universal History, the history of what man has accomplished in this world, is at bottom the History of the Great Men who have worked here" (1). For Carlyle, the ideas of Great Men, manifested in physical form, create and embody human progress: "all things that we see standing in this world are properly the outer material result, the practical realization and embodiment, of Thoughts that dwelt in the Great Men sent into the world" (Carlyle 1).

Not surprisingly, Thackeray and Kubrick, known for scathing satires of pomp and circumstance, reject the elevation of men to superhuman status. Their historical and historiographical narratives do not coalesce around the figure of the hero. Like Thackeray, Kubrick portrays leaders, experts, politicians, and other prominent men—particularly military men—as corrupt (Generals Broulard and Mireau in *Paths of Glory*), buffoonish (Captain Quin in *Barry Lyndon* and General Turgidson in *Dr. Strangelove*), or dangerously maniacal (Brigadier General Jack D. Ripper in *Dr. Strangelove* and Gunnery Sergeant Hartman in *Full Metal Jacket*).

Thackeray and Kubrick repeatedly deconstruct the myth-making process implicit within the Great Man theory, challenging the notion that individuals influence the course of history and the belief that historical change can be associated with progress. Their *Barry Lyndon* tale is a narrative of failure; this does not distinguish it from most of Kubrick's films, but it stands alone among the most obvious of this type. In *Paths of Glory*, the sympathetic Colonel Dax defends the men accused of desertion, but he is unable to save them from the corruption and self-interest permeating the military chain of command. In *Barry Lyndon*, Redmond Barry embodies an Irish and potentially democratic challenge to British imperial power, yet he ends his days in penniless, one-legged ignominy.

Redmond Barry bears a number of similarities to Kubrick's other soldier characters—including Spartacus, Colonel Dax, and Private Joker. None of these figures satisfies the criteria for the Great Man thesis, yet Barry stands alone with his brazen ambition, greed, and cupidity. Barry is no leader (as the others are); he is an unwilling conscript; and he deserts the British forces. Even Private Joker enlisted in the Marines. Barry never protects or inspires other men as Dax, Spartacus, and Joker do. He entertains fellow troops by goading a fellow soldier into a fistfight. He does undertake one apparently selfless act— carrying the Prussian Captain Potzdorf out of a burning building in the midst of a battle. Aside from that moment, Barry distinguishes himself as a soldier only through the most barbarous of activities, a fact duly noted by his superior officer when awarding Barry a medal for his valor. Seducing Lady Lyndon openly, which demonstrably contributes to her husband Sir Charles's death, Barry seeks property and position but manages only to obtain a new name, one that reflects his dependence upon his wife. A vain, ambitious figure who moves through historical events without comprehending their significance, Redmond Barry is, in every circumstance, motivated by self-interest and blind to his circumstances. He is an extreme example of ambitious upward mobility in a pre-capitalist era; he obeys neither the democratic principles that might befit his station nor any sense of *noblesse oblige* associated with the well-born.

Here, however, Kubrick's ambivalence is palpable; while Barry dismally fails the test of the Great Man, as most men do in Kubrick's universe, the film stops short of condemning him altogether. Barry's rise and fall are intimately tied to his historical circumstances. Fully invested in the culture of British aristocracy and imperialism at a time when democratic principles are on the horizon, Barry fails to understand that as an abject outsider, he is anathema to this social system. He is an Irishman, and a physically violent one, hailing from an Ireland that is about to be subsumed and incorporated into the United Kingdom in the Act of Union (1800). He will never secure his tenuous foothold within the aristocracy, despite his wife's fortune. One tragic aspect of Kubrick's *Barry Lyndon* is that this seemingly self-possessed character—a self-made man in the most literal sense, as he is literally the overconfident author of his own tale—acts in both impetuous and pragmatic ways to better his personal situation, but fails to create anything of value or to leave a legacy.

Kubrick may seem at times to torture his upwardly mobile antihero, yet he tempers the harshest notes of Thackeray's conclusion. In the novel, Barry pens his memoir in prison. By contrast, Kubrick literally arrests Barry's story with a freeze frame in the film's penultimate scene. Cinematically speaking, Barry disappears from the frame of representation, descending into visual as well as social obscurity.

Ultimately, Redmond Barry's only claim to becoming a Great Man of history is through his memoirs, his writing, his aesthetic self-construction. Here the sympathy Thackeray reveals toward Captain Freeny—another man who had to earn his living by the pen—returns in a haunting way. Only in his writing—with its fabulous linguistic fabrications—can Barry be considered a manifestation of the greatest ideas ever thought. Here, questions of identity, history, and continuity arise in relation to the aesthetic impulse, which leads us directly to the subject of Chapter 3: the way narrative form in *Barry Lyndon* articulates masculine concerns related to paternity and succession.

3

Paternal Crisis, or: History as Succession

Considered Kubrick's "most literary" film by Vincent Lo Brutto (45) and described by Frank Rich as "as far away from literary modes of filmmaking as you can possibly get" (27), *Barry Lyndon* is, in fact, both literary and abstract. On the one hand, its heightened diction, intertitles, and voice-over narration establish its lineage in Victorian literature and early cinema; on the other hand, dialogue-free interludes and long takes, paced according to the perspectival shifts of a slow zoom, situate the film within the paradigm of modernist cinema. The film's verbal and visual representational enterprises highlight the role of sequence and succession in the writing and envisioning of history.

This chapter continues the investigation of *Barry Lyndon*'s temporality by considering the ways in which Thackeray and Kubrick problematize narrative sequence. A profound concern with the order of things informs the film's plot and narration and resonates with the central theme of paternal crisis. By elaborately staging and then undermining the cause and effect flow of story information, Stanley Kubrick challenges the notion of history as a complete, chronological, and unidirectional timeline. Through measured pacing, he expands the consciousness of the present moment, which, from Aristotle through Bergson, remains a vexed concept: the present constantly threatens to slide into the past, "dragged away by what we call the flow of consciousness" as Jean-Francois Lyotard writes: "it is always both too soon and too late to grasp anything like a 'now' in an identifiable way" (24).

Barry Lyndon is not the first of Kubrick's films to take on these questions. *The Killing* and *2001* stand out as investigations of temporal alterity: the former casting the linear timeline as an impossibility and the latter depicting the vast sweep of cosmic temporality. Kubrick's inquiry into matters of time intersects with Gilles Deleuze's investigations in *Cinema 1: the Movement-Image* and *Cinema 2: the Time-Image*. The problem of linear time drew Deleuze to Henri Bergson's concept of duration, as Suzanne Guerlac notes: "duration implies a mode of temporal synthesis that is different from the linear narrative development of past–present–future. It involves a temporal synthesis of memory that knits temporal dimensions together, as in a melody" (66). The experience of duration, she argues, produces a heterogeneous multiplicity "in which states or feelings overlap or interpenetrate one another, instead of being organized into a distinct succession" (67). In their versions of *Barry Lyndon*, both William Makepeace Thackeray and Stanley Kubrick probe the meaning of duration and multiplicity by disrupting the linear timeline of history and succession.

Succession is literally concerned with what comes next and with what endures. *Barry Lyndon* addresses the problem of succession as an element of form and also as a narrative motif involving paternal legacy. Both aspects evoke a concept of temporality as a layering of extended durations that coexist rather than a series of discrete moments. Deleuze writes: "there is no present which is not haunted by a past and a future, by a past which is not reducible to a former present, by a future which does not consist of a present to come [. . .] It is characteristic of cinema to seize this past and this future that coexist with the present image" (Deleuze *Cinema 2* 36–7). In *Barry Lyndon*, the "present" remains haunted by the past and by the future, emblematized in both the killing of Redmond Barry's father and the death of his son.

These narrative events suggest the way that Kubrick explores the haunting of a nonlinear time, a durational temporality that cannot guarantee succession. Thackeray's fictional memoir presents the death of Redmond Barry's father as an historical event; the first person narrator locates that event in the past. As Chapter 2 establishes, Barry takes pains to establish his well-born status for his readers. He spends several pages discussing his heritage before mentioning his father's death. In this way, he situates his relationship with his father, and the incident that led to his death, firmly in the past, in the larger context of his discussion of the family's pedigree.

By contrast, Kubrick's film opens with the dramatization of the death of the father. Here, what's past becomes prologue. This positional shift heightens the significance of this event. Barry cannot bury the incident or explain it away within the larger family saga; in fact, the event is no longer narrated through his consciousness. This shift from Thackeray's novel places greater emphasis on the event: it forms the beginning of the son's story and founds that narrative on a traumatic moment of loss.

The opening scene introduces Redmond Barry's father, who is unceremoniously dispatched in a duel mere seconds later, verbally through the voice-over and visually through a long shot (Figure 3.1). The film frame transposes the event from the novel's recitation of Barry's oral history to the visual historicism of the eighteenth-century genre of landscape painting. The carefully distanced composition dwarfs the combatants, who stand in what looks to be an arable field, framed and separated from a lush green landscape by a curving dry stone wall; the image is the epitome of the picturesque. The visual design of the shot suggests the way that personhood and property, most notably, land, were intertwined in the eighteenth century, as the figures are embedded within, and subordinate to, the landscape. Thackeray's novel makes explicit the fact that Barry has descended from Catholic landowners who renounced their religion in order to retain their property under British rule. After the death of Barry's father, Barry and his mother become landless dependents, throwing themselves on the mercy of his father's brother.

Figure 3.1 The opening duel: violence framed at a picturesque distance. *Barry Lyndon* (1975). Produced by Jan Harlan, Stanley Kubrick, and Bernard Williams. Directed by Stanley Kubrick.

The repetition of dueling scenes in *Barry Lyndon*—this is the first of three—and their meticulous staging suggest their critical importance to Kubrick's film. For Marvin D'Lugo, the brinksmanship of the duel defines the film's "locus of meaning" (40). In the preproduction files at the Stanley Kubrick archive, numerous photographs depict different angles and positions at a number of Irish locations, attesting to the extreme care taken with the visual elements of the dueling scene. Most important is the framing of the shot. Despite the uncanny moment that emerges when it becomes clear the tiny figures are moving, viewers witness a killing on screen through a comically absurd displacement. The action is undertaken from such a great distance that the figures appear to be cartoonish miniatures.[1]

In an era in which succession meant everything, not only for the aristocracy but also for the aspirational upstart, the opening of Redmond Barry's saga symbolizes the end of patrimony, legacy, and heritage. He loses his father at the beginning of his story and loses his son and heir Bryan near the end of it. The multigenerational rhyme of this father–son dynamic is underscored through another resonance: Barry's father and son both die violent deaths that are connected with the purchase of horses, which subtly evokes the British imperial presence in Ireland.[2] Barry's conflicted relationship with his stepson Bullingdon, a fraught connection overtly marked by anxieties regarding inheritance, also culminates in a duel that takes place in a horse stable, an indoor location presumably chosen because of the taboo nature of the familial conflict.

Returning to the opening scene, the voice-over narration helps to reveal Kubrick's complex treatment of cause and effect. The narration demonstrates the ability of language to establish and disrupt sequential temporality by describing Barry's father—pictured in an extreme long shot as one of two men who are about to engage in a duel—in terms of his potential alternative future. Trained in the law, Mr. Barry "would have made an eminent figure in his profession, had

---

[1] Although rehearsed at Irish locations, ultimately, the scene was filmed in September 1974 in Gloucestershire, according to production reports.

[2] I would argue for an implicit connection between the two horse-related deaths in Kubrick's film and Eileen O'Connell's well-known Irish nationalist poem, "The Lament for Art O'Leary" (1773) about her husband, who was killed for refusing to sell his horse to the Magistrate Abraham Morris of Cork for 5 pounds. Under the Penal Laws, no Catholic could own a horse worth more than 5 pounds and could be forced to sell one to a Protestant for that sum. O'Leary, a proud Hussar, refused to do so and challenged the Magistrate to a duel; Morris refused and had O'Leary proclaimed an outlaw, to be shot on sight. Bob Quinn's Irish/English language film, *Caoineadh Airt Uí Laoire,* released in the same year as *Barry Lyndon,* is a reflective, historiographical examination of these events.

he not been killed in a duel which arose over the purchase of some horses." The pistol shot that fells Mr. Barry halfway through the sentence punctuates the line of narration with far greater dramatic intensity than the printed comma in the sentence above is able to convey.

The juxtaposition generates a startling, comic absurdity on two counts: first, the film eliminates the first character it introduces. Second, when the narrator delineates the life that Barry's father could have led, he chooses to do so at the exact moment that the bullet, with its deadly trajectory, rewrites, and in fact completely erases, that imagined future. In terms of cinematic representation, the scene introduces the film with failure, not least of which is the fact that the camera's extreme distance from its subjects makes it impossible to identify (and therefore identify with) Barry's father *until* he falls to the ground, mortally wounded. The relation between words and image is that of a punctuated moment that impedes the flow of narrative and the development of character.

The defamiliarization of sequence plays a critical role as one aspect of the challenge to historical realism posed by Thackeray's writing and Kubrick's film. Fredric Jameson writes that *Barry Lyndon* is "one of the most brilliant (and problematical) contemporary realizations of the representational ideal of the historical novel proper" ("Historicism" 91). The film undoubtedly engages with the representational ideal of the historical novel. As a lavishly appointed narrative of failure—as so many Kubrick films are—*Barry Lyndon* knowingly perturbs that representational ideal. The novel, like history writing, constructs its own terms of reference, as Gregory Flaxman writes: "Deleuze condemns history as an enterprise that stakes out origins and anticipates conclusions, the result of which is a chronological series" (24). Thackeray's novel and Kubrick's film both provide numerous instances of the failure of the carefully plotted sequence to depict time chronologically, dynamically and thus, perhaps, heroically. Time as measured through movement, which is the basis for Deleuze's movement-image, slows to near-stillness, yielding the time-image, which exposes the fact that time itself is the film's true subject. The problems introduced in relation to sequence further confound the expectation that the passage of time can be captured by historical representation in an accretion of static events, or film frames, that compile a sequentially ordered archive.

Sequence, as Bergson noted, is a construct of both space and time; it is a linear spatial ordering associated with the unidirectional temporality of "time's arrow." The ways that Thackeray and Kubrick manipulate narrative sequencing reveal the ways that social and aesthetic orders inform one another. Kubrick's

Barry Lyndon allows for the possibility of diverse experiences of time, including, but not limited to Bergson's *durée*: "states of consciousness [that], even when successive, permeate one another" (98). Calling attention to the constructedness of sequence and its formal and political implications, Thackeray and Kubrick gesture toward the possibility of other experiences of time. In doing so, they challenge the grounding assumptions of historical realism by questioning the capacity to represent history, whether through the language of a speaking subject—in Thackeray's self-revelatory narrator—or through the visual and sonic grammar of the camera and the microphone.

Kubrick adopts strategies that Gilles Deleuze describes as characteristic of the time-image, which attempts the direct representation of time. Kubrick is working within a genre that Deleuze describes as a "large form" or "SAS" (Situation, Action, Situation) genre: the historical drama. This genre appears to be fully invested in the structure of the action-image, where movement—taking the form of an event-based picaresque plot driven by romantic exploits, duels, and warfare—becomes the measure of time. But the SAS formula does not develop: *Barry Lyndon's* simultaneously interrupted and protracted narrative subverts any understanding of time as a succession of movements.

Moreover, physical movement itself becomes subdued, suppressed, and ultimately disarticulated, illegible. Even the film's conclusion undermines the possibility of establishing and registering a moment in time through movement, as the title character's death is not represented and his exit from the diegesis takes place through a freeze frame. The film's penultimate scene raises the specter of Redmond Barry's death not as an event punctuating a unfolding biographical timeline, but as an abstract temporal duration that corresponds to an absence which is a function of visual representability.

Serial becomes (his)tory

From the earliest configuration of the story as serial—one whose origins, as we saw in Chapter 2, lie in a series of earlier stories and histories—Thackeray's *Barry Lyndon* is immersed within the problematic of historical representation. Literary scholars contend that "installment literature and an awareness of history are related phenomena in the nineteenth century" (Hughes and Lund 60); in fact, the serial is understood as the form ideally suited to exploring "anxieties about historical change and periodicity" (Payne 9). The serial form embodies time's "forward moving nature" because "readers repeatedly found themselves in the middle of a story whose past was earlier installments and whose future was 'to be continued'" (Hughes and Lund 60–1). Under these circumstances, the interval—a time of waiting between installments—takes on a role within the reading process, as a period in which to reflect on the reader's intellectual and emotional engagement with the material. In fact, as Linda Hughes and Michael Lund argue, serialization imparted history to fiction because "a work's extended duration meant that serials could become entwined with readers' own sense of lived experience and passing time" (8). Kubrick retains this sense of lived experience and passing time within the film's interruptions, pauses, delays and, of course, through his unusual choice to release a film in 1975 with an intermission. The intermission is not simply an intervention in a lengthy film: it is a direct descendent of Thackeray's serial fiction, a pause that allows for history—and thought and feeling—to enter into the temporal experience of the film.

If seriality defines the genesis of the *Barry Lyndon* tale, however, neither temporal flow nor directionality can be guaranteed: the problem of succession threatens to thwart the continuity of history. The matter of textual succession affected Thackeray's versions: when he rewrote the serial as faux memoir, he "changed *Barry Lyndon* more significantly than his other republished magazine fiction" (Zygmunt vii). Succession is also intimately related to cinematic art; it's what D. N. Rodowick calls the "ineluctable linear drive of filmic temporality" (52).

Because Thackeray situates his seductive scoundrel's misadventures within the chaos of a global conflict that embroiled the major European powers on the continent and in their far-flung colonies, British colonial power and patronage drive the narrative. That power is embodied in military figures and father figures, such as Captain Quin, the middle-aged English colonialist rival for Nora Brady; the affectionate but short-lived father substitute Captain Grogan; and the initially hostile, but finally supportive, Prussian Captain Potsdorf. Mark Crispin Miller views the tale through this series of father surrogates: "throughout the film, sedentary old men confront Redmond with the fact of his own fatherlessness; he stands before them, trying in various ways to win their acceptance" ("Kubrick's Anti-Reading"). In his 1976 review in *Film Criticism*, Julian Rice argued that "Kubrick suggests that the creative vitality depends upon a man remaining a rebellious son, rather than becoming an order-preserving father" (9), but in fact, Redmond Barry's happiest moments occur when he is in the presence of his own son. The seemingly personal matter of paternal presence and absence is inextricably linked to the film's larger concern with the cycles of creation and destruction that define human history and historiography.

Destruction as negative inscription: History as palimpsest

In envisioning historical change as a temporal process of construction and destruction, Kubrick closely attends to the way that verbal and visual texts serve as partial, fragmentary, and inevitably, impermanent records of past events that will, eventually, be superseded by other texts. As I have argued elsewhere, *Barry Lyndon* alludes to and embodies the palimpsest, an ancient papyrus scroll that was repeatedly used, then washed, and even scraped clean in order to be written on again.[3] These gestures are only partially preserved, however; they are subsequently overwritten themselves, as the palimpsest becomes a tissue that reveals the layers of past and present. Despite the attempt to obliterate the past, the visible evidence of previous structures (in this case graphic or linguistic as well as architectural and social) remains.

As a figure that treats history as a sequential problem, the palimpsest is an appropriate metaphor for Kubrick's film. The palimpsest represents a simultaneously static and dynamic visual manifestation of the consequences of change. It embodies physical and temporal acts of writing and erasure that overwrite what already exists without completely eradicating what came before.

Barry Lyndon's central theme makes concrete the idea of history as palimpsest. The context for Redmond Barry's rise is the practice of modern, imperial warfare. Wars are the most literal and violent example of the human process of making and unmaking, of inscribing and erasing. The vanquishing of a society involves not only the death of its combatants on the battlefield, but also the partial erasure of its history, memories, and traditions as well as the elimination of the physical infrastructure that materially perpetuates a culture. Despite attempts at eradication, however, traces of what came before inevitably remain.

In developing the palimpsest metaphor, I have considered whether or not the chronotope might better characterize *Barry Lyndon's* theory of history.

---

[3] See "History as Palimpsest: Stanley Kubrick's *Barry Lyndon*." In *The Blackwell Companion to Historical Film*, ed. Robert Rosenstone and Constantin Parvulescu. London: Blackwell, 2013: 30–52.

The chronotope, a term that Mikhail Bakhtin borrowed from Albert Einstein, designates the inseparability of space and time; as such, is a far more dynamic concept than the palimpsest as artifact. Unlike the palimpsest, the chronotope does not remain in thrall to sequence; instead, the chronotope concept permits the sequencing and juxtaposition of different, potentially autonomous, and self-contained space-times, which can be analogized with cinema through editing's suturing capacity. The chronotope enjoys a special relationship to motion pictures, as Roberts Stam has noted, writing that the cinema provides the fullest expression of the chronotope ("Subversive" 187). Alexandra Ganser, Julia Pühringer, and Markus Rheindorf regard the chronotope as operating on two levels: "first, as the means by which a text represents history; and second, as the relation between images of time and space in the text, out of which any representation of history must be constructed" (2). My reading of the Kubrick's film concerns both of these levels, focusing on the way the film problematizes succession as a personal experience and an element of historical representation by interrupting the conventional sequencing of time and space.

However, I am not convinced that the useful tool of the chronotope—which permits discontinuities or singularities—can or should replace the palimpsest as a model for the course of history in *Barry Lyndon*. The attention paid to the film's visual surface and texture—its dependence upon the painting tradition as a prehistory of cinema—turns the film frame into a chemically etched palimpsest that intervenes in, but does not erase, a previous history of images. If the palimpsest seems to be too static a figure, I would argue that it nevertheless implies a process—that of incomplete erasure—that stands as a conceptual, aesthetic, and graphic counterpart to the colonial experience of Redmond Barry that *Barry Lyndon* alludes to as well.

Kubrick's palimpsest permits elements of Thackeray's written text to "show through" in the form of the intertitles and the voice-over narration. One element of Thackeray's work that Kubrick inherits a century later is the foregrounding of the narrative frame and the cause and effect sequence through which events are represented. Thackeray's obvious frames—the serial publication, the mock editorial persona of Fitz-Boodle, and the diaristic memoir—are Victorian literary devices that call attention to the process of constructing fictional and historical narratives. Kubrick adapts these stylized elements—for example, using text to frame the sections of the film—inserting them into a film culture in the 1970s that seemed bent on rejecting this type of visible artifice.

Since Thackeray's work deals, also in a palimspestic manner, with eighteenth-century subject matter, the novel has been referred to as "an archaeological dig" (Krohn 68). Originally published in 1844 and set in the 1760s–1780s, *Barry Lyndon* is a work set within the lifetime of its date of publication and deals with "turbulent" events. According to Jason Jones, texts in this category "dramatize how conventional historical explanations blind us to causal factors that do not mesh well with society [. . .] [and critique] our fantasies about historical meaning and their implication for social order" (Jones 14). Thackeray's novel and Kubrick's film not only critique our fantasies about the historical meaning of the British Empire and implications for social order, but also delve more deeply into the meaning of order itself in relation to historical representation.

Narrative undone

Although *Barry Lyndon* initially seems to conform to Robert Rosenstone's description of history as drama, the film actually challenges the distinction Rosenstone draws between Hollywood history and experimental approaches. For Rosenstone, historical films made according to Hollywood's traditional mode of representation rely upon the codes of cinematic realism to personalize history by constructing a plausible, coherent, and closed world organized by the story of an individual; experimental films disrupt those conventions (Rosenstone 1995:7–10). While *Barry Lyndon* initially appears to draw upon the character and plot-centered Hollywood tradition, the film manipulates time and space in ways that undermine narrative progress and preclude audience identification with the characters, making the personalization of history and psychological historicism difficult, if not impossible. These interventions in narrative form and visual style, which link the film to traditions of art cinema and art history, are also critical to the film's discourse on history and temporality.

For Kubrick and Thackeray, narrative is a property of both literary fictions and historical accounts, neither one of which can be counted on to be complete or accurate. Establishing the narrative norm, or framework, and then producing the deviation, in the mode of Rudolf Arnheim's definition of caricature, destabilizes realist representation. One way that the deviation is achieved, in Thackeray's writing and Kubrick's film, is through a strategy of what night be called *narratus interruptus*.

More precisely, both Thackeray and Kubrick foreground the cause-and-effect sequence through which the events are represented, providing a particular experience of narrative time while at the same time asking readers and viewers to think about that form of time. They call attention to the way aesthetic techniques create the meaningful structures of fictional and historical representation. Finally, these techniques remind readers and viewers that both fictions and histories are inseparable from the aesthetic practices used to represent them.

Frames and interruptions

The very title of Thackeray's 1844 serial—*The Luck of Barry Lyndon: A Romance of the Last Century*, edited by George Savage Fitz-Boodle—announces its complex status as both fiction ("a romance") and history ("of the last century"). Since his 1856 revision is a first-person memoir, the novel is also a hybrid; it purports to combine fact and fiction to produce a genre that is now commonly referred to as creative nonfiction. Robert Fletcher notes,

> By creating a speaker who tells a tale by not telling it, Thackeray explores the boundaries among fiction and belief, knowledge and power; in effect, the novel undermines as naïve the common sense distinction between truth and fiction, and exposes the dangers of a wholehearted belief in any language game. (493–4)

In the original serial version, Thackeray's fictional editorial persona, Fitz-Boodle, who was known to readers of *Fraser's*, acts as a frame distancing Thackeray's contemporary audience, and all subsequent readers, from the Redmond Barry narrative. His commentary provides an interruptive temporality that creates pauses for reflection within the text. Fitz-Boodle intervenes throughout the story, moving beyond the specific circumstances surrounding Redmond Barry to muse on aspects (both formal and ethical) of representation. At the conclusion of the serial, he defends his decision to publish this tale of a "lucky" scoundrel by appealing directly to readers. He asks whether the poetic justice that novelists mete out corresponds in any way to reality:

> Justice, forsooth! Does human life exhibit justice after this fashion? Is it the good always who ride in gold coaches, and the wicked who go to the workhouse? Is a humbug never preferred before a capable man? [. . .] Sometimes the contrary occurs, so that fools and wise, bad men and good, are more or less lucky in

their turn, and honesty is "the best policy," or not, as the case may be. ("The Luck" 227)

He legitimizes his editorial choices by arguing for the importance of moral beauty in representation, the pursuit of which would include what is "ill-favored":

> [T]hose persons who find their pleasure or get their livelihood by describing its manners and the people who live in it are bound surely to represent to the best of their power life as it really appears to them to be [. . .] if not bounden to copy nature, they are justified in trying; and hence in describing not only what is beautiful, but what is ill-favored too [. . .] I believe for my part Hogarth's pictures of "Marriage à la Mode" in Trafalgar Square to be more moral and beautiful than West's biggest heroic piece. ("The Luck" 227)

In addition to sharing Fitz-Boodle's taste in artists—*Barry Lyndon*'s visual design draws specifically from William Hogarth's (1697–1764) engravings—Kubrick adapts the voice of Thackeray's original moralistic editor–narrator in the film. The film narrative is organized into three parts—Part I, Part II, and the Epilogue—which are introduced by intertitles containing textual commentary. Their contents may seem straightforward: Part I's intertitle reads: "By what means Redmond Barry acquired the style and title of Barry Lyndon," and the Part II title reads: "Containing an account of the misfortunes and disasters which befell Barry Lyndon." Yet these intertitles borrow a graphic textual element from literature, enforcing a literal reading practice in relation to the cinema. They also make it clear that the unfolding events and images have been selected and arranged to provide narrative coherence.

Since the intertitles adopt the eighteenth-century convention of boldly forecasting future events, they provide more information than is now customary for authors of fiction to reveal at the beginning of a narrative. This foreclosure of a narrative's potential future developments corresponds more closely to the technique used in historical narratives that cover a period in history whose "end point" is well recognized and can be represented as the logical culmination of a series of events than it does to fictional story-telling procedures. This backward-looking strategy can also be found in the frame narration of *Killer's Kiss* and *Lolita*.

Here, the intertitles signal the film's intent to intervene dialectically in the representation of history in several ways, some of which produce temporal repercussions. First, the intertitles legitimize the narrative's ability to embody and explain history in terms of cause and effect, signaled by the use of language such as "by what means" and "containing an account."

The intertitles also call forth cinema's own history. Prior to the advent of synchronous sound, textual inserts, and supplements—now variously termed titles, subtitles, and intertitles, depending upon their function and the specific time period under discussion—included film titles, descriptive and explanatory material, and lines of dialogue. They were intended to help viewers new to the medium navigate plot twists and interpret character behavior. Their reappearance in a late twentieth-century film about the precinematic eighteenth century muddles the historical linearity of literary and film representation and the relation between the two.

Until this point, I have followed convention in using the term intertitle. But film historian André Gaudreault argues for the careful examination of the textual matter film scholars routinely refer to as intertitles. He proposes that, in many cases, what we refer to as intertitles in very early cinema are more properly referred to as subtitles because, first, the term intertitle did not come into use until 1955. Second, he points out, the very idea of inserting something in between shots did not develop until the 1910s. What was in place in very early cinema was the notion of the title of the film as distinct from the subtitle, which functioned as a heading for different sections of the film. For Gaudreault, the critical element is the meaning of the placement of the cards in relation to the narrative. "To be an intertitle," he writes, "a title card must not only be sandwiched between two image segments, but must bridge what came before (which it completes) and what comes after (which it announces). It must become an element of [. . .] *editing*" (90 emphasis in original). What is useful about Gaudreault's parsing of the terminology of titling for *Barry Lyndon* is the fact that Kubrick's placement of the text functions in a static manner as a bridge, not between shots, as with the dynamic mode of editing, but between the representational modes of literature and film. These textual bodies are in fact subtitles, announcing the large sections of narrative to come.

The subtitles bridge semiotic processes by introducing a potentially reflexive practice of spectatorship integrating the processing of graphic and linguistic information. Reading words on screen, the viewer scans the film frame in order to process the linguistic information. This reading practice may appear to be similar to, but is not the same thing as, the way the spectator imbibes visual information from the film frame. Reading words as screen images affords an opportunity to reconsider the visual practices of spectatorship, including those depicted within the diegesis. Laura Frost reminds us about an often-forgotten yet "passionate debate about titling" (293) in early cinema. In her examination of *Gentlemen Prefer Blondes*, she emphasizes the way that Anita Loos's novels "borrow visual properties from film and her films borrow textual strategies from literature" (293). Both forms of appropriation according to Frost, "show how words exceed their contexts and signify not only though their meaning but also through their literal status as objects: letters printed on the page or projected on the screen" (293). The subtle suggestion that words are meaningful aesthetic objects comports with Kubrick's film's wider discourse regarding the imbrication of politics and aesthetics, which I examine in Chapter 5.

Finally, the subtitles insert *Barry Lyndon* the film into its own historical narrative, marking it as an artifact of its time. They act as traces of the Thackeray novel, reminding or informing viewers of the story's origins in a literary source and are indelibly marked by a 1970s visual sensibility through the curlicued font selection. The subtitles participate in the historical palimpsest: initially, they may suggest film's appropriation of and overwriting of Thackeray's text as the successor that supercedes literature and makes it obsolete. However, there is a tension between cinema's usurpation of textuality and cinema's dependence upon the written word. As Kamilla Elliott notes, "intertitles were a constant reminder of the failure of film visuals to be the universal language they claimed to be" (88). Cinema, the medium that seems to have replaced literary narratives—thus moving forward in time—has done nothing of the sort. The narrative failure of the character Redmond Barry to secure his legacy has a counterpart in this formal failure.

Kubrick similarly draws viewers' attention to the temporal aspects of narrative construction and erasure through the unidentified voice-over narration: the film's Fitz-Boodle, as it were. This narrator functions as an *acousmetre*, Michel Chion's term for a disembodied voice whose very invisibility confers mysterious powers. The narrator is never seen and his investment in the situations and characters depicted is never made clear, but his commentary powerfully shapes the narrative. For the most part, his comments accomplish two things. He interrupts Redmond Barry's narrative as it unfolds, and he revises official historical accounts of the Seven Years' War. Since the narrator possesses more information than the characters or viewers, the narration embodies a backward and forward movement through time, although it never ventures beyond the time frame of the tale, which concludes in 1789. The narrator's interventions represent one important way in which the film rejects cinematic realism and presents history as an open-ended project under construction. The narration draws attention to temporality while explicitly undermining the unidirectional timeline that is the hallmark of Hollywood narrativity. In some ways it mimics the distancing frame and the cognitive back and forth embodied in Thackeray's faux memoir, with Barry's narration undercutting itself within the time and space of a single sentence. The reading process becomes a suspension rather than a serial progression.

Although an early commentator on the film noted that the voice-over "provid[es] the necessary information to bridge gaps between shifts of time or pace and thus to insure hypotactic continuity" (Klein 99), I would disagree. The narration repeatedly creates lacunae and/or draws attention to them. For example, when the narrator describes young Redmond Barry's infatuation with his cousin Nora, the use of the phrase "first love" implies that the romance is ephemeral, destined to be superseded by future amorous encounters. Young Barry's emotional investment, which exists in the present tense of the narrative, is minimized even as the narrator seems to magnify its importance by singling it out for discussion. Here, Kubrick denies the audience an emotional connection with Barry in the very act of calling attention to his feelings. Further, he rejects the realist cinema's presentism by implying that the narrated events, which are just unfolding, are less significant than those to come. This temporal morass also challenges the viewer's expectation that the past (which is the cinematic present tense at this moment of narration) and the future can be readily distinguished through spatial and temporal distancing.

Although Barry is represented as a youth of strong will and action, a courageous boy who challenges Nora's British suitor to a duel, the narrator frequently alludes to destiny and fate as the true authors of Barry's tale, thus obviating the role of temporal progression altogether by invoking the foreclosure of fate. "How different Barry's fate might have been had he not fallen in love with Nora and had he not flung the wine in Captain Quin's face. But he was destined to be a wanderer"—intones the narrator, barely allowing the audience to take in the events that precipitate the duel between Barry and Quin before suggesting that the story might have had a different outcome. The narrator advises viewers that, had Barry not performed the actions that they have just witnessed, he might yet live (from their perspective; or have lived—from the perspective of the narrator, who has knowledge of Barry's entire life story) a different life. Here Kubrick asks viewers not only to imaginatively rewrite Barry's narrative *in medias res*, but also to bend the rules of cinematic realism. Viewers should not only dismiss the events dramatized on screen in favor of an imagined counterfactual but also juggle multiple narratives simultaneously. Finally, however, they are counseled to relinquish these vain attempts at configuring the story, since Barry was destined to be a wanderer, and thus his actions are ordained by fate.

The narrator not only rewrites Barry's life story by mentioning potential alternative outcomes while simultaneously alluding to ineluctable fates, but also questions the truth claims of official accounts of history, a practice which also implicates the way that seriality and succession are the foundations of such histories. When Barry deserts the British forces and is forced to join the army of Frederick of Prussia, the narrator makes it clear (with language that originated with Thackeray's work) that historical narratives are at best incomplete and at worst misleading. "Gentlemen may talk of chivalry, but remember the ploughmen, poachers, and pickpockets whom they lead. It is with these sad instruments that your great warriors and kings have been doing their murderous work in the world." His sympathetic characterization of Barry's desertion seems motivated by a perceived discrepancy between the experiences of ordinary men like Barry and those of gentlemen who never engage in battle. "It is well to dream of glorious war in a snug arm chair at home," he cautions, "but it is a very different thing to see it first hand."

The experience of "seeing it first hand"—witnessing historical events rather than planning, imagining, or reconstructing them after the fact—emerges as an important motif within the film's discourse on the Seven Years' War. The narrator makes his most powerful statement about the deficiencies of recorded history after Barry's first battle in British uniform. "Though this encounter is not recorded in any history books," he declares, "it was memorable enough for those who took part." The sequence in the film that depicts what the narrator describes as a mere "skirmish" includes dynamic scenes of soldiers marching as well as tableau shots of wounded and dying British Redcoats. As such, it serves as a performative utterance and as an intervention in history. The sequence overwrites the deficient historical accounts the narrator alludes to, and it does so by staging the experiences of those who lost their lives in a battle that was not deemed important enough to be recorded. It points to Walter Benjamin's observation that: "History deals with [. . .] arbitrarily elaborated causal chains" ("Selected Writings" 403). As part of the film's political critique, this scene and narrational passage embody Hayden White's observation about the imperialism of historical thinking: "this 'history' of 'historical' cultures is by its very nature, as a panorama of domination and expansion, at the same time the *documentation* of the 'history' of those supposedly 'nonhistorical' cultures and peoples who are the victims of this process" (32). By "nonhistorical" cultures, White refers to the nonindustrialized cultures of the twentieth century that were treated to historical and anthropological discourses of primitivism. My contention in Chapter 4 will be that Redmond Barry's Ireland is presented as just such a place and that the panorama of domination and expansion is clearly marked as English colonialism in Ireland.

The narrator's interventions are only the most obvious means by which Kubrick suggests that historical narratives are not fixed events embedded in an unchanging timeline, but are instead subject to constant erasure and revision. The story events are reversed and rewritten. The fact that Barry's decline and fall are already embedded within the rising action is signified through a specific temporal disjunction. Barry and Lady Lyndon's wedding appears after the Part II subtitle; however, the marriage, as part of Barry's acquisition of "the style and title" of Barry Lyndon, had been announced in the opening subtitle as the culmination of Part I. The scene that dramatizes Barry's attainment of the title is thus displaced structurally and chronologically. The event serves both as the climax of the rising action and as the initiation of the falling action. This double function highlights a contradiction that informs the model of history as a linear timeline: a single event like this one may occupy more than one position of narrative significance, and it bears a particularly important meaning because it contains both the zenith and the nadir of the story arc.

This complex placement of the wedding scene reiterates one attribute of historical narratives that the narrator has already hinted at: when written from a temporal vantage point after the events have taken place, which they must by definition be, all narratives, with their supposedly stochastic potential, are in fact bound by inevitability. The characters that populate any fictional narrative theoretically possess many potential futures, yet those possibilities must be dispensed with, erased, or written over. The knowledge of what actually ensued and the need to demonstrate causality overdetermine the narrative from the outset, rendering it a foregone conclusion. Under these circumstances, the pleasure of the text derives almost entirely from style: that is, from the telling of the tale, whether through words or images, or through both.

Finally, a significant narrative motif emphasizes Barry's repeated attempts at refashioning and overwriting himself: he is a character whose stability as a figure through time is called into question. Since Thackeray's 1856 revision of the serial presents itself as an eighteenth-century memoir of an adventurer, it invokes Jonathan Swift's *Gulliver's Travels* (1726/35), a memoir that, like Barry's, devolves into the bitter, delusional rant of a misanthrope. In *A Social History of Madness*, Roy Porter calls the autobiography a "form [that] demands a solipsism which might be seen as inherently pathological. To tell one's story: what could better establish one's veracity, or provide more conclusive symptoms of utter delusion?" (29). For Walter Benjamin, "autobiography has to do with time, with sequence, and what makes up a continuous flow of life" (*Reflections* 28). Thackeray's protagonist's discontinuity culminates in madness; in Kubrick's film, that problem of continuity is elaborated through a tone of sadness. Part of that sense is structural, as Klein's discussion of the adaptation suggests: "Although less than a tenth of Thackeray's novel is devoted to Barry's downfall, Kubrick devotes more than a quarter of the film to his 'misfortune and distress'" (Klein 97–8).

Barry himself is a text whose past traces are still visible even as he undergoes radical revision. Redmond Barry erases and rewrites his own identity on numerous occasions, at times to ensure his survival and at other times to secure social advantage. The names he acquires and dispenses with reflect this process: he is born Redmond Barry, but briefly acquires the identity of Lieutenant Jonathan Fakenham, the gay officer he impersonates as he deserts the British army. As Lazlo Zilagy, the valet to the Chevalier, he acts as a double agent, pretending to deliver information to the Prussians while secretly working on behalf of the Chevalier. The misleading reports he delivers may provide insight into Kubrick's views of historical reportage: the narrator notes that "the information he gave was very minute and accurate, though not very important." When the Chevalier is in danger, Barry assumes his beloved mentor's identity in order to effectuate his escape. When he marries the countess of Lyndon, he becomes Barry Lyndon, with, in palimpsestic fashion, his previous identity as Barry remaining in evidence linguistically. His resentful stepson Bullingdon insults him by addressing him as "Mr. Redmond Barry." Through a range of devices that involve the film's structure, narration, themes, and motifs, the notion that stories, histories, and identities are constantly subject to revision over time, through the temporal process of interruption and reversal, permeates the sensibility of Kubrick's *Barry Lyndon*.

Lust, longing, and the long take: Masculinity and failure

Judith Halberstam's *The Queer Art of Failure* describes failure as "a story of art without markets, drama without a script, narrative without progress" and "an art of unbecoming" (88). Halberstam's example of "unqueer failure," developed through a reading of Irvine Welch's novel *Trainspotting*, explores the disaffection of young male Scots, at least one of whom directs his venom toward the Scottish people for allowing themselves to be colonized by English "wankers." Since they lack a queer vision of alternatives, the characters in Welch's novel "cannot imagine the downfall of the white male as part of the emergence of the new order" (92). Hence "failure is the rage of the excluded white male, a rage that promises and delivers punishment for women and people of color" (92).

As Halberstam argues more generally, the act of losing "has its own logic; its own complexity; its own aesthetic" (93). Indeed, the aesthetic of interruption and failure in *Barry Lyndon*—a film that also deals with the rage of the excluded white male, this one a colonial Irishman—extends from the formal problematics of narration and identity to the themes of war and history, and finally to the premature and tragic interruption of the life of the indulged Lyndon heir, Bryan.

Barry's ascent, failure, and fall is a gender-marked process. His coterie of father surrogates is not a homosocial posse or entourage; each father figure is encountered individually and seems to bear no connection to the next one. His trajectory from Captain Grogan to Colonel Potsdorf to the Chevalier traces his attempts at securing filial relationships with powerful mentors. The one hint that Barry may be seeking the wrong kind of male relationship is the passage involving Lieutenant Fakenham and his lover. Despite the potential for humor embedded in the scene of the two gay soldiers professing their love for one another with a seemingly characteristic British reticence—and I am certain that some audience members have snickered at the scene—this pairing stands apart from the film's backdrop of troublingly instrumental relationships. This pair of gay men is singular in the way it refuses the relational failures that plague Barry and pervade the film: this romanticized relationship suggests a balance of power, the possibility of respect, and the ability to express emotion.

By contrast, Barry's encounters with women and romance mark femininity as dangerous business. His cousin Nora Brady leads him on, then participates in the deception around the duel with Captain Quin so that she and her family gain access to the Captain's money. Lady Lyndon, Barry's naïve mark, transforms into an enervated nag whose disappointment must be turned inward, as she is only briefly permitted to complain about his smoking shortly after their marriage in the scene in the carriage. This scene—and the subsequent breakdown of the marriage—comports with Todd McGowan's observation that, "whenever a character takes up a position of authority in one of Kubrick's films, he inevitably finds an obscene enjoyment in the role" (47).

It is worth looking closely at two remarkable portions of the narrative—two long takes during Barry's pursuit of Lady Lyndon at Spa—to examine the way the film circumscribes the dynamics of sexual desire and produces sexuality as failure. The scenes are evidence not only of the diversity of temporal frameworks in the film but also of the anticlassical impulse at work. Realist films generally render scenes of romantic pursuit and consummation with dynamism and momentum: sexual coupling, as Bordwell and Staiger's research in *Classical Hollywood Cinema* revealed, was the most important narrative goal of the vast majority of Hollywood films. In *Barry Lyndon*, Barry's lust for power is enacted through sexual conquest which itself is depicted as an excruciatingly slow process.

Most accounts of Kubrick's work emphasize his signature tracking shots, symmetrical compositions, and use of the wide-angle lens. His long takes are mentioned primarily in relation to his penchant for tracking movement. *Barry Lyndon* might be remembered as particularly laborious, but, in fact, many of his films exhibit average shot lengths of two to three times the average in American films of the period.

What's so notable and also memorable about the long takes in *Barry Lyndon* is not simply their duration but also their static nature. *Lolita's* longer average shot length may be perceived very differently, given the dynamic figural behavior within the scenes; for example, Lolita with her hula hoop; Humbert and Lolita's automobile travel; Claire Quilty's playfully sinister, then finally desperate, freneticism; and so on. But there is no mistaking the long takes in *Barry Lyndon*, deployed as they are in conjunction with static tableaux compositions, where even characters who move must do so directly toward the camera, or they are tracked so that they occupy the same position in the center of the frame despite their movement, or they are engulfed in space through the use of the reverse zoom.

The effect of this entombed movement can be seen in these two long takes in the middle of the film; they act almost as counterweights on either side of the important halfway point of Barry's conquest. They reveal Barry making his bid for power and prestige through marriage. The first take is 1-minute long and represents an important turning point: at this moment, Redmond Barry first encounters his meal ticket, the Countess of Lyndon, at Spa in Belgium. In this scene, the narrator introduces the Lyndon entourage as the group makes its way slowly across a garden area, closely watched by Barry and the Chevalier. The means by which the thwarting or redirection of movement becomes palpable and uncomfortable in this scene is the masterful stroke of placing Sir Charles in a wheelchair. Movement is orchestrated in conjunction with the camera zoom such that no progress appears to be made by the group being observed. Time passes, but no progress is made, despite the fact that a machine, the wheelchair— which is both an emblem of paralysis and yet a device designed for progressive and sequential movement—appears in the scene.

In the second long take, Lady Lyndon waits outside on the balcony, motionless, as Barry slowly approaches her. Mark Le Fanu uses the work of Andre Bazin to draw a distinction between the mobile shots of Murnau, Wyler, and Welles and the static, deep focus long take, which is based on "simplicity . . . integrity, and the patient intensity of [the artist's] gaze" ("Metaphysics"). Here the distinction between these types of the long take is artificial: Kubrick's long takes combine both mobility and deep focus. They ask the viewer to reconsider the definition of motion and stasis, hence the question in *MAD* magazine as to whether or not *Barry Lyndon* was even a moving picture. These definitions must be challenged at not only the visual but also the narrative and thematic level. For example, one of the most important narrative events takes place at the end of the painfully slow movement across the frame as Barry reaches the Lady Lyndon's side. A full minute of barely perceptible moment—staged as a perversely anticlassical progression across the screen from left to right—sets the stage for the first kiss between Barry and the Countess.

The technique used to render the early moments of the Lyndon's rarefied romance is also used to capture the world coming to a standstill after their son Bryan's death. During the funeral scene, as Jason Francois notes, "the only object in the film able to outpace Kubrick's zoom out is a coffin, which moves inexorably toward the moving camera" ("The Vanity"). The movement toward the camera emphasizes the tiny, foreshortened coffin that bears the young boy's remains. The parallel drawn between sexuality (the scenes of early romance) and death (as they mourn Bryan's passing) is unmistakable. Rather than endorse cinema's long-standing reliance on sexuality for narrative drive and emotional investment, Kubrick slows and interrupts progress toward pleasure (which, despite the sumptuous surroundings, is nowhere in evidence among the characters in this film). Apart from the creation of a brief mock family unit with Lischen, the young mother Redmond Barry meets and beds shortly after his desertion, delight eludes his grasp as he increasingly encounters emptiness and loss.

Barry's monstrous humiliation of the fragile, passive Lady Lyndon with servants and nannies is met with her increasing withdrawal, silence, and stillness. One of the few scenes in which Kubrick interrupts his own measured pace takes place immediately after Bryan's death, when he employs a handheld camera to capture the dynamic grief that overwhelms Lady Lyndon. She becomes hysterical, wailing and thrashing around her bedroom, alone and presumably unheard, as there is never any mention made of her behavior. This use of the handheld camera draws a parallel with several scenes of Barry's spontaneous violence with Captain Quin and with O'Toole in the army. The primary difference here is Lady Lyndon's solitude: her excitement, grief, and anger are dissipated within the confines of her bed chamber.

Mother figures fare far better in *Barry Lyndon* than objects of passion (the nannies and maids) or patrimony (Lady Lyndon). Barry indeed seems to be an anti-Oedipus figure, as there is no contest for his mother's love with his dead father. Barry's infatuation with Nora is perhaps a challenge to his uncle as it interferes with his plans to rise in the world, or at least to pay off his debts with Captain Quin's sinecure. Barry's mother remains a dutiful caregiver and advisor throughout his life, living beyond the ending of his story in the novel in an unseemly reversal in which the parent outlives the child. In the film it is unclear who outlives the other, as both are treated as living characters who become immobile in time and space; they are relegated to an invisible off-screen space at the conclusion of the film.

The second mother in the film, the Prussian girl Lischen, is one of the most idealized women in all of Kubrick's films. In the mutual seduction scene—a static dinner table scene in her humble cottage—Lischen holds her infant son, who is clearly as much a part of the relationship as the two adults. In fact, the three comprise an ideal family unit visually rhyming with a later scene, after the Fall (marriage), where Barry adulterously embraces a woman with a baby carriage in full view of Lady Lyndon on the grounds at Castle Hackton. Through this visual progression, the family unit itself is undone, foreshadowing the singular focus on the nuclear family in Kubrick's subsequent film, *The Shining*.

Bathed in warm candlelight, this pseudo-family with Lischen presents itself as the healthy counterpoint to the improper, perverse family units, also lit by candlelight, at the gaming tables at Spa. These include the duo of Lady Lyndon and her cleric, Mr. Runt; the gambler Prince and his manservant, whom Barry must defeat with swordplay in order to be granted the Chevalier's ill gotten winnings; and the entourage of old men who attend Sir Charles Lyndon at Bath. (Sir Charles certainly represents an Oedipal conflict, as his grotesque death after a coughing fit is instigated by his knowledge of Barry's affair with Lady Lyndon.) There is a clear implication that the modest and earthy coupling of Barry and Lischen offers the only hope of generational continuity, as the aristocratic couples and families are queerly nonreproductive. Barry and Lischen's relationship is doomed, however, as it is both created and destroyed, its future foreclosed, by the cultural upheaval of war.

In sum, these gendered and sexual dynamics highlight the conflicted masculinity of Barry's character. Kubrick is recognized as a critic of phallic masculinity with films such as *Dr. Strangelove*; here he conducts an examination of the womanizer, a figure that can simultaneously invoke (hyper)masculinity and femininity and thus "conjures up the contradictory, paradoxical discourses of sexuality under patriarchy" (Mulvey 77). More precisely, Barry harks back to the characters of Max Ophuls, as explicated by Laura Mulvey, in the way he singularly embodies "two iconographies of masculinity" (76). In Ophuls, according to Mulvey, the military man and the womanizer/libertine confront one another; in *Barry Lyndon*, those figures are conjoined in Redmond Barry. The boundaries of masculinity have slackened; the existence of feminine attributes in the manliest of men becomes a possibility.

Barry Lyndon displays a remarkably astute understanding of diverse modes of masculine performance, more than a decade before Judith Butler's *Gender Trouble* appeared. These performances may not be socially authorized, as evidenced by the addition of an openly gay romance to the story in the subplot where Barry steals Lieutenant Fakenham's identity papers in order to desert the British army. Here, the military man's sexuality is rendered complex, as the two officers lament their forthcoming separation, but pledge their devotion to one another and to their country in a scene that is, somewhat surprisingly, given the conventions of the 1970s, not entirely played for humor. The name of Fakenham suggests that Barry shares a form of the closet with the gay soldiers; his secret in the most immediate sense is his desertion and it remains intact until he begins to unwisely and confidently toss about ridiculous references with Captain Potsdorf. In a later iteration of unauthorized masculinity, Barry's physical abuse of Bullingdon in public earns him no admiration for masculine vigor or authority but instead causes the landed gentry to turn against him.

In a final act of antisequence, the male figures return to the maternal realm, as Jean-Paul Dupuy has observed. "At the end of the film," he writes, "both Barry and Bullingdon return to their respective mother, thus revealing their symmetry" (61). James Naremore writes that Kubrick "made three films about the American nuclear family, all of which are satires of patriarchy" (4). Although not concerned with American nuclear families, *Barry Lyndon* satirizes patriarchy nevertheless, contemplating its structure of domination through a negative poetics. The paternal figure's loss, rather than his threatening presence (as in *The Shining* or *Eyes Wide Shut*), creates a tension with the structural codes of patriarchy itself. In *Barry Lyndon*, the father is Christian Metz's imaginary signifier: present and absent, reimagined within an impossible timeline that moves forward and backward with a recursivity that defies progress and succession.

The implication that cycles of creation and destruction are inevitable informs the conclusion to *Barry Lyndon*. Thackeray situates the sobering finale to the narrative of Redmond Barry's tale within a temporal framework that transcends the everyday concerns of characters and audiences. Kubrick retains this element as a voice-over that establishes a coda to the film. *Barry Lyndon* concludes with this statement: "It was in the reign of King George III that the aforesaid personages lived and quarreled; good or bad, handsome or ugly, rich or poor, they are all equal now." It's instructive to note that this phrase appears at the beginning of Thackeray's novel, during Barry's opening salvo regarding his origins, and describes ancestors of Barry's who lived during the reign of King George *II*. Kubrick displaces and elevates this statement, confounding the layering of pastness that already looms large over the film—a (twentieth-century) film based on a nineteenth-century novel about an eighteenth-century subject. In the long run, history's winners and losers occupy the same stratum, or, to be precise, sub-stratum. Implicit in the idea that this leveling leads to equality is the notion that the legacies of the victors might possibly be superseded by subsequent generations, just as the traces of the vanquished (whose histories are less well-documented) may be capable of being recovered. In short, history is a hostage to time; the only positive interpretation for Kubrick's narratives of failure, including *Barry Lyndon*, in the context of a palimpsestic history is that ideas, objects, and accomplishments relegated to obscurity in the historical moment might reemerge at a later moment in time.

Sequencing reality

One of the remarkable aspects of the contemporary critical response to *Barry Lyndon* is the way that Kubrick's attention to detail, evidenced in his research for the Napoleon project, and his interest in experimenting with new film technologies such as front projection in *2001* contributed to a discourse of historical authenticity around *Barry Lyndon*. There are numerous examples of this perspective, from *TIME* magazine critics Martha Duffy and Richard Schickel, whose comment that the film seemed to be "a documentary of the eighteenth century manners and morals" (163) was cited earlier, to Ken Adam in his interview with Michel Ciment, to *Irish Times* blogger Donald Clarke, who wrote in 2013 that "the picture really seems to laze along at the pace of eighteenth century society" ("50 years, 50 films"). Any understanding of *Barry Lyndon* as documentary, or as a straightforward costume drama or historical epic must be questioned in light of what is clearly an artful and artificial first person narration in Thackeray's memoir and in the context of Kubrick's own work.

In all of his films, and particularly in those that immediately precede *Barry Lyndon—Dr. Strangelove, Lolita, 2001*, and *A Clockwork Orange*—Kubrick laid claim to a narrative and visual style blending realism and surrealism rather than hewing to a representational ethos of Hollywood continuity and narrative transparency. Kubrick's heightened interest in the aesthetic environment of *Barry Lyndon*, which translated into copious preproduction research on eighteenth-century British and European painting, and what might be called the technology fetishism of the much ballyhooed extremely fast 0.7f Zeiss lens (which, in 2014, remains the fastest lens ever used in film production) should, instead, be understood as contributing to Kubrick's exploration of the uncanny, not as part of a realist–historical project. As James Naremore notes, "much like Franz Kafka, [Kubrick's] most bizarre effects emerge from the very clarity with which his imagery is rendered" (40). In a 1971 interview with Penelope Houston, Kubrick voiced his own thoughts on this subject in this manner: "I have always enjoyed dealing with a slightly surrealistic situation and presenting it in a realistic manner" (Houston 114).

Thackeray and Kubrick's rejection of historical realism is also a realization that history is an aesthetic endeavor; primarily, but not exclusively, a narrative one. This focus unmasks both the experience of temporality and the concept of history as by-products of aesthetic form rather than as "raw materials." The aesthetic forms of interest to Kubrick not only assume the shape of narrative sequencing, the subject of this chapter, but also the visual conventions of painting, photography, and cinema, which are subjects addressed in Chapter 5. In the next several chapters, my analysis departs from an examination of narrative form to address the visual and spatial implications of Kubrick's temporal experiments. Chapter 4 looks at the notion of the cycle as counterpoint to sequence, while Chapter 5 interrogates the concept of stasis and slowness in the film in relation to painting and cinematography.

4

Transnational Topographies:
Barry Lyndon as Irish Odyssey

A little bit of Hollywood has fallen off the merry-go-round and landed in Ireland.

Cos Egan, "Kubrick's Irish Odyssey"

An innovation every day.

Bernard Williams, on producing *Barry Lyndon*

In Chapter 3, I argue that succession—which is both a temporal ordering and a process of exchange between generations—structures important elements of the narrative design and themes of *Barry Lyndon*. Although the serial framework quite literally originates with Thackeray's writing in Victorian England, it acquires a heightened self-consciousness through Kubrick's interest in the reflexivity of fictional and historical construction. The theme of paternal crisis informs the halting progress of this ostensibly action-oriented picaresque tale, infuses its slow pace with profound reversals, and links these aesthetic and phenomenological experiences to the politics of class, nation, and gender.

Two contemporary reviewers of *Barry Lyndon*, Judith Crist and Cos Egan, detect another regime of temporality at work, describing the film as an odyssey ("Kubrick as Novelist"; "Kubrick's Irish Odyssey"). The term makes reference to Homer's tale of the voyage of Odysseus and links *Barry Lyndon* to Kubrick's previous work in *2001: A Space Odyssey* (1968). In this chapter, I propose that the rhetoric of the odyssey that Crist and Egan employ is far from superficial and deserves further investigation. I am not alone in holding this view. Fabrice Jaumont has pointed out that the Odyssey myth recurs in Kubrick's work, arguing that the "transcription of the Odyssean archetype and of its implied circularity into a cinematographic language allows [Kubrick], simultaneously, to question the possibilities of cinematic spatio-temporality and movement" (10).

In short, to grasp the significance of time to *Barry Lyndon*'s formal and political commentary on history and images, we must not only consider the way it constantly calls linearity into question but also pay careful attention to its repetitive, circuitous substructure. Repetition contributes to the production of the uncanny and the process evokes the familiar—a line of dialogue, a composition, a setting, a sound cue—whose difference is marked primarily by time. No repetition is "pure," as Bergson reminds us, because we must account for the difference that time makes.

This quality of doubleness is a critical feature of the Odyssey's voyage and return structure, a characteristic that marks it as the province of the death drive. The return might be conceived of as a return to origins, a return to a previous state of being, or even nonbeing. Jaumont suggests, however, that Odysseus's return "tends towards the Eternal Return, which is a questioning of time, and a refusal of death common to most heroic myths" (4). In Kubrick's film, Redmond Barry is expelled from England and returns to his origin in his mother: there is a possibility that he returns to his Irish origins. In the novel, he explicitly dies with his mother in England, but the film does not depict or allude to his actual death, it only stages his representational death.

The philosophical concept of the eternal return (or the eternal recurrence) emerges in the ancient Hindu Vedas, can be found in Pythagoras, and has been explored in the modern era by philosophers from Nietszche and Schopenhauer to Ricoeur. In the twenty-first century, theoretical physicists vigorously debate the question of origins and ends. Physicists Paul Steinhardt and Neil Turok, whose book, *Endless Universe*, cites Kubrick's *2001*, argue for a cyclic, "ekpyrotic" model of the universe ("A Cyclic Model" 1438) and propose that the Big Bang may not be "a beginning of time, but rather a transition to an earlier phase of evolution" (*Endless Universe* 2). On a more prosaic level, for the nonphysicists, the implication is that even major cosmic events may not represent a movement forward in time.

Repetitive cycles are not merely the province of philosophers and physicists: social theorists have developed ideas about circular temporalities as well. Karl Marx's much-cited observation about the character of historical change from the *Eighteenth Brumaire of Louis Bonaparte* refers to repetition and difference: "Hegel remarks somewhere that all the great, world-historic facts and personages occur, as it were, twice. He forgot to add: the first time as tragedy, the second time as farce" (5). Giambattista Vico, a key source for Marx, had emphasized repetition and difference in the course of history. In *The New Science* (1725), he proposes that human history progresses by moving repeatedly through three distinct periods: the ages of gods, heroes, and men. The *ricorso*—a break or return—represents a recurrence of an earlier social institution that perpetuates this cyclical development.

The notion of the eternal return has inspired aesthetic developments as well. The gothic sensibility of Walpole, Maturin, Le Fanu, and Stoker utilizes problematics of interrupted succession, family secrets, and haunted environments—in short, the cyclical reappearance of what, after Freud, would be called the return of the repressed. This dimension of the concept of the return imagines the continued existence and the reanimation of what was meant to be eradicated, or expunged, but which has been repressed through trauma.

This chapter examines the repetitions, returns, and circularities that counterpoint the precise yet disfigured sequentiality of *Barry Lyndon*. I begin by situating the question of return within the Irish context of the film's production. Examining the film's relationship to Irishness, particularly in light of theories of Irish postcoloniality and alternative temporalities, grants a richer understanding of this film's aesthetic and political stakes. Bliss Cua Lim has written that "colonialism and its aftermath underpin modern historical time," a temporality that is epitomized by both the assumption of homogeneity and an ideology of progress (12). Following in the footsteps of theorists such as Fredric Jameson and David Harvey, Lim argues that the "temporal logic of colonialism" founds a "linear, evolutionary view of history that spatialize[s] time and cultural difference" (13). Lim sets the cinema of the fantastic in opposition to colonialist cinema, asserting the existence of "multiple times that fail to coincide with the measured, uniform intervals quantified by clock and calendar" (2) (and, one might add, the film projector). Lim argues that the supernatural "discloses the limits of historical time" (2).

My premise is that *Barry Lyndon*, while it does not attempt to approach the realm of the supernatural film, nevertheless discloses the limits of our concepts of historical time. After examining the film's production history, and asking to what extent Kubrick's production participated in the material reenactment of colonialism, I turn to a discussion of the film's melancholic and nostalgic dispositions, connecting that sensibility to the temporal and affective logic of colonialism.

On the most fundamental level, the overall structure of *Barry Lyndon*—like Kubrick films such as *Lolita*, *Full Metal Jacket*, and *Eyes Wide Shut*—conforms to a repetitive, cyclical pattern. *2001* may be the film of Kubrick's whose temporal structure *Barry Lyndon* most closely resembles. Whereas *2001* embeds the quotidian and repetitive experience of daily life within the arid cleanliness of space technology, *Barry Lyndon*'s temporality emerges from the tension between the grim succession of lost fathers and sons and the repetition of the duels, the brawls, and untimely deaths. *2001* is certainly the Kubrick film most strongly associated with cycles and evolutionary leaps, as Philip Kuberski observes, writing:

> This primordial symbolism of the circle and the cycle reminds us that the movement forward and up must also accommodate itself to recursiveness; there is a limit to linear progression, at which point lines begin to turn and time to bend. It is the cyclonic tedium of technological existence, this parody of eternity, which will be broken once the third Monolith is discovered. (69)

In *Barry Lyndon*, what is erected (or written) in Part I is dismantled (and unwritten) in Part II. Kubrick tightly orchestrates the plot events so that every event or persona Barry encounters in Part I reappears as an uncanny double in Part II, reexperienced as an ironic reversal. In Part I, Barry's father's fatal duel opens the film; it is followed by the faked duel between Barry and Quin, the marriage of Nora and Quin (which Barry hears about after the fact), and the death of Barry's surrogate father, Captain Grogan, in the skirmish. During Barry's tenure as a soldier and gambler, he acquires two surrogate fathers, Captain Potzdorf and the Chevalier, and that same period of his life concludes with his loss of both of them. In Part II, the sequence of events is reversed and inverted. When Barry marries Lady Lyndon, he becomes a surrogate father to Lord Bullingdon, then a father to Bryan. Bryan's death echoes Barry's father's demise, as it is connected to the purchase of a horse. The final duel with Bullingdon pits ersatz father against son, Barry occupying the role of the former. The structural certainty of the rise-and-fall narrative—what goes up must come down—becomes a powerful meditation on the cycles of creation and destruction, of acquisition and loss, both on an individual and on a cultural scale.

Repetition and the cycle, which, I shall argue, are related to the history of colonialism, shape the production process and the text of *Barry Lyndon*. Writing specifically about repetition and history, Vivian Sobchak states: "repetition foregrounds configuration rather than linearity, circularity rather than teleology. Thus, when 'historical events' are taken as its object, repetition works against their objectively known 'finishedness,' their 'overness,' their 'pastness'" (38). Cyclical historical narratives detach events from history and intervene in the process that would relegate history to an enclosed, hermetic pastness, left behind in the wake of the progress represented by modern, linear time. Below, I begin with *Barry Lyndon*'s production history and its relation to colonial time before moving to the film's discourse of melancholia and its temporal implications.

Irish Odyssey

This film is without doubt the most important film ever produced in Waterford.

Donald Brady, *Film and Film-Making in Waterford: Preliminary Studies*

Between July 1973 and the end of January 1974, Stanley Kubrick spent 7 months in Ireland shooting *Barry Lyndon*. I examine *Barry Lyndon* in this Irish context, which encompasses the film's production history and textual attributes, because both aspects speak to important debates within the study of national and transnational cinema and within the emerging field of film geography. Investigating the Irishness of *Barry Lyndon* also offers important insights into the film's multiple temporalities.

In many ways, *Barry Lyndon* both clarifies and confounds the national cinema paradigm that continues to shape our understanding of cinema, despite the globalization of media industries in the twenty-first century. My goal here is certainly not to reclaim *Barry Lyndon* for an Irish cinema canon (or an American or British canon). Instead, I want to consider the way national identities and transnational geographies informed the production process and offer new vantage points from which to consider the film's temporal regimes.

On the face of it, the *Barry Lyndon* project speaks to the inherently transnational character of many cinematic endeavors: it involves the literary adaptation of Irish fictions and histories by Calcutta-born (and well-traveled) British writer William Makepeace Thackeray and the cinematic adaptation of Thackeray's work more than a century later by Stanley Kubrick, an American film director who, by the 1970s, had been living and working in the United Kingdom for nearly a decade.

On the narrative level, the film examines a transnational culture of warfare, including the associated social and military hierarchies—topics that recur throughout Kubrick's *oeuvre*. On the formal level, the film explores the way that aesthetic technologies—manifested most prominently in Kubrick's use of eighteenth-century portraits and landscape paintings—produce national identities, making visible British national subjects who must also be understood within a global context of domination. For my purposes here, the Irishness of *Barry Lyndon* has little to do with a purist vision of national identity or cultural integrity; instead, I am interested in exploring the film's discourse on the untidy, compelling, and often troubling social and aesthetic processes, and their imbrication with temporal regimes, that produce and sustain national identities.

Irish time

Ireland's peculiar relation to temporality has long been a subject of interest to scholars of Irish literature and culture. In *Inventing Ireland: The Literature of the Modern Nation*, Declan Kiberd writes, "what was modern about the 1916 thinkers was precisely their disruption of chronology, their insistence on the revolutionary idea of tradition" (294). In *Transformations in Irish Culture*, Luke Gibbons describes a dissonant relation to modern temporal regimes when he calls Ireland a "First World Country with a Third World memory" (*Transformations* 3), a formulation so resonant that it has been cited by Irish politicians (Haslam n41). Joe Cleary has proposed a rethinking of Marxist historical trajectories because "Irish history had evolved in ways that did not conform in some decisive respects to developments in the metropolitan cultures that inform Lukács's or Jameson's works" (208–9). In his work on the Irish novel, Gregory Dobbins points to the "temporal heterogeneity of Irish culture—a condition that signals an alternative to a more dominant conception of modernity" (87). Peter Hitchcock reminds us that, "in every space of postcoloniality, [. . .] culture refracts duration; not just that colonialism was endured, but that its figures of time did not absolutely displace or dismantle local forms of temporality" (4). Finally, in *Irish Times: Temporalities of Modernity*, David Lloyd writes about the ruin as a symbol of continuing violence in Irish culture, asserting the certain figures of time persist, not as Romantic possibilities for retrieving a precolonial past, but as unassimilable, resistant hauntings: apparent as "symptoms of an obstinate backwardness" (3), they are "recalcitrant for capitalist modernity" (88). His case study of the contemporary photographs of Allen de Souza offers a glimpse of an alternative history, "not rendered as the record of a gradually imposed civility but as transforming the melancholy of loss into the refusal to let go of the possibilities of the past" (5).

Homogeneous temporality and orderly sequence may comprise the official scheme as proclaimed by imperial power, attempting to align the social order with scientific progress, as Giordano Nanni documents in *The Colonisation of Time*, his study of nineteenth-century British settler colonialism in Australia and South Africa. Repetition, cyclicality, and heterogeneity are more likely to be associated with premodern and postmodern temporalities. In the text of *Barry Lyndon*, and in its production process, the linearity of modern, colonial time encountered the cyclicality of the refusal to let go of the possibilities of the past, and what might be called a return of the repressed.

Irish cinema and the 1970s

When Kubrick brought his production to Ireland in 1973, he, perhaps unwittingly, entered into a set of long-standing disputes regarding representations of Irish landscapes and identities. As Ruth Barton has established, the story of Irish national cinema is, in large part, a story about international filmmaking in Ireland. Lance Pettit views this history as imbued with "complicated forms of economic and cultural domination" (45) and, more specifically, with Anglo-American neocolonialism. Since Ireland served so often as a location for films produced by British and North American directors, "an image of Ireland on screen emerged out of the national industries of other countries" (Barton 4). The images of Hibernia captured and disseminated by the creative machinery of globalized cinematic encounters prior to Kubrick's arrival came from films shot in Ireland, from Sidney Olcott's *The Lad from Old Ireland* (1910) and *The Colleen Bawn* (1911), to Robert Flaherty's *Man of Aran* (1937), John Ford's *The Quiet Man* (1952), and David Lean's *Ryan's Daughter* (1970).

In this regard, the images that grace the "Green Screen"—a term for media depictions of Ireland and Irishness that was coined prior to the advent of green screen production technology—serve as an important example of the "inescapable truth" that "cinema itself has contributed to the imagining and definition of national landscapes and communities" (Harper and Rayner 24). By 1973, US and British productions had created a vision of a magical, pastoral Emerald Isle and Kubrick's *Barry Lyndon*, intentionally or not, engaged in a dialogue with that construct.

As Luke Gibbons, John Hill, and Kevin Rockett argued in their groundbreaking collection in Irish cinema studies, *Cinema and Ireland*, Ireland has been made visible to film spectators around the world as a rural, primitive, nostalgic, and supernatural terrain. The origin of these stereotypes can be traced back to the writings of the earliest British colonizers of Ireland, from Gerald of Wales's *Topographica Hibernica* (1188) to Barnabe Rich's *A New Description of Ireland* (1610) and Edmund Spenser's *A View of the Present State of Ireland* (1633). Rich, Spenser, and other observers viewed the populations living in Ireland as wild, uncivilized, and primitive people who could not be trusted to properly husband the available natural resources, especially the vast, seemingly empty, landscape—a view that justified the British plantation of the island. As a result of this centuries-long contest over the land, which culminated in the recruitment of Irish pastoralism by the post-Independence government of Éamon de Valera, the Irish landscape emerged as the premier emblem of Irishness within political and cultural nationalist discourses (McLoone *Film* 137).

This ancient and early twentieth-century history had by no means been forgotten by, nor was it irrelevant to, the nationalist politics of the 1970s, when the Troubles were reignited after Bloody Sunday (1972) and when anxieties about Britain's military presence in the North revitalized the Irish Republican Army (IRA). The link to landscape remained salient: numerous nationalist ballads of the era cite locations both specific and general, including "Four Green Fields," "Only Our Rivers Run Free," and "Fighting Men of Crossmaglen." By the 1980s, plays such as Brian Friel's "Translations" (1980), developed within the context of the politically attuned Field Day Theatre Company, would explicitly present the British ordnance survey map of Ireland as a practice of both material and linguistic colonization.

Questions of colonization loom large in the history of the film industry in Ireland as well. Underscoring the point that national cinema industries are produced by transnational flows of people and capital, it was American director John Huston—who had become an Irish citizen—who led the call for the Irish government to develop financing mechanisms to support Irish filmmakers. The Irish Film Board/*Bord Scannán na hEireann* was established as a direct result of his lobbying. As the IFB geared up in the late 1970s to provide financing mechanisms, its charge became complex and potentially contradictory, reflecting the realities of establishing a "local" national-cultural art practice within a global industry structure. "In so far as it considers it appropriate" reads one provision of the 1980 law that established the Board, "the Board shall have regard to the need for the expression of national culture through the medium of filmmaking": another provision empowers the board to "participate and promote participation in international collaborative projects" ("Irish Film Board Act").

While the promise of the Film Board slowly moved toward fruition during the 1970s, an Irish cinema developed independent of government support that seemed bent on exploring the less salubrious and quaint elements of Irish life that international directors had ignored. The pristine, nostalgic, and rural vision of Ireland embodied in the beautiful landscapes that Ford and Lean had exploited became an object of derision. This rethinking of Ireland's Green Screen is evident in Bob Quinn's *Poitín* (1977), with its unvarnished perspective on economic deprivation in a rural village; Joe Comerford's *Traveller* (1981), a film in which a traveler couple's honeymoon is simultaneously a cross-border smuggling trip; and Cathal Black's *Pigs* (1984), which depicts a group of squatters in squalid, inner-city Dublin.

Against the backdrop of a burgeoning Irish art cinema of alternative images and narratives—and, importantly, amidst the return of the repressed in the form of the political violence that would be known as The Troubles—Stanley Kubrick began shooting *Barry Lyndon*. He followed almost immediately in the footsteps of another American director, Robert Altman, who had recently shot his seventh feature, *Images* (1971), in the Wicklow mountains south of Dublin.[1] Like Kubrick's film, Altman's project reveals the complexity associated with the national cinema paradigm, and, specifically, the increasing difficulty of reconciling global cinema industries with the continued existence of nation states. Despite the fact that the film was made by an American director and production company, *Images* was entered as Ireland's first official entry at Cannes in 1971, where Susannah York, the star of the film, won the award for best actress.

Although Kubrick joined in a tradition of international filmmakers who ventured to Ireland, *Barry Lyndon* has not been assessed in terms of its relationship to the Irish economy and film industry or its contribution to screen representations of Ireland; Arthur Flynn's *The Story of Irish Film*, which gives a brief account of the production side, is one exception. This scholarly indifference stands in stark contrast to the considerable attention paid to films such as *The Quiet Man* and John Huston's *The Dead* (1987), both shot in Ireland by American directors. The

---

[1] Coincidentally, *Images*, like *Barry Lyndon*, descended into obscurity. It was considered lost; rumors that Columbia had destroyed the negative were quashed when MGM released a DVD version in 2003.

fact that Ford and Huston claimed Irish heritage and that their films were sourced in short stories by Irish writers Maurice Walsh and James Joyce, respectively, may endow these projects with a patina of Irishness by genotype that partially explains their prominence. The early events of Thackeray's *Barry Lyndon* are explicitly set in Ireland and Kubrick's film was widely understood in popular and critical discourses as the tale of an Irish rogue; a special screening of the film was made available to President Cearbhall Ó'Dálaigh of Ireland at the film's release.[2] In short, *Barry Lyndon* claims to represent something about Irishness, from a perspective that emanates not from the sentimental Irish-American heritage of Ford and Huston but, in the first instance, from Thackeray's mid-Victorian reading of Irish history and, finally, from Kubrick's interpretation of that angle of vision.

Finally, when it comes to the national cinema paradigm, Stanley Kubrick seems to enjoy the status of a man without a country. "In a remarkable way," Penelope Houston wrote in 1971, after Kubrick had been living in the United Kingdom for almost a decade, "he has kept himself apart from all worlds, appearing neither as an expatriate American filmmaker nor as a resident British Director" (108). After Kubrick's death, Warner Brothers' Vice President Steve Southgate reinforced this view in a statement in Peter Bogdanovich's omnibus eulogy in *The New York Times*. Kubrick was "one person in the film industry who knew how the film industry worked—in every country in the world" ("What They Say"). James Naremore offers another perspective, comparing Kubrick's work to that of Franz Kafka and endorsing Tom Gunning's view of the director "not simply as the last modernist but also as the last of the Viennese *auteurs*" (4). Thomas Elsaesser, by contrast, emphasizes his American sensibility: "the move to Britain [. . .] did not dent Kubrick's resolve to be an American mainstream (rather than a European art cinema) director" (137). In my view, it would be antithetical to the film's complex transnational character to limit *Barry Lyndon* to the context of a national cinema paradigm. What interests me is the way that the problematic character of national identity is embedded in the production history and text of *Barry Lyndon*, contributing, in both compelling and perhaps problematic ways, to its richness and complexity.

Ireland has experienced cinematic colonialism on two fronts: through transnational economic processes and through cinema's representational regimes. Questions about the *Barry Lyndon* project's relationship to these dynamics

---

[2] Letter, Correspondence file, SK14/6/18. Stanley Kubrick Archive, London College of Communication, London, UK. Subsequent references to material in the archive will refer to specific files.

remain. How was Kubrick's *Barry Lyndon* production informed by, and how did it intervene in, the financial realities of location filmmaking in Ireland and what sorts of figurative (and potentially colonialist) constructions of Ireland and Irishness does the film put forward?

Landscapes of production

Details surrounding the *Barry Lyndon* production may offer some surprises to Kubrick fans, given the biographical conventions that now attend his directorial persona. In an often-cited metaphor drawn from his enjoyment of the game of chess, Kubrick is frequently cast as the ultimate chess master, anticipating and controlling every possible contingency. In fact, the production of this film posed numerous unanticipated challenges, including the change of venue from the United Kingdom to Ireland very close to the start of shooting; a spate of bad weather in Ireland in the fall of 1973; an emergency appendectomy for one of Kubrick's daughters; and an unplanned and hasty retreat back to the United Kingdom in February 1974.[3] The unusual circumstances that seemed to plague the location shoot affected every level of the production, resulting in numerous delays, which, in turn, contributed to a discourse of excess that informed the film's theatrical release. After moving to Ireland, the production went over schedule and over budget, a fact made evident from producer Bernard Williams's daily recalculations on production call sheets. Williams's report for January 10, 1973, for example, calculates the shoot in Waterford as taking 10 days more than had been scheduled (39 as opposed to 29), but he then subtracts 8 days from the planned Dublin shoot without explanation, arriving at a total number that is just 2 more than the original budgeted period of 79 days.[4] Paul Hitchcock, the

---

[3] The fact that the decision about changing the venue from the United Kingdom to Ireland in 1973 may have been a fairly precipitous one is reflected in correspondence housed in the Stanley Kubrick Archive at the London College of Communication (SK 14/6/1–21). On July 6, 1973, Jan Harlan wrote a letter to British customs and excise regarding the importation of a specially outfitted Arriflex II camera from Cinema Products in Los Angeles in which he specifically stated the film was being shot in England. On July 19, 1973, Kubrick signed a letter that discusses the scouting of locations in Castletown, Ireland which also states that he and the scouting crew were staying at the Ardree Hotel in Waterford. A letter of August 24, 1973 from William O'Kelley, Kubrick's production liaison to the office of the Irish *Taoiseach* (Prime Minister), explains that the decision had been made to shoot the entire film in Ireland.

[4] Stanley Kubrick Archive, SK 14/3/1.

Warner Brothers liaison on the production, estimated an overage of more than $3 million as early as April of 1974 and, in notes from July of 1975, estimated the cost of finishing the film at $10.2 million.[5]

In the Warner Brothers press kit for the film, an anonymous article entitled "Kubrick's Irish Odyssey"—later attributed to Irish writer Cos Egan, who was credited as a set dresser on the production—characterizes the director's arrival in Ireland in the grandiose and sexualized terms of first contact. He marks in particular the spatial and, implicitly, temporal difference between the backwardness of Ireland and the modernity of England: "No one ever panned a camera in Tipperary before, so it was virgin land for Stanley. Through his eyes we see the innocent beauty of Ireland as in contrast to the rich material wealth of England" ("Kubrick's"). These publicity materials reinvigorate familiar tropes associated with the Irish landscape that originate in the earliest texts of British colonization, notably the undiscovered, primitive quality of the terrain and the evident failure of its inhabitants to convert it into a useful economic resource.

Initially, Kubrick had planned to make the entire film on location in the United Kingdom. According to the financial records contained in the preproduction files at the Stanley Kubrick Archive in London, he rented an airplane hangar at the Handley Page aircraft company complex in Radlett, Hertfordshire, where he had shot some scenes for *A Clockwork Orange*, in order to employ the front projection process he had pioneered in *2001*. He also considered using Shepperton studios for this process.

Kubrick biographer John Baxter writes that production designer Ken Adam, line producer Bernard Williams, and producer Jan Harlan persuaded Kubrick to consider shooting in Ireland because of its well-preserved eighteenth-century structures (285). However, the timeline of the scouting of Irish locations suggests that the decision to shoot in Ireland may have been based upon not architectural differences but economic differences and, specifically, the strategies the British trades unions adopted to protect the UK film industry. British unions were reluctant to cooperate with foreign productions that intended to shoot outside of studios—unless they were shooting at sites that were seen as necessary locations—because they aimed to preserve the UK's high cost facilities and maintain its skilled workers. In *The British Film Industry in the 1970s: Capital, Culture and Creativity*, Sian Barber characterizes the era's unions as "militant"

---

[5] Correspondence File #3, Warner Brothers Archives, Burbank, CA.

and considers the film industry unions to be "partially responsible for the failure of co-production agreements" in the 1970s (59).

The unions' motivations are apparent in a letter written by Michael Relph, Chairman of the Film Production Association (FPA), published in "Cinema, TV, Today" on December 30, 1972 relating an internecine dispute between the FPA and the Federation of Film Unions (FFU). The latter was proposing a policy that all films—with very few exceptions—should be made in a studio. Relph praised the major studios, whose "onerous" burden he defined as trying to maintain "as large a force of skilled labour as possible as well as providing high quality studio and technical facilities when required" ("Letter"). He cites a situation that seems very close to the disagreement that would arise during the summer of 1973 with Kubrick's production. "It is recognized that certain producers and directors prefer the autonomy that working in a freelance situation outside a major studio gives to them, but this must be weighed against a responsibility to our national industry" ("Letter").

According to production notes housed at the Warner Brothers archive, at a June 7, 1973 meeting with representatives from three British unions, the Association of Cinematograph, Television and Allied Technicians (ACTT), the National Association of Theatrical Television and Kine Employees (NATTKE), and the FPA, the representative of the latter expressed displeasure at Kubrick's plan to shoot in the United Kingdom outside the studio facilities, especially for the front projection process.[6] The unions seemed to accept shooting outside the studios as warranted only when specific locations were critical; Kubrick's high-tech front projection process seems to have been a major sticking point. A letter dated June 18, 1973 from the General Secretary of the ACTT to the FPA requests the Head of the FPA to use his authority to encourage Kubrick to use the studios.[7] On July 11, further discussions between the production team and the unions revolved around the use of Handley Page as a base and the potential use of Shepperton studios for the front projection element.[8]

A July 9, 1973 production note states that Kubrick had sent staff to Ireland to scout locations, and a July 16 update affirmed that Kubrick himself was in Ireland and liked Waterford.[9] Warner Brothers' official position regarding the decision to

---

[6] Warner Brothers Archive, Correspondence File #3.
[7] Correspondence File #3, Warner Brothers Archive.
[8] Correspondence File #3, Warner Brothers Archive.
[9] Correspondence File #3, Warner Brothers Archive.

move the production to Ireland was that it would save money; this public stance may well have reflected the primary motivation for the relocation, or it may have been adopted to exercise leverage with the unions. In a letter to the editor of *New York* magazine dated September 26, 1975, about 3 months before the film's release, Kubrick defends the decision to shoot in Ireland, arguing that making the film in the United Kingdom and, in particular, the high cost of taking the crew away on location (which would have added 20% to the cost of production) and the insufficiently interesting sites located within working distance of London were primary reasons for the move.[10] *Barry Lyndon* ultimately cost 11 million dollars, a figure which was seen as excessive and may explain why Kubrick felt he had to publicly defend the decision to move the production to Ireland. For comparison purposes, *Jaws*, a film also touting location shooting and innovative technology (the mechanical shark), was budgeted at $3.5 million and went over by about $3 million. In the case of *Jaws*, the producers were able to "parlay those problems into positive publicity" (Schatz 18). This was not the case for the *Barry Lyndon* production, whose process ultimately consumed 300 days over a span of 2 years. Principal photography took place in six counties in Ireland and at several stately homes in England, while a second unit shot scenes at castles in Germany.[11] Warner Brothers' executive John Calley alludes to the prodigious shoot in "Kubrick's Grandest Gamble," the *TIME* cover story released just before the film's premiere (Duffy and Schickel 167).

Thus, although it might have been "accurate" in some sense for Kubrick to shoot the film's early scenes in Ireland because Thackeray's fictional narrative of Redmond Barry's rise and fall begins there, he seemed to have moved the production to Ireland in order to produce the visual spectacle he was planning on his own terms, while also reigning in costs. As it happened, the production went over schedule and over budget, and the lore of the long shoot and budget overruns became a part of the public discourse about the film.

It is important to consider not just motivations for the Ireland shoot, but also its effects, and one way to measure *Barry Lyndon*'s impact—the production's footprint, as it were—is to examine patterns of employment. In the summer and fall of 1973, the production was based at the Ardree Hotel in Waterford, but it relocated to Dublin after a holiday break in late November; shooting recommenced in Dublin in January 1974. Kubrick used a large cast and crew

---

[10] Unpublished draft; Correspondence File #2, Warner Brothers Archive.
[11] Daily call sheets, Stanley Kubrick Archive, SK 14/3/1.

on *Barry Lyndon*, one totaling more than 160 individuals. He employed Irish actors, extras, and craftspeople; an unattributed production note in the Warner Brothers archive estimated the cost of the Irish crew at $12,000 per week. According to letters of correspondence between the production and the Irish Army as well as call sheets which list the numbers of cast members expected for lunch on the set, 250 men from the Irish army were hired as soldier extras for battle sequences. Although a claim has circulated that Kubrick established a costume factory in Waterford, no evidence for one exists in the production files available at the Stanley Kubrick or Warner Brothers archives. There is documentation that indicates the production maintained one building at the Handley Page complex in the United Kingdom until October 1973; this unit was a costume shop, where seamstresses and tailors made the period costumes, and served as a props department.[12]

Kubrick brought with him a number of British crew members to Ireland for the shoot, and rented or purchased certain props and costumes—guns, swords, chandeliers, and the film's ubiquitous wigs—from sources in London, having made most of these arrangements before moving the production from Handley Page to Waterford.[13] Kubrick hired men with whom he had worked before for several key roles, including Tony Lawson, the editor, and John Alcott, the cinematographer, who were both British. Still, production files reveal that 26 of 55 cast members (47%) and 46 of 106 crew members (43%) listed home addresses in Ireland, mainly in Dublin and Wicklow.[14] Whether these individuals were Irish citizens or residents is difficult to determine, but it is clear that the production contributed to local Irish economies through production expenses (hotels, meals, car hire) and payroll for about 8 months, from the initial scouting of locations in the summer of 1973 until the production left Dublin in February of 1974.

One reason Kubrick's production fell behind schedule in Ireland was that it was caught up in dramatic historical events that testified to the continuing relevance of imperial warfare, one of *Barry Lyndon*'s primary thematic touchstones. In 1972, the IRA expanded its campaign of violence beyond Northern Ireland, instigating bombing campaigns in Britain and in the Republic of Ireland. Kubrick's film, whose subject matter concerned a global imperial conflict and whose production

[12] Stanley Kubrick Archive, Production, Daily call sheets, SK 14/3/1 and Correspondence, SK 14/6/19.

[13] Stanley Kubrick Archive, Pre-production, Costumes—Acquisition and Hire, and Properties, SK 14/2/5 and 14/2/10.

[14] Stanley Kubrick Archive, Pre-production, Cast and Crew SK 14/3/21.

required hundreds of Irish soldiers to march, dressed as British Redcoats, across Irish fields unwittingly and perhaps even ironically found itself swept up in the drama of current events related to British colonial history.

The return of The Troubles to the Irish Republic—the term originally was used to describe the war years of 1919–22, a period of both anticolonial resistance and civil war—instigated Kubrick's return to England. On Wednesday, January 30, 1974, a scheduled day of shooting in Dublin's Phoenix Park was canceled due to the widespread chaos created by 14 bomb threats that disrupted the entire city. The cast and crew reported that they were not able to get to the location until mid-day, but it was too late to film. Kubrick filed a routine insurance claim to compensate the production for time lost.[15]

Within a week, and apparently in response to circumstances related to a different kind of threat, possibly emanating from the IRA, the entire production had relocated to the United Kingdom. A February 12, 1974 production report signed by associate producer Bernard Williams indicated that the schedule for the Irish location shoot had been completed on February 6, and that the cast and crew had left for England, resuming filming there on February 12.[16] Kubrick and his family had left Ireland several days before the 6th, however, with some haste, in response to what was later described as a second threat, communicated via a phone call. The details of the second threat were never made public; in the September 1975 letter to *New York* magazine, Kubrick assured his readers that the Irish had no quarrel with Americans. The authorities assumed the threat was a local response to his British crew, Kubrick wrote, and cited "British Go Home" graffiti that appeared throughout the Republic. The insurance company refused to compensate the production for the time lost to the move back to England, which has contributed to lingering speculation regarding the second IRA incident as to whether or not it actually took place, or whether it was a hoax instigated by a crew member.

Pavel Barter's 2013 radio documentary on the production, "Castles, Candles and Kubrick," revisits this mystery. Crew members on the shoot provide conflicting testimony that ultimately fails to resolve the controversy surrounding the hasty retreat from Ireland. Claims are forwarded that the second incident involved a specific threat, conveyed by a phone call to Dublin Castle, and that, when Kubrick heard about it, he left Ireland immediately. Other commentators

[15] Stanley Kubrick Archive, Production, Progress Reports, SK 14/3/2.
[16] Stanley Kubrick Archive, Production, Progress Reports, SK 14/3/2.

reject that explanation, however, suggesting that the second incident was unrelated to the IRA bombing campaign and was possibly the work of parties disgruntled with the production, perhaps even an extra who had been fired.[17]

These incidents speak to the influence of twentieth-century anticolonial resistance in Ireland, manifested in part by a renewed campaign of violence in the early 1970s, on the *Barry Lyndon* production. This is the case, despite the circumstances of the second threat, because anticolonial politics served as either a motivation or a cover story.

Returning to the question of economics, it would seem that *Barry Lyndon* had a substantial direct economic impact on the Irish economy, both as a presence and as an absence. The contribution was mainly concentrated in the employment provided to professionals and extras in Dublin, Wexford, and Waterford. In addition, individuals whose homes and property were used as locations were compensated at mutually agreeable daily or weekly rates: the production paid 25 to 50 pounds a day for fields and meadows.[18] Equipment was rented from Mole Richardson in Dublin and from Ardmore Studios.[19] When Kubrick left Ireland, Arthur Flynn estimates that 22 days remained on the shooting schedule (134); this counters the scenario presented in the production reports, where daily recalculations strain credibility. Even Cos Egan complained about the probable financial impact of the production's early withdrawal: "Barry Lyndon's premature departure from his native shores had probably cost the country millions of pounds in all sorts of spin offs, from an epic film production such as this" ("Kubrick's Irish Odyssey"). The scenes that were cancelled would have employed 500 extras, according to Flynn: blaming the IRA's bombing campaign for an overall decline in filmmaking in the Republic in 1974, Flynn nevertheless calculates that the profit shown by Ardmore Studios in the first part of 1974 was due to Kubrick's visit (134).

This survey of the film's production history reveals that Kubrick employed Irish people, while relying heavily on British suppliers and a British team with whom he had previously worked. The production certainly infused some financial support into local economies, while becoming embroiled in the return

---

[17] *Castles, Candles, and Kubrick* (Pavel Barter 2013). "Documentary on Newstalk." www.newstalk.ie. Aired October 19, 2013 (accessed December 3, 2013).
[18] Stanley Kubrick Archive, Correspondence, SK 14/6/1.
[19] Stanley Kubrick Archive, Financial Papers, SK 14/11/2.

of the repressed, or what today would be called blowback from historical events that were ironically and intimately related to the narrative Kubrick was filming.

Kubrick's wild colonial boy and Celtic melancholy

Not surprisingly, assessing the text of *Barry Lyndon* in terms of its relationship to screen Irishness proves to be at least as complicated as recounting the project's economic contributions and political entanglements. In terms of textual matters, the question of the return—in a temporal rather than a financial sense—is intertwined with the same tropes of Irishness that we have seen emerging from the long history of British writing on Ireland, including in Thackeray's own work.

In envisioning *Barry Lyndon*, Kubrick both indicts and participates in a colonialist figuring of Ireland's geographical and social landscapes by deploying two ideological frames. Kubrick relies heavily on two affective and aesthetic frameworks. The first such framework is melancholy; as critics and scholars have noted, the film is almost overwhelmingly elegiac and ridden with grief. Peter Cosgrove notes, "Kubrick's adaptation becomes an elegy for the destruction of the low-born hero by an unyielding class system" (22) and Robert Kolker calls the film " a ceremony of loneliness" (163).

The second structuring element—more literally a work of framing—formally contextualizes the film's subject matter within eighteenth-century debates regarding the beautiful, the picturesque, and the sublime. This aesthetic discourse is explored in relation to the temporality of the interval in Chapter 5.

The prominence of mournful emotions in the film and its overall melancholic disposition are partly achieved through the slow pace, the subdued facial and physical expressiveness of Ryan O'Neal and Marisa Berensen's performances, and Kubrick's sorrowful musical choices. The latter include, prominently, Handel's "Sarabande," Seán Ó Riada's "Women of Ireland," and, perhaps especially poignant, Schubert's "Piano Trio No. 2 in E Flat Major." The piano trio was a late work completed during the composer's final illness and it was subjected to "considerable alteration" (McQuiston 108), adding to its melancholy tone.

Mise en scène plays a role in establishing the film's melancholic tone as well, especially as the setting and cinematography contribute to the increasing isolation of Redmond Barry after his marriage. Numerous shots in the second half of the film depict Barry alone, overshadowed by his environment to begin with, and singled out through the movement of the reverse zoom (see Figure 4.1). This tonal despondency, I will propose, has everything to do with the same historical complexities related to national identity and imperialism that made the production of *Barry Lyndon* an odyssey and an ordeal, with its voyage to Ireland and retreat to Britain. Ireland's history as a British colony stands at the center of this frame, metaphorically and literally. That history animates the film's temporalities and provides the occasion for the return of the repressed. The melancholia that supplies the affect of film has its roots in a nexus of politics and psychology that contemporary scholars have variously referred to as postcolonial or racial melancholia.

Scholars of race and postcoloniality in both American and British contexts have generated new, politically inflected understandings of melancholia, a condition typically relegated to the "apolitical" realm of psychoanalysis. In *Postcolonial Melancholy*, Paul Gilroy argues that "the racial and national fantasies that [British] imperial and colonial power required were [. . .] predominantly narcissistic" and proposes that "it is the infrahuman political body of the immigrant rather than the body of the sovereign that comes to represent all the

Figure 4.1 Barry, alone, engulfed by his surroundings. *Barry Lyndon* (1975). Produced by Jan Harlan, Stanley Kubrick, and Bernard Williams. Directed by Stanley Kubrick.

discomforting ambiguities of the empire's painful and shameful but apparently nonetheless exhilarating history" (x).

Using this approach, it is Redmond Barry's colonial Irish body—as racialized in terms of the "scientific" discourses of the eighteenth and nineteenth centuries—that becomes the site of discomfort and ambiguity. Anne Anlin Cheng agues in *The Melancholy of Race* that racial identification itself is a melancholic act because it is associated with the dynamics of loss and compensation—dynamics that we have seen in operation in Redmond Barry's first person testimony as to his origins. Laura O'Connor draws upon Cheng's analysis of racial melancholia— the "deep-seated, intangible, psychical complications for people living within a ruling *episteme* that privileges that which they can never be" (quoted in O'Connor 43)—to develop her characterization of the Anglicized Celt. This figure is defined doubly by a thwarted ambition to acquire an unattainable Englishness and a repressed identification with a Gaelic culture that is reviled and revered (O'Connor 43). The Anglicized Celt "expresses this ambivalence as grief" (43).

Barry Lyndon's delicate yet tangible connection between Irishness and mournful emotions stems partly from the film's source material, produced by a British writer with his own ambivalent relationship to Ireland. Thackeray's writing on Ireland encompasses not only the installment version of *Barry Lyndon*, published in *Fraser's* in 1844, but also his *Irish Sketch Book* travelogue, published in 1842. His personal connection to Ireland was mediated through his marriage to Isabelle Shawe, an Irish woman who experienced severe mental health problems throughout their marriage. In "A Box of Novels," from the early 1840s, Thackeray constructs an Irish national character heavily freighted with melancholia:

> A characteristic of the Irish writers and people, which has not been at all appreciated by the English, is, I think, that of extreme melancholy. All Irish stories are sad, all humorous Irish songs are sad: there is never a burst of laughter excited by them but, as I fancy, tears are near at hand. (46)

In his reprinted edition of the *Irish Sketch Book* as *Miscellanies* in 1871, Thackeray commits to a geographically inflected paradigm of national identity by connecting the sadness of the Irish landscape—even amidst sunshine—to Irish music:

> I think the Irish scenery [is] just like the Irish melodies—sweet, wild and sad even in the sunshine. (*Miscellanies* 429)

He further conflates the emotions of the Irish people with the physical environment. About the landscape, he writes:

> You may walk all Ireland through, and hardly see a cheerful [landscape] [...] the finest and richest landscape in Ireland always appeared to me to be sad, and the people corresponded with the place. ("A Box of Novels" 47)

For Thackeray, it is an inevitability that cheerfulness will be wed to tearfulness: "[The country], it always seems to me, like the people, to look cheerful in spite of its wretchedness, or, more correctly, to look tearful and cheerful at the same time" (*Irish Sketch Book* 92). Luke Gibbons has identified the construction as a long-standing stereotype defining Ireland as the location where the "tear and smile seem twin-born" (*Quiet* 47).

Once sadness and cheerfulness are conjoined in double-edged poignancy, which is particularly effective at eliciting an emotional response, it seems impossible to decouple them. Even the verdant countryside between Dublin and Cork seems to Thackeray to be tinged with sadness:

> The country is well-tilled, well peopled; the hay-harvest on the ground, and the people taking advantage of the sunshine to gather it in; but in spite of everything—green meadows, white villages and sunshine—the place has a sort of sadness in the look of it. (*Irish Sketch Book* 26)

To ground this travelogue in Irish history, it should be noted that Thackeray's writing ascribes a melancholic disposition to an economically distressed population. His visit took place 5 years before the Great Famine, a period in which a number of "lesser" famines that were precursors to the major crop failure of 1845–51 took place. He notes that there are "twelve hundred thousand people in Ireland—a sixth of the population—who have no means of livelihood but charity" (*Irish Sketch Book* 38). He further remarks that, in the south and west of Ireland, "the traveler is haunted by the face of the popular starvation. It is not the exception, it is the condition of the people. In this fairest and richest of countries, men are suffering and starving by millions" (*Irish Sketch Book* 85).

In addition to his eyewitness experiences with Irish people and places, Thackeray's writing on Irish subjects was informed by his personal circumstances. His wife, Isabella Shawe, fell into a depression after the birth of their third daughter and attempted suicide by leaping off the ship when she and Thackeray sailed to Ireland in 1840. Her illness meant that, instead of traveling with her husband during the writing of the *Irish Sketch Book*, she was committed to a mental institution near Paris, where Thackeray's mother was living. Robert Morris speculates that the "hysterical" Isabella may have been a model for the "frenetic" Lady Lyndon (xxi).

Thackeray's contemporaries ascribed his downbeat tone to the author's temperament. Theodore Martin observed: "It is not cynicism, we believe, but a constitutional proneness to a melancholy view of life, which gives that unpleasing colour to many of Mr. Thackeray's books which most readers resent. He will not let his eye rest upon a fair face, without thinking of the ugly skull beneath" (Martin 183). Reportedly, when an Irishman reproached Thackeray for his treatment of the Irish, "Thackeray's eyes filled with tears as he thought of his wife—born in County Cork—and turning away his head, he exclaimed, "God help me! all that I have loved best in the world is Irish" (Cunliffe and Watt 29–30). S. S. Prawer believes that Thackeray intended to "counter the accounts of those who saw nothing in Ireland but *la grande misere*" (180). John McAuliffe disputes this claim, pointing out that the narrative voice of the traveler in the *Irish Sketch Book* is as tonally inconsistent and intentionally self-parodic and ironic as that in a number of Thackeray's works, including that of *Barry Lyndon* (26).

Regardless of Thackeray's ambiguous or ambivalent feelings and motivations, film reviewers invariably describe Kubrick's film as melancholic. Alexander Walker compares its tone to John Ford's "misanthropic melancholy" (253). Andrew Sarris writes about both the tone and the film's indebtedness to painting: "every frame is a fresco of sadness" (quoted in Miller 229). Homay King focuses on acts of seeing in the film, treating the gaze itself as imbued with melancholy (123). This dominant emotional valence permeates the film's narrative and visual style as well as its musical score.

At the narrative level, as we have seen, the plot documents Redmond Barry's multiple losses—that of his father, his first love, his Irish home, his son, his wife, his status, fortune, and, finally, his leg. A brash upstart at the opening of the film Barry's losses, and particularly the death of Bryan, progressively empty him. At the same time, his proto-capitalist version of retail therapy in the form of the acquisitive overconsumption of liquor, women, clothing, and paintings—all of it financed by mortgaging his wife's fortune—fails to assuage his grief.

Moreover, the film's expert depiction of remoteness—not only in the overly spacious, even cavernous, interiors that provide an inhuman scale for the action, but also through the minimal dialogue—is consistent with the phenomenology of melancholy, as described by psychologists Sass and Pienkos: "with the dimming down of emotional life, everything loses the intensity of its motivational valence and consequently appears both dull and distant" (4).

Melancholia describes a profound and prolonged process of grieving that precipitates a loss of identity; it is "perhaps the quintessential symptom of an ailing spirit" (Ruti 639). Indeed, identity loss is a motif in the film, as Redmond Barry assumes a number of names and disguises over the course of his life, with stints as a soldier and a gambler and with the assumption of his wife's name when he marries. The well-known formulation from Freud is that melancholia is a self-destructive turning inward to emptiness: "In mourning, it is the world which has become poor and empty; in melancholia, it is the ego itself" (246). Melancholia signifies a continual return to, and the impossibility of overcoming, traumatic loss and suggests a debilitating lack of closure or resolution.

As a trope relating to Irish national identity, it implies a pathological inability to recover from the losses suffered under centuries of British colonial rule. Luke Gibbons positions melancholia within a group of medical conditions—his primary interest being the disease of nostalgia—arising among individuals who were displaced during the wars of the late eighteenth century:

> As originally diagnosed in the late eighteenth century, nostalgia was placed alongside conditions such as melancholia, hypochondria, and bulimia, and first came to prominence in the 1790s when acute experiences of dislocation and homesickness were identified as causes of desertion in the highly mobile French armies in the aftermath of the revolution. (*Quiet* 48)

A specifically Celtic melancholia is associated with fatalism and resignation (*Quiet* 49) in the face of irrecoverable losses and inevitable endings.

Mari Ruti has begun to address the power dynamics of mourning and melancholia, rejecting the implication that they are passive states of victimhood and reclaiming them as political rather than pathological responses:

> in the context of hegemonic realities that impose loss as an inherent condition of minoritarian subjectivities, the subject's refusal to "get over" its losses cannot be regarded exclusively as a pathological response but must instead be recognized as an attempt to preserve what is most valuable about the past. (641)

In fact, melancholia might be seen as a political gesture of the continuing value of the troubled past, an act signifying the subject's "militant refusal to allow certain objects to disappear into oblivion" (Eng and Han quoted in Ruti 641).

Furthermore, melancholia describes a temporal relation to pastness that reconfigures the past, present, and future: "melancholia dwells in the past in ways that hold this past open and unresolved" (Ruti 646). Jennifer Radden also identifies a temporal dimension to melancholia in *The Nature of Melancholy: From Aristotle to Kristeva*. Radden identifies three particularly salient aspects in the historical literature on melancholia: it is founded upon feelings of fear and sadness *without cause*; it is associated with cyclical temporalities and affective polarities; and, finally, it is linked to idleness and boredom.

Going back to the Greeks, melancholia was first viewed as a temperament rather than a disease, understood within the medieval system of the four humors and associated specifically with the black bile excreted from the spleen. In the eighteenth century, William Hogarth and Samuel Johnson illustrated the melancholic person visually and verbally. In his "Rake's Progress" series, the former depicts a man sitting alone, separated from the expressively articulated madness surrounding him in "Bedlam" (Figure 4.2). The latter defined the condition in his famous dictionary in relation to black bile, hypochondria, and obsessiveness (61). Across the centuries, symptoms of melancholy have included fear and sadness, dejection and gloom; "frequently portrayed without sufficient cause" as a misery in excess of what circumstances justify (Radden 12–13). Melancholia has also assumed diverse forms, according to Radden. "The question of one or many," she writes, "is also complicated by the humoral, astrological, and supernatural explanations of melancholy offered through the ages" (9).

Humoral and astrological theories, the latter emphasizing a link between bouts of depression and the planet Saturn, viewed melancholy as episodic or cyclical. By the nineteenth century, terms such as "circular insanity" and *la folie circulaire* were employed in Britain and France, although, as Radden points out, the connection between melancholia and circularity largely faded during the twentieth century as the condition became associated with women and with idleness (16–18).

The connections between Irishness and melancholia in *Barry Lyndon* may seem subtle or allusive, but it should be remembered that the film was clearly marked by its Irish associations at the time of its release. Warner Brothers was interested in presenting the film as authentically Irish, as evidenced by its promotional materials. In the production facts released at the premiere, statements touted Kubrick's use of "authentic Irish settings" where he "found qualities of landscape untouched since the eighteenth century, as well as aspects

Figure 4.2 Hogarth's Bedlam: the mad, melancholic end of the rake's progress. *A Rake's Progress*, Plate VIII, c. 1763. Source: Bridgman Art Library.

of the natives (and their weather) that fitted Thackeray's realistic depictions" ("Production Facts").

Warner's executive Julian Senior emphasized the production's Irishness in the United States by asserting the usefulness for marketing purposes of using Cos Egan's name in the by-line of his "Irish Odyssey" article, noting that Egan had traveled with the production throughout the Irish location shoot and also on some English locations (Warner Production Files).

In terms of the scholarly approach to the film, early essays by Mark Crispin Miller cite the Thackeray novels, remarking that "Barry Lyndon is a stage Irishman" ("Kubrick's Anti-Reading").

Miller also asserts, somewhat contradictorily, that Kubrick's film, in contrast to Thackeray's work, emphasizes Barry's passivity: "Kubrick's changes in Thackeray's plot enhance the protagonist's enigmatic quality by making him a passive figure" ("Kubrick's Anti-Reading"). It is this dynamic between passivity and violence that will conclude my discussion of the Irish Odyssey.

The circular movement of Redmond Barry, from hotheaded boy, to dissolute soldier, to steely swordsman, to stately gentleman, and back again to brawling beast, retraces an embodied history of Irish postcolonial or racial, masculine melancholy. On the one hand, Kubrick seems to sympathize with his outsider protagonist, a pretender who does quite well for himself, given that his only talents are swordplay and womanizing. On the other hand, the means by which he conveys Barry's outsider status, and the (non-) location to which he consigns Barry at the conclusion of the film, reiterates the racial melancholy of Irish coloniality and postcoloniality. Jaumont understands the freeze frame that marks Barry's exit from the scene of representation—and the literal freezing that concludes *The Shining*—as a form of fixation that represents the possibility of atemporal return:

> The Eternal Return of the hero is also attained through a process of fixation, like the photogrammic permanence which immobilizes one point of *Barry Lyndon*'s circular Odyssey, after he has stepped into a coach for ever. Both examples [from *Barry Lyndon* and *The Shining*] project the heroes out of their story's temporality, their return—to Ireland or to 1921—being halted, fixed, rendered unchangeable: the atemporal return of Kubrick's Odysseus. (27)

As we have seen from the origins of the story in Thackeray and in prior Irish histories, Barry is an equivocal hero. Drawing in part on those intertexts as well as on the 1970s star text of Ryan O'Neal as both lover boy and hothead, Kubrick reanimates the stereotype of the violently emotional Irishman in Redmond Barry.

Kubrick uses handheld cameras to depict Barry in two moments in the film— during the brawl with army mate O'Toole, and in the attack on Bullingdon at the concert (Figure 5.1). These scenes demarcate and repeat experiences of one-on-one violence. They reveal that Barry has doubled back on himself, returning in later life to his younger aggression. They also enliven the film's normative depiction of frontally composed still and tracking shots (Figures 4.1 and 4.4), thus formally calling attention to Barry's emotional instability and cultural difference.

Michael Shapiro and Bille Wickre have remarked upon this aspect of the film, the latter observing, "Despite his pursuit of a peerage through bribery, lavish spending and entertaining, Barry is unable to gain the status he desires because he fails repeatedly to control his emotions" (168). These emotions mark Barry as a force of nature, a wild colonial boy who literally introduces movement, asymmetry, and disorder into the frame, and who is decidedly out of place in the static environments through which he is forced to move.

Kubrick's cinematography delineates the space of imperial imagination with all of its contradictions: on the surface, nature is allied with culture—the landscape naturalizing social hierarchies. The tension between the picturesque, in which the natural world is contained and quaint, and the sublime, which is associated with Barry himself, primarily through scenes of violence, comes to define the central conflict of the film. Kubrick's camerawork, which is typically linear in its use of tracking shots and reverse zooms to demarcate the appearance of orderly space and time, eventually, and often quite literally, circles back on itself to reveal Barry's patent unsuitability within the social and spatial environments of Castle Hackton and Lady Lyndon's aristocratic world.

If *Barry Lyndon* can be understood as an Irish Odyssey, it follows the shape of Homer's narrative primarily in the sense that Redmond Barry wanders the world, in a perverse reenactment of a gentleman's Grand Tour on the Continent, as a result of the culture of war. Unlike Odysseus, Barry's repetition produces loss and failure: he is unhomed on numerous occasions in the process of his voyage. The only Penelope who waits for Barry is his mother. He is left in an indeterminate space and time—literally the last image of Barry is of arrested movement of his damaged—some would say castrated—body. Barry loses his leg to an amputation as a result of Bullingdon's bullet and is last seen entering a carriage, a means of conveyance that, like Sir Charles Lyndon's wheelchair, ought to signify motion but which, instead, becomes a prop of paralysis within a *tableau vivant* (Figures 4.3 and 4.4). As Kubrick's production became caught up in the cyclical temporalities of postcolonial conflict, its own forward momentum was arrested by the IRA bombing campaign.

To conclude, I summarize the issues at stake in this examination of *Barry Lyndon* as Irish Odyssey. Kubrick brought his production to Ireland, including a creative team, and drew upon UK businesses with whom he had worked before; the shoot infused some capital into the economy. While the irony with which Kubrick (and Thackeray before him) addresses British and European imperialism in the narrative can be seen as politically sensitive to the history of colonialism, their deployment of Irish melancholia reiterates the trope that understands Ireland's relationship to modernity as backward and pathological rather than dissident, defined by an incapacity to recover from loss.[20] Furthermore, in its

Figure 4.3 Barry enters the carriage, a static conveyance. *Barry Lyndon* (1975). Produced by Jan Harlan, Stanley Kubrick, and Bernard Williams. Directed by Stanley Kubrick.

Figure 4.4 Sir Charles Lyndon: the visual dialectics of immobility. *Barry Lyndon* (1975). Produced by Jan Harlan, Stanley Kubrick, and Bernard Williams. Directed by Stanley Kubrick.

rendering of the British colonial landscape through the frame of aesthetics—a subject to which I turn in Chapter 5—the film reinforces the Burkean distinction between the sublime and the picturesque in a manner that supports notions of the naturalness of Irish violence. Kubrick's rhetorical strategy—while seemingly marshaled in order to reveal Barry's plight as a colonial outsider—also comes close to reiterating the need for imperial policing and military measures to suppress a spontaneous and threatening emotionality, particularly when Barry abuses his wife and stepson.

Kubrick seems to understand Redmond Barry as a hot-headed Irishman with a proclivity toward violence who has become trapped within an artfully arranged, picturesque landscape, a land to which he has no claim and a place where he does not belong. This presumption carries implications for Irish claims to land in Ireland as well. Kubrick may have come to sympathize with this figure; Barry's rebelliousness and his social aspirations certainly speak to American values of iconoclasm and independence. Kubrick ultimately places the character in a much more favorable light than Thackeray had done—making him more pathetic than venal—and creates a more sympathetic character in Barry than he does in Barry's cinematic siblings from the 1970s, Alex de Large (*A Clockwork Orange*) and Jack Torrence (*The Shining*). Kubrick may sympathize with the upstart Barry against the assembled force of the British military and aristocracy, yet in doing so may also have recapitulated a mode of Irishness as sublime violence that emanates from colonialist ideologies and persists in contemporary representation.

[20] Kubrick's awareness of Irish stereotypes is evident in both *The Killing* and *A Clockwork Orange*, where Irish characters are subjected to drunken abuse, or are abused because they are drunk.

5

The Rhythm and the Rest:
Painting, Cinema, Stillness

Three hours and four minutes of pictures.

Stanley Kauffmann, review of *Barry Lyndon* for *The New Republic*

There is no work which does not have its beginning and end in other arts.

Gilles Deleuze, interview with Melissa McMuhan

We expect photographs, like paintings, to be transparent in the manner that is captured by the term "looking through" and this expectation carries over into our experience of cinema.

Richard Allen, *Projecting Illusion*

Chapter 4 considers the way that the Odyssey's cyclical temporality informs the production history and the melancholic affective register of *Barry Lyndon*. There I argue that the framework of voyage and return, the epic version of the return of the repressed, is a temporal mode that is properly associated with (post)colonial melancholia which represents a potentially dissident challenge to linear and colonial conceptualizations of time. This challenge gains no purchase, however, within Kubrick's contained and picturesque environment.

In *Barry Lyndon*, the cycle does not actually trace out a "complete" return, but produces a downward spiral, as Redmond Barry is left in an indeterminate, unhomely time and space at the film's conclusion. In the closing moments of his narrative—one based upon his autobiography—Barry becomes a structuring absence, an emblem for the emptiness at the heart of melancholia. In keeping with his self-made status in Thackeray's novel (and in the world), he survives representationally only *as* text, in the script that appears on the new technology of the bank check. He is nothing more than a debt to be paid.

In their analyses of the temporal structures of sequence and cycle, Chapters 3 and 4 explore the way *Barry Lyndon* renders two modes of temporality that historian Reinhart Koselleck associates with the project of modernity: the sense of before and after and the repeatability of events. This chapter turns to an examination of Koselleck's third temporal mode: the contemporaneity of the noncontemporaneous.[1] In *Futures Past: On the Semantics of Historical Time*, Koselleck argues that imperialism brought to light various coexisting cultural regimes that were, through the (imperialist) process of synchronous comparison, ordered diachronically. "This fundamental experience of progress," Koselleck writes, "embodied in a single concept around 1800, is rooted in the knowledge of noncontemporaneities which exist at a chronologically uniform time" (238).

In the historical, political, and anthropological terms of modernity, noncontemporaneities form the basis for the hierarchies established to distinguish between more and less developed cultures. Koselleck's framework thus begins to address the "temporal elitism" (Lim 111) that underlies the view that European modernity brought advancement to the rest of the world. Cultural practices of and relationships to temporality become political matters. "The modernity syndrome," writes historian Wolf Schäfer, "creates unmodern people and repudiates their right to be part of the present" (114). *Barry Lyndon's* cinematic entombment of Redmond Barry as a sublime Irishman in a picturesque landscape, discussed in Chapter 4, captures this dialectic of the modern and the unmodern.

Barry Lyndon engages with noncontemporaneity—the coexistence of different temporalities—within its aesthetic register, and it does so in two ways. First, through the device of anachronism, and, second, through the staging of an encounter between painting and cinema that foregrounds the different spatio-temporal experiences, or space-times, afforded by each medium. This latter intervention contributes to a potent critique of progress and periodization within art history. Kubrick's aesthetic translation of noncontemporaneity does

---

[1] The concept of the contemporaneity of the non-contemporaneous was originally developed by Marxist theorist Ernst Bloch in *Heritage of Our Times* (1935) as part of his thesis regarding the multi-temporal and multilayered contradictions that exist at any given moment in history. In his analysis of Fascism, Bloch considered certain social groups in Germany—youth, peasantry, and the impoverished middle class—more susceptible to the Fascist propaganda that fabricated a mythical German past because of their non-synchronous relation to modern experience. Bloch famously observed, "not all people exist in the same Now" (62).

not erase its political significance. As we have seen, the politics of history and aesthetic form are bound together throughout the film. Rather than diverting the political critique by a seeming displacement to the regime of visuality, *Barry Lyndon* expands the capacity of Kubrick's historical critique by incorporating both logical/analytical and affective registers through captivating images and by providing opportunities for a temporal experience that solicits critical intellectual investment as well as emotional engagement.

Barry Lyndon provides viewers with a means of contemplating the competing temporalities of modernity through its treatment of movement and stasis, or, rhythm. The rhythmic juxtaposition that governs the way painting and cinema are integrated in the film, which is developed through carefully orchestrated musical cues as well, draws our attention inexorably toward the interval, toward stillness, and toward the end of time rather than the forward march of progress. Just as the narrative interruptions and repetitions carry political implications, these powerful rhythms come to inform the film's discourse on British imperial history. After a careful examination of the politics and poetics of visuality in the film, a coda at the end of this chapter extends the discussion to the film's musical score, which becomes another mode through which Kubrick engages multiple temporalities.

Affect and anachronism

My contention that *Barry Lyndon* treats temporality in a reflexive manner, providing opportunities to be drawn into the sensual slow pace as well as possibilities for critique, accords with the widely shared view of Kubrick as a modernist filmmaker, one whose work combines abstract, contemplative, realist, and surrealist approaches to the indexical, photographic image. This view is not universally held among scholars of *Barry Lyndon*, however, and probing the divergence of opinion on this topic is helpful for furthering my argument regarding Kubrick's creation of an aesthetic time that recruits both intellectual and affective responses.

In "*Barry Lyndon*, Paintings, and the Archive," Tatjana Ljulic disagrees with the view that Kubrick's style promotes detachment. For Ljulic:

painterly reference, rather than being aimed at frustrating narrative continuity and inducing a detached viewing mode, reflects a concern with immediacy, which translates into both the film's narrative method and its visual mode of rendering people and spaces on view. (3)

Although my contention in this chapter will be that Kubrick's use of paintings moves beyond the level of reference in very complex ways, I share Ljulic's interest in the film's relationship to immediacy. My argument is that the temporal strategies in the film produce an aesthetic time of contemplation that solicits and enables feeling and thinking; as such, my thinking intersects with Ljulic's observations. In contrast to Ljulic, I emphasize Kubrick's ability to construct a sense of emotional and temporal immediacy while also allowing for critical contemplation in a double movement.

Immediacy offers the experience of immanence, of presence in a "now" moment in time, one that then can be seen to stand apart from the flow of time. It thus represents a mode of temporality that depends upon stasis, or more precisely, on the distinction between the stillness of now versus the passage of homogeneous time. Immediacy can create the circumstances for aesthetic time, evoking the exercise of emotion and critical contemplation, but in and of itself immediacy is only one step in the process.

For Ljulic, the issue of immediacy is linked to the problem of anachronism in the film. Intentional anachronism is one obvious way for the film, and for any work, to signal the noncontemporaneity of certain of its elements. Anachronism also contributes to the confounding of linear time. The critical discussion of anachronism in *Barry Lyndon* focuses on two issues: Kubrick's citation of the work of nineteenth-century painter Adolph Menzel in the candlelight scenes, and the use of Franz Schubert's "Piano Trio in E Flat," which was composed in 1827, several decades after the events depicted in the film. Ralf Fischer considers the anachronisms to be part of Kubrick's larger project of reflexive historical critique, proposing that he "blocks access" to the eighteenth century partly "through the art of the nineteenth century" (177); this, for Fischer, is one means of conveying the sedimented history of this work, which assumes the form of a twentieth-century film that adapts a nineteenth-century novel about an eighteenth-century figure.

Challenging Fischer's view, Ljulic argues that Kubrick blends references to eighteenth- and nineteenth-century sources in *Barry Lyndon* in order to convey greater immediacy. The nineteenth-century's Romantic version of melancholia, she suggests, better conveys the affect the director sought to portray and she cites as evidence Kubrick's comments to Michel Ciment regarding the dearth of tragic love themes in the music of the eighteenth century (22).

Ljulic draws an analogy between this anachronistic musical choice—selected for its expressive capacity—and the visual depiction of Lady Lyndon, whose depressive emotional state closely mirrors that of nineteenth-century visual sources found in the *Barry Lyndon* production files (20–2). Ljulic may overstate the case when she asserts, "there are no melancholy images of women in eighteenth-century painting" (22). In fact, images do exist prior to 1800 that convey the romanticized version of despair that became commonplace in the nineteenth century.[2]

Ljulic's larger point regarding the mood established by Kubrick's compositions remains valid, however. As medical historian Erin Sullivan writes, "it was in the Romantic era that melancholy enjoyed its second dawn" (884). The nineteenth-century glorification of melancholy, Sullivan argues, culminates in its close association with beauty in Baudelaire's iconic confession: "I can barely conceive of a type of beauty in which there is no misfortune" (217). An aura of tragic beauty does indeed cling to Lady Lyndon's depiction, particularly after the marriage, and it is useful to remember the conjecture on the part of Thackeray scholars that the figure was drawn from the example of the author's own depressed wife. For that matter, Barry himself conveys a similarly depressed affect when, slumped at the table amidst a depraved scene of gaming and whoring, he physically recreates the same debauched and depressed scenario within Hogarth's *Rake's Progress* (1732–5).

Ljulic argues that Lady Lyndon serves as a portrait of absorption, and therefore immediacy. Michael Fried's term absorption, which he contrasts with theatricality, signifies the self-sufficient and the self-contained work that does not betray any awareness of its audience. "The emotive poignancy of the practically wordless figure of Lady Lyndon," Ljulic writes, "testifies to the affective absorption which Kubrick's cinematic portraits emanate" (23). Affective absorption is present here; within the framework of Lady Lyndon's character and the narrative, however, that absorption rapidly becomes self-absorption, which may not be read as a form of immediacy that invites spectators to invest in the image. Barry's status as an ambivalent, grief-ridden, Anglicized Celt in part reflects his failed masculine self-construction; in contrast, the melancholia that afflicts Lady Lyndon occurs for entirely different reasons. She has lost her autonomy, not to the vagaries of war and empire, but to an abusive husband who

---

[2] One such example is Joseph Wright of Derby's *Maria and Her Dog Silvo* (1781), in which Maria's figure and facial expression rhyme with the composition and emotional sensibility of the nineteenth-century images of melancholy to which Ljulic refers. Wright's is an image in which "melancholy [can be seen] as a condition in which we express our deepest and most human feelings" (Ingram et al. 12).

is more a vampire than a partner (the vampire being another Irish reference, but one that I cannot pursue here).

I return to the question of eighteenth- versus nineteenth-century representation to suggest that the film does in fact move outside romanticized, nineteenth-century rhetoric in its depiction of Lady Lyndon's melancholia, with implications for the question of temporal immediacy and aesthetic time. Lady Lyndon descends into grief-stricken madness in the bedroom scene after Bryan's death. This scene provokes thinking and feeling because it makes the neat categorization of absorption and theatricality—and, specifically the distinction of the inner orientation of absorption from the audience awareness of the latter—difficult. This "moment" of breakdown, which plays out dynamically over several minutes, represents the acting out, or the externalization, of an extreme subjective, inner state. In other words, it is a state of utter self-absorption and inwardness, despite its vigorous physical expression. Moreover, that demonstrative display draws Lady Lyndon's character back into the eighteenth-century understanding of melancholy as disease.

The insightful and provocative question of immediacy that Ljulic raises cannot, I believe, be fully explicated without reference to the film's overall program of stillness and activity, two processes that fail to fulfill their role as proxies for the inner and outer worlds of the characters, as seen in the example of Lady Lyndon. For example, the isolation and stasis used to frame both Barry and Lady Lyndon at Castle Hackton after their marriage alternates with notable bursts of explosive energy in scenes shot with a mobile, and even slightly out of control, camera. Barry's public attack on Bullingdon in the music room is a return to his youth as a brawler and soldier; it conveys the repressed emotion that undermines the seeming stability of his composed and even mild-mannered persona (Figure 5.1). Lady Lyndon's outburst occurs when she is by herself in the bedroom; she is subject to the gender expectations of the era, signified by a very specific type of architectural confinement—she is increasingly pictured in interior spaces—and ultimately silenced within the film's representational regime (Figure 5.2).

My point here is that it is the *oscillation*, or the mobile dialectic, that the film establishes between stillness and motion, interiority and exteriority, decorum and indecency, and, as I discuss later, portrait and landscape, that contributes to an understanding of the characters' entrapment within their social milieu and within the aesthetic forms they inhabit. The oscillation affords moments of identification and emotional connection but also creates space and time for the

Figure 5.1 A handheld camera captures Barry, brawling, in motion. *Barry Lyndon* (1975). Produced by Jan Harlan, Stanley Kubrick, and Bernard Williams. Directed by Stanley Kubrick.

Figure 5.2 Lady Lyndon mourns, violently, alone. *Barry Lyndon* (1975). Produced by Jan Harlan, Stanley Kubrick, and Bernard Williams. Directed by Stanley Kubrick.

viewer's thoughtful contemplation of the situatedness of these characters within history and fiction.

The degree to which passivity defines the lives of both Barry and Lady Lyndon, for example, is made clear in ways that are tied to the film's rhythms. The overt brutality that *Barry Lyndon* addresses is associated with the mindless slaughter of the Seven Years' War, which, in the opening of the film, is linked visually and musically to dancing, marching, and dying. Katherine McQuiston and Christine Lee Gengaro detail the painstaking work of arranging the musical cues and the attention paid to their careful repetition—especially "The Sea-Maiden" and "British Grenadiers" in the film's early scenes (Gengaro 159–64).

A more implicit violence enfolds the protagonist as he circulates among those on whose behalf the soldiers' lives are sacrificed. The brutal artifice of the British aristocracy is the source of unseen, yet palpable violence; that violence has been displaced onto their colonies, including Ireland and the Americas. The game of war, as practiced at the time, is presented as a slightly surreal ritual, a temporal experience of marching and falling. By contrast, Redmond Barry's enforced passivity is marked by the oscillation between Kubrick's signature tracking shots, confined to interiors in the latter half of the film, and the use of the slow zoom, the latter dampening the feeling of movement in space. The tension of this containment, with brief moments of resistance—marks him as fundamentally different in character from the landed gentry. Kubrick establishes in a similar way the oscillation between the Countess's evolving state of near-catatonia and her violent articulation of emotion when she is at her most helpless, in the face of the death of her child.

Finally, I return to the question of distance and theatricality; for, in accordance with what I have argued thus far, this remains the dialectical context for the experience of immediacy. In a classic demonstration of the apparatus theories of the 1970s in "Postmodernism and Consumer Society," Fredric Jameson objects to "the cult of the glossy image" in the nostalgia film (*la mode retro*) contending that, "from time to time such sheer beauty can seem obscene" (1960). By virtue of its beauty, Jameson argues, the image endorses and authorizes its own consumability, consigning itself to the logic of late capitalism: "It is the triumph of the image in nostalgia film which ratifies the triumph over it of all the values of contemporary consumer society, of late capitalist consumption" (1962).

That cinematic beauty, however, is subject to a politics of its own. In *Pretty: Film and the Decorative Image*, Rosalind Galt convincingly argues, "the rhetoric of cinema has consistently denigrated surface decoration, finding the attractive skin of the screen to be false, shallow, feminine, or apolitical" (2). Galt's interest in the way that aesthetics constitutes a problem in and for cinema—from a decidedly different angle than Jameson's—is pertinent here: the characterization of *Barry Lyndon* as a beautiful film has contributed to its treatment as an anomaly within Kubrick's *oeuvre* and within American cinema of the 1970s. It may have therefore restricted its consumability under the auspices of the film auteur. The film was too decorative, too feminine, and too apolitical to be a Kubrick film: its marked departure from his three previous films capable of being measured by its extremely oblique angle on masculine violence and the way it co-constructs the artful world of the aristocracy in eighteenth-century Britain.

I would propose that, despite the numerous accolades they garnered, the beautiful images do not triumph in Kubrick's film, nor are they meant to. Instead, as with the narrative, the image system is designed to fail at the task it has been assigned. The series of beautiful film images is no more suited to capturing (a) time or representing history than a series of sentences. This is why Redmond Barry must exit the scene of representation: last encountered as a frozen image, he becomes a virtual photograph, signifying the immobility of death. In the process of elaborating these failures, Kubrick provides opportunities for modes of engagement that permit aesthetic and political reflection and that allow the viewer to enter into his historical critique.

Inanimate images

Returning to our focus on the film's painting-like images and the paintings that appear in the frame, I want to make the case that the rhythmic alternation of movement and stasis through the use of paintings within the *mise en scène* and *as mise en scène* enables diverse temporalities—Koselleck's noncontemporaneities—to coexist in the film. The arena in which the viewer can engage with diverse times is the aesthetic realm; opportunities for absorption and reflection evolve in relation to the visual and aural systems at work. As historical artifacts, the paintings are endowed with a heightened materiality while, at the same time, they remain in thrall to the same representational processes that even the film's (animate) characters must face: like Barry, the paintings are subject to movement (particularly in relation to the zoom lens) and stillness. They move between visibility and invisibility, yet also participate in a third possibility: when the paintings themselves become absorbed, like tissue, into the *mise en scène*.

One of the three important eighteenth-century genres of painting with which Kubrick works is the conversation piece (Figures 5.3 and 5.4). By virtue of its formal properties and its history, this mode calls attention to a heightened materiality and lends itself to the experience of an aesthetic temporality that

Figure 5.3 Thomas Gainsborough's *Mr. and Mrs. William Hallett* c. 1785. Source: Bridgeman Art Library.

Figure 5.4 The Lyndon Entourage: staging a conversation piece. *Barry Lyndon*
(1975). Produced by Jan Harlan, Stanley Kubrick, and Bernard Williams. Directed by
Stanley Kubrick.

joins cognition and contemplation, analysis and affect. The conversation piece
is painting's translation of the *tableau vivant*, the still life or living picture, a
hybrid form that draws together sculpture, painting, and theater. *Tableaux
vivants* became especially popular in the late eighteenth century in a number of
amateur and professional contexts, from parlor games to stage melodramas to
the *pose plastique*. One potential source of inspiration for Kubrick's distinctive
deployment of paintings in *Barry Lyndon* was Denis Diderot's (1713–84)
theatrical aesthetic, which advocated that stage productions incorporate *tableaux
vivants* based on contemporary paintings for use at dramatic climaxes (Jacobs
88). Popular in Britain and among the royal family for centuries, *tableaux vivants*
remediated painting; the difference between original and adaptation was murky
at best. "Carefully posed and lit tableaux," writes Stephen Jacobs, "were often
staged behind large gilt frames with a layer of gauze that imitated the effects
of the varnish of an old painting" (Jacobs 90). *Tableaux vivants* survived well
into the twentieth century in the cinema of Griffith, Dreyer, Bresson, Antonioni,
Tarkovsky, Akerman, Warhol, and Kubrick.

The *tableau vivant* is a static representation of aesthetic noncontemporaneities:
it blends modes from different genres of art and periods in history. In *The*

Material Image: Art and the Real in Film, Brigitte Peucker calls the *tableau vivant* a "palimpsest of textual overlay" and "the 'embodiment' of the inanimate image" (30). As an accretion of several aesthetic modes (sculpture, painting, and drama), the "impure" *tableau vivant* (Jacobs 94) orchestrates a "collision" of sorts. Peucker writes:

> Film is a medium in which different representation systems may collide, may replace, but generally supplement one another, suggesting that those moments in films that evoke *tableaux vivants* are moments especially focused on film's heterogeneity. (31)

Numerous *tableaux vivants* in *Barry Lyndon*—one of the most memorable being the Lyndon entourage at young Bryan's birthday party—underscore the film's heterogeneity in terms of temporality and aesthetic forms: film, in a sense, moves backward and forward across genres of visual representation, from paintings to pictures to drama, each of which possesses a specific temporal mode of address. For my purposes, it is of greater interest to consider the way the sensibility of the *tableau vivant* permeates the entire visual order of the film, establishing the ground upon which the visual discourse operates.

Justin Remes argues that static films go beyond commentary on mere physical movement to address the movement of time and consciousness as well. "By foregrounding stasis," he claims, these films "make the spectator more aware of the movement of time and consciousness, neither of which can be apprehended in the same way when one is absorbed in the movement of a cinematic image" (265). He concludes: "the majority of works within the cinema of stasis aim to create a space for meditation, for immersion in an image, for sober reflections on the nature of movement and stasis, time and space, cinema and art" (268).

The type of prolonged engagement that is required of a film such as *Barry Lyndon* is "often only encouraged by traditional visual art," in Remes's view (267). Painting is a traditional visual art that permits prolonged engagement and, although clearly a committed narrative filmmaker, Kubrick radically, even experimentally, foregrounds the relationship between painting and cinema in *Barry Lyndon*. He uses strategies similar to those adopted by the *Nouvelle Vague* when they incorporated photography in their films: "inserting stills into his film, freezing the frame, or composing his films of photographs" (Elsaesser "Stop/Motion" 120). The incorporation of photographs yields a specific temporal relationship between indexical images: stillness interrupts the illusion of movement. Incorporating paintings as Kubrick does in *Barry Lyndon*—not merely as props—produces a completely different visual and temporal encounter. The visual experience of a painting provokes a slow reading process that unifies stillness and motion.

Thomas Elsaesser reminds us that the photograph underwent a reconceptualization during the 1970s—the decade of *Barry Lyndon*—as it moved into the canon of Western art history ("Stop/Motion" 118). The overall shape of my argument regarding competing and comparative temporalities in *Barry Lyndon*, manifested in oscillations between genres of painting, between and among painting, photography, and film, and between movement and stasis, is informed by Thomas Elsaesser's discussion of the temporal relation of photography and cinema. He addresses the question of the "tense" of the photograph—which both freezes a moment as a signified of the past and establishes a "future perfect"—by arguing that the unique temporality of the photograph is "unthinkable without the cultural experience of cinema against which it formulates a silent protest" ("Stop/Motion" 119).

Kubrick's *Barry Lyndon* forces us to reconsider what is thinkable within the technological and cultural parameters that circumscribe the modes of painting, photography, and film. The film reflects his technological ambition and emotional reach—for example, in the decision to use a lens from the space race to capture the delicacy of the human face lit by candlelight—while also serving as a harbinger of the transition to the digital age. Every era produces its particular regimes of visuality, Kubrick suggests with *Barry Lyndon*. In the eighteenth century, quite specifically, he reflects on the politics of the genres of landscape and portraiture, which engage in an oscillating dialectic of their own.

Painting pictures

I think Stanley wanted to create a kind of documentary of the eighteenth century. The only traces left were paintings by artists such as Gainsborough, Hogarth, Watteau, Rowlandson and Chodowiecki. He did not want to accept that these artists had stylized the eighteenth century and had not always reproduced the world of their day faithfully.

Ken Adam, interview with Boris Hars-Tschachotin

In *Barry Lyndon*, Kubrick probes the relationship between textuality and time, refusing to limit his inquiry to language and narrative form. He evokes the notion of history as palimpsest—a figure that incorporates both sequence and simultaneity—in relation to narrative and in terms of the visual texts produced by painting and film. In many ways, *Barry Lyndon* rehearses Deleuze's postwar transition from the movement-image to the time-image, when "a cinema of seeing replaces action" (9).

This cinema of seeing involves the title character, as he increasingly appears to be acted upon by events. It also implicates the viewer, as Kubrick slows the film's forward momentum through numerous visual techniques, denuding the screen of movement-images in a variety of ways. In terms of editing, he relies upon long takes; with cinematography, he relies upon the reverse zoom as well as centered compositions in which figures move toward the camera (in part, calling attention to the way each frame can be contemplated as an individual photograph or canvas). This film's particular cinema of seeing resonates quite literally with Guy de Bord's society of the spectacle, a regime in which, "the spectacle is capital accumulated to the point where it becomes image" (x). While de Bord wrote of the society of the spectacle as an outgrowth of capitalism, still nascent in the eighteenth century, Kubrick recognizes land and art as properties that can provide the basis for capitalism and the commodity form. As the "negative expression of living value," the paintings that line the halls of the Lyndon estate, Castle Hackton, "have become exclusively abstract value" (de Bord 35). More specifically, the decorative portrait and the landscape paintings of the eighteenth century become social documents of capital accumulation. W. J. T. Mitchell has asserted that "the relation of genres like poetry and painting is not a purely theoretical matter, but something like a social relationship" (108) and I draw upon that argument to examine the relationship between landscape and portrait painting that *Barry Lyndon* develops, within the context of eighteenth-century aesthetic debates regarding the beautiful, the picturesque, and the sublime.

William Gilpin's *Essays on Prints* (1768) is credited with introducing the idea of the picturesque—which is inherently linked to landscape—and also for identifying particular picturesque locales as appropriate sites for British tourism. The British lakes district and the Irish Lakes of Killarney were both marketed as scenic alternatives to the Grand Tour of Europe during the 1790s, when the French Revolutionary wars compromised travelers' mobility and safety. Landscape painter John Constable described the notion of the picturesque best when he remarked, "'Tis a most delightful country for a landscape painter. I fancy I see Gainsborough in every hedge and hollow tree" (quoted in Bermingham 111). The picturesque is defined in a circular, reflexive manner such that an encounter with the picturesque in nature means that the experience can be compared to pictorial representation. In contrast to the quaint, manageable, and touristic regime of the picturesque, the beautiful, as Kant and Burke characterized it, offers the quasi-mathematical satisfaction generated by pleasant proportions. Finally, the sublime manifests itself as the overwhelming awe-inspiring encounter that threatens the loss of the self.

Kubrick develops his cinema of seeing through the citation of eighteenth-century British paintings within the film's *mise en scène*. Kubrick exploits this visual art tradition in two ways: first, in and of themselves, these paintings hold a lingering fascination, as aesthetic objects that embody history. Second, Kubrick draws from the paintings to create the environment that his characters inhabit, suggesting that painting, which offers one approach for envisioning the world, may seem to have been superseded by newer technologies, including motion pictures. In both instances, Kubrick defies cinematic realism by drawing attention away from the story, asking viewers to recognize the painterly quality of the individual film frame, and staging a visual and temporal interchange between painting and cinema, neither of which is presented as an objective or unmediated form of realist representation.

One important way Kubrick employs the art history tradition in *Barry Lyndon* is through mimesis: he makes specific reference to well-known paintings. One of the best-known portraits of this period is Thomas Gainsborough's *Knabe in Blau* (*The Blue Boy*, c. 1770), presumed to be a portrait of Jonathan Buttall (Figure 5.5). This iconic painting serves as the basis for costume choices in several scenes. On more than one occasion, O'Neal wears a blue velvet coat, either paired with gray breeches or as part of a complete blue velvet suit (Figure 5.6). By drawing upon a painting from an era that continues to hold a cultural fascination, it may seem that Kubrick seeks to forward a claim to historical accuracy.

This mimetic logic contains some gaps, however: the viewer's sense of recognition is likely based upon the memory of seeing *The Blue Boy* or, even more likely, a photographic image of it. Thus, this recollection may function as the gauge of verisimilitude. But seeing or, more accurately, having seen a painting, which is a kind of historical experience, is certainly not the same thing as experiencing the historical era from which it originated.

Multiple and competing temporalities are implied here. They are associated with the time of the creation of the painting; the time of its (original and subsequent) acquisition; the circumstances in which it has been encountered in a museum or gallery; and possibly its ubiquity as an emblem of high art in books, calendars, or on the internet. All are implied by if not embedded in

Figure 5.5 Thomas Gainsborough's *The Blue Boy*, c. 1770 (oil on canvas). Source: Bridgeman Art Library International/©The Huntington Library, Art Collections & Botanical Gardens.

this material image. It should be noted that Kubrick is well aware of the status of art both as guarantor of status and as degraded commodity in the film. He gestures toward the proto-capitalist rise in mercantile commerce which would replace aristocratic patronage when he creates scenes in which Barry purchases

Figure 5.6 Barry as Blue Boy. *Barry Lyndon* (1975). Produced by Jan Harlan, Stanley Kubrick, and Bernard Williams. Directed by Stanley Kubrick.

paintings from fawning dealers, remarking fatuously about his appreciation of the use of the color blue in one painting.

In this way, *Barry Lyndon* relies upon the mediation of art and memory to establish a sense of history, calling forth the Bergsonian idea of pure recollection, which, the philosopher theorized, can be solicited in moments of disinterestedness or boredom. Ken Adam reveals his own understanding of the dynamic when he describes Kubrick's apparent commitment to treating art as neutral or documentary visible evidence, which perplexed Adam.[3]

The role of memory in history has been vigorously discussed in contemporary historical studies. A "fruitful indeterminacy," as Geoff Eley puts it, has enveloped contemporary historical inquiry. This indeterminacy upsets an earlier approach to conceptualizing the boundary between "memory" and "history" where the latter was understood as the professional organizing and contextualizing of the former. History literally "disciplined" memory in that older understanding (Eley 560).

---

[3] Adam's understanding seems to me unlikely to have been the full story on Kubrick's approach. Kubrick's wife Christiane has been an accomplished painter since the 1960s. In fact, she painted an impressionist canvas depicting Kubrick rehearsing with an actor during the production of *Barry Lyndon* (see Pramaggiore 2014).

History and memory operate at different temporal, cognitive, and affective registers: memory is fragmented, elusive, and subjective. Without the discipline of history—the professional organization of material—the enterprise of remembering might have little to offer beyond the uncanny parapsychology of déjà vu, the experience of having already seen something. The sense of having seen something—at the art museum, in a book collection—blends emotion and thought in "the impression that something is stored in memory, but the only accessible vestige is a feeling about its existence" (Brown 5).

The uncanny effect of Kubrick's citations in the context of *Barry Lyndon* is far reaching: these are not merely individual images, but an entire 3 hours of film frames composed to look like art works that viewers may have encountered. It is no surprise at all that reviews praised and condemned the film alike on the grounds that it evoked the sensibility of the museum (Kael 49). Historian Frank Ankersmit addresses the complexity of this scenario:

> to put it in terms of the word "resemblance": we are dealing with a realistic representation if the work of art concerned represents reality in a way that *resembles* the way that the works of art familiar to us represent reality. (*New Philosophy* 220; emphasis in original)

Paintings bear a multifaceted relation to history: they are historical objects that reflect not only the materials and favored techniques, but also the visual culture and aesthetic assumptions of the period in which they are made. If certain styles of portraiture signified "the real" in the eighteenth century—by accurately capturing the details of human subjects—they can no longer be understood in terms of transparent realism when Kubrick situates them in relation to visual technologies such as photography and motion pictures. History may be lodged in physical artifacts (paintings) and in memory (the viewer's experience of those paintings), but neither is an unmediated mode of representation or experience. The complex relationship between the "real" *Blue Boy* painting and viewers' potential associations, and the temporalities associated with those moments, calls into question the way in which this film, or any film, "recreates" or captures time or history and seems to suggest that the only possible relationship that cinema can forge with time is that it produces temporalities (which belong to the order of fantasy, dream, memory, and what I have been calling aesthetic time), not that it can represent time, or even a time.

Kubrick both presents and analyzes his experience of duration in the still and moving images. Suzanne Guerlac describes Bergson's concept of duration as implying "a temporal synthesis of memory that knits temporal dimensions together, as in a melody" (66). The temporal synthesis of memory here is the only means for establishing a historical experience in *Barry Lyndon*: we (may) remember our experiences with the eighteenth-century British paintings and the film calls upon us to historicize that remembrance. These works are foremost entries within the Western canon of visual art, and Kubrick might reasonably have expected audience members to have encountered them. By establishing the reality of the eighteenth century through art, Kubrick proposes that realism itself must be called into question, a process that anthropologist Alan Feldman has associated with the faux documentary, which "compels the viewer to ask teleological questions about the ends of realism and the end of realism. Realism was once the narratological milieu in which historical representation luxuriated; now realism itself is revealed as having a history and one that is ideologically skewed" (494–5). If realism is revealed as merely one more aesthetic regime with its own history, questions of ideology may take on a greater importance.

As we have seen, critics have interpreted Kubrick's penchant for period detail as evidence of a realist aesthetic. The film's lavish and meticulously wrought *mise en scène* seems to support this assertion, yet the models Kubrick used to establish a sense of verisimilitude were paintings that, like *The Blue Boy*, obeyed the rules of their genres. In short, I propose that Kubrick deliberately copied art, not nature, in creating the world of this film. In an interview for the film *Stanley Kubrick: A Life in Pictures* (Harlan 2001), actor Jack Nicholson recalls a conversation in which Kubrick said, "in movies, you don't try and photograph reality, you try and photograph the photograph of the reality." Without the same indexical relationship existing between painting and reality—which is the case for *Barry Lyndon*—the process acquires still greater complexities.

Vincent LoBrutto points to the director's use of period paintings as straightforward mimesis: "As Kubrick began a meticulous study of the paintings of the period, he intended to exactly re-create the images from the masters of the time, using the paintings to render the precise look of sets, props, and costumes" (381). This process yielded a paradoxical "painterly documentary reality" (380). Had photographs of the period existed, Kubrick probably would have used them, but the point remains the same: visual art forms reflect specific historical, technological, and ideological conditions. Within the film's "relentless procession of impeccable, museum-piece compositions" (Kael 49), *Barry Lyndon* conveys ideological content. Viewers are immersed in a social world defined by the two most important genres of eighteenth-century British painting: the portrait and the landscape. Put another way, Kubrick uses period paintings as *mise en scène* to rhythmically and visually reproduce the dialectic between the property-owning individual and the property that endorses that individual's validity as a subject of representation.

Following the footsteps of an important painter of the period, Thomas Gainsborough (1727–88), Kubrick's shot scale alternates between the genres of the portrait and the landscape. It may simply be a coincidence that Gainsborough was an artist who accepted, if not celebrated, the dialectic between nature and artifice—a subject that animated eighteenth-century debates about aesthetics. In fact, Gainsborough's relation to realism was equivocal at best. Although rivals such as Joshua Reynolds often disparaged him as a sketch artist, Gainsborough himself frequently denied that he merely "copied real views." He was known to draw using candlelight, and for using model landscapes—substituting broccoli for trees, for example (Buchwald 367). "Although his earliest works are indeed quite literal recordings of nature," writes Emilie Buchwald, Gainsborough "proceeded to evolve a method of depicting [nature] which is as general, ideal, and abstract in its way" (361).

Gainsborough was also something of an experimentalist with visual technologies. He was fascinated with the effects of light and in the 1770s, he began painting landscapes on glass and then projecting light through the transparent images using candlelight and a magnifying frame contained in a wooden box (the box can be seen at the Victoria and Albert Museum in London). John Hayes writes, "his usual practice in later life was to bring whatever he required to draw from nature into the studio, whenever it was practicable to do so, rather than sketch out of doors" (31). By modeling his landscapes on Gainsborough's "general, abstract and ideal" compositions, Kubrick's moving pictures not only repurpose a traditional style of painting for a newer medium, but also perpetuate the aesthetic dilemmas that those paintings exemplify regarding the relation between art, reality, nature, and artifice.

Kubrick reenvisions eighteenth-century practices of visuality—the portrait, the landscape, and the conversation piece, genres that link the aristocracy with the landscape to naturalize their social hegemony—through cinematography. His layering and juxtaposition of aesthetic modes questions the realism of painting and cinema, rather than producing a sense of full immersion in the *mise en scène*, in part because the "original" pro-filmic material is itself visual art. This visual rhetoric presents the cinematic apparatus as a medium linked to a historical period and a realist regime of its own.

When Kubrick references the paintings of German-born painter Johann Zoffany (1733–1810), a founding member of the Royal Academy, in the film's interior spaces, he asks viewers to contemplate the implications of the genre for which Zoffany is best known. A favorite of George III and Queen Charlotte, Zoffany was celebrated for his mastery of the conversation piece, a sub-genre of portraiture that features groups of individuals engaged in leisure activities that reflect their privileged social position. Kamilla Elliott draws a linkage from the conversation piece to the cinema through the live tableau: "the evidence indicates that if film replaced any aesthetic form to the point of extinction, it was *tableaux vivants* in which live actors held poses after famous paintings" (Elliott 120).

In *Barry Lyndon*, Kubrick cites Zoffany's *Portrait of Sir Lawrence Dundas and his Uncle Lawrence* (1775) in several shots that depict Barry reading with his son Bryan (Figures 5.7 and 5.8). The decorous interaction between family members—whether uncle and nephew or father and son—is informed by the painting's title, which alerts viewers to the fact that the titled figure is the child rather than the adult. This is the case for Redmond Barry as well: Barry's son Bryan and his stepson Bullingdon, not Barry himself, are heirs to Lady Lyndon's fortune. Cutting from a close up of Barry and Bryan to an extreme long shot of the two figures—a notable departure from the frequent use of the reverse

Figure 5.7 Barry and Bryan: Intimacy. *Barry Lyndon* (1975). Produced by Jan Harlan, Stanley Kubrick, and Bernard Williams. Directed by Stanley Kubrick.

Figure 5.8 Barry and Bryan: Isolation. *Barry Lyndon* (1975). Produced by Jan Harlan, Stanley Kubrick, and Bernard Williams. Directed by Stanley Kubrick.

zoom—Kubrick interrupts the intimacy established by the first shot in a clinical fashion. In doing so, he provides a larger visual context for family intimacy and makes manifest the isolation of father and son within the lavishly appointed Castle Hackton. The wide shot also reveals large paintings, whose geometrical frames dominate those of the film. The frame is a visual trope in Zoffany's work, which often depicts rooms with walls literally covered by a jumble of framed works of art. The inclusion of these frames, along with the frontal staging of characters and the film's slow pace, emphasizes that performance and display form part of the daily experiences of the characters. Here again, reality and artifice are not so readily distinguished from each other.

In designing the walls in the interior of Castle Hackton, Kubrick pays respects to works such as Zoffany's *La tribuna degli Uffizi* (1772–8), a painting that Queen Charlotte commissioned (see Figures 5.9 and 5.10). The work, still held in the British Royal Collection, is a startlingly complex conversation piece depicting British tourists at the Uffizi Palace in Florence which was criticized for improperly portraying real individuals—as well as for its unruly, overcrowded frame. According to one source, Zoffany's error was so egregious that the Queen would not "suffer the picture to be placed in any of her apartments" (Shawe-Taylor 133).

Figure 5.9 Johan Zoffany's *Tribuna of the Uffizi*, 1772–8 (oil on canvas). Source: Bridgman Art Library International/The Royal Collection copyright 2011 Her Majesty Queen Elizabeth II.

Both in the painting and in Kubrick's cinematic remediation of it, the profusion of visual scenarios overwhelms viewers with objects that cease to function either as images that signify reality or as art and become instead mere decoration, connoting nothing more than the owner's ability to acquire such treasure. In this example, the rewriting of visual texts takes on a new meaning, as paintings become artifacts of conspicuous consumption within other paintings (in Zoffany's work) and ultimately serve as visual texture and historical citation within Kubrick's cinematography.

Kubrick's program of referencing the paintings of Gainsborough and Zoffany suggests that paintings, like cinema, function as artifacts of history and memory. Allusions to specific paintings provide an occasion for viewers to acknowledge the role that visual art of all kinds plays in the construction of history. If viewers recognize *The Blue Boy* or views of the English countryside and, in doing so, embrace a sense of the film's historical accuracy, then history is intrinsically tied

Figure 5.10 Art for art's sake at Castle Hackton: Red walls covered with paintings. *Barry Lyndon* (1975). Produced by Jan Harlan, Stanley Kubrick, and Bernard Williams. Directed by Stanley Kubrick.

to the Western canon of visual art. In short, the visual world that Kubrick creates in *Barry Lyndon* emphasizes that written and visual histories are produced as effects of specific perspectives. The official history of the British imperial project is recorded in tales of heroism and in hagiographic paintings of the landed aristocracy. In *Barry Lyndon*, Kubrick's interventions in narrative form and visual style rewrite and reenvision this narrative, using the latter's own most prized aesthetic forms: the romance tale and the British painting tradition.

Kubrick employs narration and visual culture in *Barry Lyndon* in a manner that goes beyond simply challenging the received wisdom or official history of this period. He stages encounters between narrative and history and between painting and cinema, raising larger questions about the way narrative and image—creative processes of mediation rather than practices of transparent reportage—construct history. In fact, the film's elegiac tone can be partly attributed to the way the narrative and the images face the constant threat (and promise) of the palimpsest: they are subject to being dismantled, partially destroyed, lost, overwritten, and subsumed to new technologies of language and vision. The newest or most technologically advanced art form is not necessarily positioned to withstand the processes of history better than archaic or anachronistic forms.

In fact, *Barry Lyndon* foregrounds the relationship between the artificial and the natural as an aesthetic and as a social phenomenon, proposing that aesthetic technologies, including the conventions of visual art forms such as painting, photography, and cinema, are historically rooted and ideologically bound. Kubrick immerses the viewer in an eighteenth-century landscape whose aesthetic conventions are laid bare through a succession of technologies from painting to photography and cinematography. Kubrick transforms British paintings into a *mise en scène* that encases and ultimately encloses his Irish protagonist, just as actual physical enclosures radically altered the British landscape during Gainsborough's era. That sense of foreclosure becomes obvious through visual choices that demarcate the film's first and second halves, corresponding to the narrative rise and fall, wherein Barry is far more likely to be shot in an interior in the film's second half than in its first. The long takes and fast lenses allow Kubrick, in Bazin's words, to explore the "geological" stratum that the latter associated with painting: "the sequence of a film gives it a unity in time that is horizontal and, so to speak, geographical, whereas time in a painting, so far as the notion applies, develops geologically and in depth" (Bazin 221).

Within the foreshortened depth of the image, Kubrick's camerawork reveals Barry's unsuitability to the physical and social environment of Castle Hackton and Lady Lyndon's aristocratic world. Kubrick's cinematography delineates the space of imperial imagination with all of its contradictions: on the surface, nature is allied with culture—indeed the landscape naturalizes particular social class and national divisions. As Ann Bermingham has argued in relation to the development of the landscape garden in the eighteenth century: "by conflating nature with the fashionable taste of a new social order, it redefined the natural in terms of this order, and vice versa" (14). "In the outdoor conversation piece"—a term that might be applied to a large portion of Kubrick's film, beginning with the opening duel—"nature becomes a sign of its owners' status and privilege and also the primary source of that status" (15).

Kubrick's attention to aesthetic details is less compelling as a mode of documentary realism than as a means of probing the historically contingent dialectic between what can be understood as real, authentic, or natural versus what is believed to be artificial, social, and constructed. When we consider the idea of progress through the historicity of painting and cinema, and therefore, attend to the difference between still and moving images, we grapple with a set of issues that Thomas Elsaesser associates with the era of digital technology;

I would argue, however, that these concerns were already fully operative during the 1970s within the contemplative aesthetic of *Barry Lyndon*.

Elsaesser attributes changes in the relationships between motion and stillness and between cinema and photography to shifts brought about by digital technology. In his view, the digital format erases the material differences between still and moving images, and thus directs attention to "the degrees, the modulations and modalities of stillness, arrest and movement" (118). One result is that photography and cinema must be rethought in terms of "particular historical 'imaginaries,' rather than being defined by properties inherent in each medium" (120). That is, digital technology forces us to shift from a formal to an historical understanding of the concept of the medium:

> Such an idea of photography and cinema as merely different applications or culturally coded uses of a new (or rather, age-old) mode, namely that of the graphic image (including the photographic image), of which the digital image · would merely be the latest installment, as it were, no doubt challenges our concepts of the photographic and the cinematic in all manner of ways. (120)

Barry Lyndon proposes such a challenge to our concepts, not only of the photographic and cinematic, but also the painterly: paintings, (still) photography, and cinematography are revealed as culturally coded and technologically based uses of graphic images, images whose beauty does not exempt them from their implication in ideologies of personhood and status within particular contexts of social power.

Kubrick's "painterly realism" displaces viewers by revealing that its own representational ethos is bound up in the complex history of visual media, a history inseparable from colonialist representation. Angela Dalle Vacche argues that films that use art can be read as "self-conscious meditations on what is at stake in the encounter between painting and cinema, art and technology, tradition and modernity" (3). Kubrick's absorption of period paintings into the film's *mise en scène* signifies much more than a desire to get the period details right. It suggests a formal method for reproducing the rhetoric of colonization in the realm of the visual, and a desire to understand the aesthetics of the visual image both through and beyond its incarnation as a technology of modernity.

With *Barry Lyndon*, as with *2001*, Kubrick flirts with the cinematic taboos of slowness and stillness, engaging with cinema as a "time-based medium," in Maya Deren's terms, and probing the status of the moving image as index. Laura Mulvey writes of a "delayed cinema" which "brings the temporality of the index and its uncertainties [. . .] out of stillness into the further complexity of movement and then back again" (182). The possibilities afforded American audiences by the opportunity to experience a contemplative gaze seem to have been overshadowed by the denial of the movement imperative (a desire that, in contrast, Kubrick fed in *2001* with the trippy Stargate sequence), by the threat of boredom, and by the confrontation with a sedimented and thus potentially illegible image of pastness. All of these alternatives are embedded in *Barry Lyndon*'s citation of art history through painting and film.

In his 1968 *Playboy* interview with Kubrick, Eric Norden summarized the critical view of *2001* as "dull, pretentious, and overlong," terms that were later applied to *Barry Lyndon* (49). However, no one called upon *Barry Lyndon* to be "exempted from the category of art," a sentiment Norden attributes to Renata Adler, John Simon, and Judith Crist in their assessment of *2001* (49).

If Kubrick's cinema was "made and received in the aura of art" (Naremore 9), then *Barry Lyndon* represents the apotheosis of auratic reception (for better and for worse in terms of commercial matters). Miriam Hansen writes of Walter Benjamin's famously elusive concept: "aura is a medium that envelops and physically connects—and thus blurs the boundaries between—subject and object, suggesting a sensorial, embodied mode of perception [that combines] contemplative distance and haptic nearness" (115). Hansen continues, characterizing Benjamin's concept of "technological and social modernity" through "the ascendance of multiplicity and repeatability over singularity, nearness over farness, and a haptic engagement with things and space over a contemplative relationship to images and time" (116). These elements of aura are precisely what is at stake in the temporal discourse of *Barry Lyndon*; it explains my own experience of disjointed time, what Hansen calls the "psychophysiological state of Rausch or ecstatic trance" (116). The play of stillness and motion gestures toward but cannot be reduced to a digital binary, as it resists the on/off switch and, instead, depends upon the illusion of analog continuity.

Coda: The musical image

Rhythm is to be understood as something utterly fundamental, i.e., as the most primary sensation of time, as the very form of time

Friedrich Nietzsche, *Kritische Studienausgabe*

Time enters mechanics as a measure of interval.

Peter Lynds, *Time and Classical and Quantum Mechanics*

When it is said that cinema is dead, it's particularly stupid, because cinema is at the very beginning of an exploration of audio-visual relations, which are time relations, and which completely renew its relationship with music.

Gilles Deleuze, Interview with Melissa McMuhan

Every dialectic—including those founded upon motion and stillness, or absorption and theatricality—implies rhythm. Marxist social scientist Henri Lefebvre was so taken with the idea, he invented a science grounded in the analysis of rhythms. In *Rhythmanalysis: Space, Time and Everyday Life*, Lefebvre writes that rhythms are "simultaneously natural *and* rational, and neither one nor the other" (9; emphasis in original). In this way they capture the flavor of an aesthetic project like Kubrick's, which attempts to move beyond the subjectivity of an individual character as an entry point into an historical narrative. Rhythm may be experienced as both external and internal, individual and social, a structured process and a spontaneous response to it; ultimately, however, rhythm creates a comforting sense of system and also signals change within a system as well as its potential undoing.

Consistent with Kubrick's interest in the emotional forces that underlie—and undermine—the human quest for rationality, rhythm may embody both temporal order and disruptive chaos. As Lefebvre argues, "rhythm appears as regulated time, governed by rational laws, but is in contact with what is least rational in human being: the lived, the carnal, the body" (9). Providing a description of the phenomenological experience of rhythm that carries rich implications not only for *Barry Lyndon*'s time signature, but also for film representation in general, Lefebvre writes that, "to grasp a rhythm, it is necessary to have been grasped by it, one must *let oneself go*, give oneself over, abandon oneself to its duration" (27; emphasis in original).

Rhythms are individual and social. Emile Durkheim recognized that individual experiences of temporality are "conditioned by the collective rhythms of society" (Flaherty 2). In *Barry Lyndon*, collective rhythms emerge not only from the literal drumbeat of warfare and the stately cadence of the "Sarabande," but also from the visual rhythms created by the juxtaposition of landscape and portrait paintings.

Rhythm represents yet another alternative temporality, as it produces both linear and cyclical temporal schemes. Further, rhythm is felt in the body, which thwarts our ability to spatialize and disembody time. In her discussion of rhythmic time in *Sequel to History: Postmodernism and the Crisis of Representational Time*, philosopher Elizabeth Deeds Ermarth cites Vladimir Nabokov, who worked with Kubrick on the adaptation of *Lolita*, on the issue of rhythm. Nabokov argues that the moment between the beat, the gap, which he called the "Tender Interval," offers an experience of time that cannot be reduced to mere measurement. He writes:

> Maybe the only thing that hints at a sense of time is rhythm. Not the recurrent beats of the rhythm but the gap between two such beats, the grey gap between the black beats: the Tender Interval. The regular throb itself merely brings back the miserable idea of measurement, but in between something like true Time lurks. (quoted in Elden xiv–xv)

Nabokov's understanding of interval as a resistance to time as measurement echoes Deleuze's time-image. Unlike movement-images, where time is subordinated to the imperatives of movement, in time-images, the interval assumes the power to produce unpredictable movement. Philosopher Stephen Crocker considers the implications of Deleuze's argument for the productive potential of the interval: the "inert interval" is no longer "a space to be overcome" but rather a "site of an active ability to determine experience" (47). The interval becomes a "period of determination" (47) "[assuming] a central role in the determination of the whole of movement" (Crocker 54). Thus, the interval or rest—visually and sonically—may productively be understood not as the absence of movement or sound, but as the site of the determination of movement and sound, and as the generative locale for temporality itself.

The curious case of the intermission, also called the interval, in *Barry Lyndon* becomes an occasion to consider the generative possibilities of the interval as stasis, silence, and rest. As a period for a viewer to consolidate and reflect upon the affective and intellectual response to the first half of the film, at the time of its release, the audience would have presumably exited the theater, found the restroom, and would have withdrawn physically and affectively from the film. (Kubrick instructed theaters to play soundtrack music during the intermission.) This pause might enable a different relation to the film than the one that accompanies a screening of the DVD or blu-ray version—during which a short interlude of black screen is accompanied by Handel's "Sarabande." The concept of the interval as a highly productive time of waiting shifts its status from that of (disruptive) interruption to that of a restorative, creative, and potentially contemplative period of aesthetic time that grounds the practice of integrating critical appraisal and emotional investment.

The orchestration of multiple temporalities in *Barry Lyndon* obviously extends beyond its visual design to its soundtrack, with rhythms and melodies that "knit temporal dimensions together," to recall Suzanne Guerlac's observation (66). Kubrick's musical choices are not the unheard melodies of classical Hollywood cinema; in fact, the music functions in the same way as the paintings do, as another sensorially and materially rich layer of discourse. Leonard Rosenman and Jan Harlan's scoring, adaptation, and arrangements contribute to the repetitive, circular structure of the film. They use three pieces of music, in particular, again and again: the traditional "Women of Ireland," performed by the Chieftans, Franz Schubert's "Piano Trio," and Handel's "Sarabande." That the repetition is critical to the film's design is made clear by the work of Christine Lee Gengaro and Katherine McQuiston on music in Kubrick films. In *We'll Meet Again*, McQuiston writes that the film's requirements meant significant modifications were made to the music: " 'Sarabande's' structural components are repeated well beyond the length of Handel's original composition" (87).

The repetitive use of these three pieces establishes the time signature of the film, a term I use metaphorically. Just as the temporality of reading paintings, the juxtaposition of portrait and landscape, and the slow zooms define the visual regime, the music's assertive presence encourages both emotional intimacy and critical distance. Historian Frank Ankersmit—perhaps taking a page from film theorist Christian Metz on the attributes of the aural image—remarks upon the way sound promotes an especially material connection to mood:

> The mood of a time is something we can only hear and not see—although it is no less real for this [. . .] the objects we see are at a distance from us, whereas the sounds we hear are right in our ears. (*Sublime* 274)

In terms of the narrative trajectory, Katherine McQuiston describes the music as accompanying the movement of Redmond Barry in a fairly straightforward way from the "functional" and "joyful" music of the "lower classes" early in the film toward the "stylized, still, restrained music of the aristocracy" (93). I would suggest that further complexity is at work here, as Kubrick juxtaposes folk and formal musics throughout the film, notably with the repetition of the Irish traditional "Women of Ireland" and the "Sarabande," as he establishes a rhythmic encounter between these two works and the Schubert piece.

In fact, the music itself does not sustain the opposition McQuiston draws. A case in point is the "Sarabande," which refers not to a title but rather to a form. The sarabande comprises one part of the baroque suite, which developed in seventeenth-century France in standard form as the sequence of allemande, courante, sarabande, and gigue. The baroque suite was strictly ordered (probably as a result of the needs of music publishers rather than the desires of composers), with overtures preceding dances. The Handel "Sarabande" Kubrick selected for *Barry Lyndon*, the keyboard suite in D minor (HWV 437), derived from 1 of the 22 suites the composer wrote. This particular suite contains five rather than four movements: a prelude, allemande, courante, sarabande, and gigue. Although it is widely reported that Handel's "Sarabande" was used by Ingmar Bergman in *Cries and Whispers* (1972), and thus may have influenced Kubrick's choice, Bergman in fact used Bach's "Sarabande" for cello.

What's most interesting about the sarabande is the cultural positioning that it evokes. Like Redmond Barry, the music is a colonial import, smuggled into the stultifying halls of the British aristocracy and gussied up. The music originated in a form that was exotic, sensual, and irregular. The *zarabanda* is a provocative dance of Moorish or Spanish origin that was first documented by travelers in South America. Scholar Rainer Gstrein favors the idea of its Spanish origins (Brainard 193). The music originated in the twelfth century, was made popular in Spain's colonies, and, finally, was banned by Phillip II in 1583 because it was considered indecent. The Inquisition's punishment for singing or dancing the sarabande was 200 lashes and expulsion from the kingdom for women; men served 6 years in slavery.

The sarabande was popular in France, Italy, Germany, and in the England of Charles II, where it became a ballroom dance that resembled a country dance (Brainard 195). Originally, danced by women using hopping movements in a "rapid, dotted pulse," the form slowed to a "grave meter" (Brainard 195) after 1650 so that, by the eighteenth century, it was appropriate for formal and ceremonial occasions.

Moreover, the cultural import of the traditional Irish music must be acknowledged—the preservation of certain colonial musics taking place against all odds. "Women of Ireland"—*Mna na H-Eireann* in Gaelic—began as a poem by Peadar O Doirnin, an eighteenth-century poet from Ulster. It would have been lost, had not Seán Ó Riada set the poem to music in 1969—contemporary history in relation to the *Barry Lyndon* production in the early 1970s.

The sentimental and sorrowful Irish tune and the stately "Sarabande" parallel the fortunes of Kubrick's hero: he is a low-born Irishman associated with an excess of sensuality who seeks to acquire the trappings of aristocratic reserve while hiding the dirty secret regarding his origins. When McQuiston analyzes the particular arrangement of the "Sarabande" used in *Barry Lyndon*, she emphasizes the way the arrangement foregrounds repetition. Her conclusion regarding the effect of those changes resonates with my assertions regarding Thackeray's prose and Kubrick's narrational and visual interventions as presenting a foreclosed future. McQuiston writes, "the clear repeating pattern exacts a fateful, forward-driving sound and a sense of destiny" (96). Thus, the music forms an essential, yet alternative, aesthetic register for the enactment of multiple temporalities. To McQuiston, "the music represents both the endless, nonnegotiable flow of time, and the numbered days of the characters" (98). In this way, the linearity and repetition in the music functions as counterpoint to the narrative and visual design of Kubrick's *Barry Lyndon*.

This brief examination of the *Barry Lyndon* soundtrack returns us once again to the question of historical representation. For Deleuze, sound disincarnates the body, whereas painting incarnates the body; the latter form "has the power of rendering visible the sensations that traverse the human body and connect it to the world" (Bogue 190). Just as paintings provide a means for Kubrick to materialize history in the image, a way of bringing the weight and density of the medium into cinema, the music dematerializes and undoes that sedimentation, threatening a discourse of failure yet again, and raising the prospect of history left unfinished.

This fear haunts the ending of the film, as Barry retreats from view, yet continues to drain the Lyndon coffers. It's tempting to see this as an allegory for the filmmaking process, and perhaps it is. What this motif connects the film to, in a larger sense, is the failure of the project of modernity itself. In "An Unfinished Project," Fredric Jameson considers Walter Benjamin's massive, unfinished Arcades project and pronounces it an emblem of modernity's unfinished business. For Jameson:

> modernity can be distinguished from our own postmodernity as a space of "unevenness" (the theory of Bloch in *Erbschaft dieser Zeit*), in which the most modern uneasily coexists with what it has not yet superseded, cancelled, streamlined and obliterated. Only from the vantage-point of the postmodern, in which modernization is at last complete, can this secret incompleteness

of the modernization process be detected as the source of modernity and Modernism alike. (193)

Barry Lyndon's unfinished business relates to his construction of self: his inability to achieve the status of the heroic, or even the historical; his failure to leave behind a structure, an idea, or a person. In short, the only evidence of his own materiality that he might leave behind would be his language, his memoir, and his image. Regardless of the temporal mode he encounters, his incapacity to achieve completion—signified by his amputation—is the final source of sorrow in the film.

6

Untimely Cinema:
Barry Lyndon and the 1970s

Perhaps when everything is beautiful, nothing is beautiful.

Stanley Kubrick, Interview with Eric Norden, 1968

The preceding chapters have explored key aspects of the discourse of temporality within *Barry Lyndon* (1975), including the way it counters narrative sequence with a disruptive anxiety about succession, the way it animates the affective cycle of colonial melancholia through repetition and a circular plot, and the way it generates visual and aural rhythms both to personalize and objectify the dialectics of empire. These strategies, based upon Thackeray's and Kubrick's interests in experimenting with the temporally inflected relationship between words and images, provide us with opportunities to engage with the text and to reflect upon it critically.

To conclude this inquiry, I examine the discourse of temporality surrounding *Barry Lyndon*, and, particularly, its place in cinema history. I want to situate *Barry Lyndon* in the context of its time, within the cinema of the 1970s in the United States and Britain. This is not motivated by a desire to secure its claims to masterpiece status within the film historical firmament or the Kubrick *oeuvre*. Instead, I wish to look at the environment surrounding the film's release, focusing in particular on genre and stardom, to learn whether a reconsideration of the film's supposed untimeliness, an exercise of retrospection, might tell us something about the time of *Barry Lyndon* that the analyses in the previous chapters have not revealed.

I return first of all to the question of time and timing. In "Evolutionary Imagineer: Stanley Kubrick's Authorship," Thomas Elsaesser considers *Barry Lyndon* proleptically as somehow belonging to the 1980s. He argues that Kubrick's film was a generic revision and a prototype that appeared on the scene too early to benefit from the resurgence of the costume drama after films such as *Chariots of Fire* (1981), whose immense popularity paved the way for the rise of the British heritage film. This observation overlooks the fact that a large number of popular period dramas were available on British television from BBC and ITV—some of which, including *Upstairs/Downstairs* (1970–5), migrated to US television and enjoyed immense popularity there as well. In terms of Kubrick's *oeuvre*, Elsaesser contrasts *Barry Lyndon* with *The Shining* (1980) and *Full Metal Jacket* (1987), films that he believes were released at the appropriate moment to capitalize on the interest in their respective genres (140).

Fredric Raphael proposes a different temporal scheme for the reception of *Barry Lyndon*. His assertion is that, instead of being ahead of its time, the film was behind the times, at least for its target audience. The audience whose appetite had been whetted by *2001: A Space Odyssey* (1968) and *A Clockwork Orange* (1971), writes Raphael, scorned the Kubrick who gave them *Barry Lyndon* and saw him as "a kind of artistic Benedict Arnold ungratefully leaving their present for the antique world of European classics" (153).

Compounding these temporal conundrums is Kubrick's own place within the firmament as a celebrity director in the 1970s. David Cook characterizes Kubrick as someone not quite of his time: Kubrick was a "non-film generation director of the 1970s" (35). Like Cook, Elsaesser distinguishes the older postwar generation of Aldrich, Altman, Penn, and Peckinpah from the New Hollywood directors Scorsese, de Palma, Lucas, and Schrader. Kubrick's apparent untimeliness keeps him out of either camp and Elsaesser will ultimately label the dynamic duo of Robert Altman and Stanley Kubrick as "survivors" ("American Auteur" 54). For him, Kubrick's importance to new Hollywood rests primarily upon his influence on younger directors, such as Spielberg, who would go on make blockbusters using his formula.

Clearly, there is a case to be made that *Barry Lyndon* was something of an anomaly and an anachronism in the 1970s. I plan to pursue a different tack, however, in attempting to account for the peculiar temporalities of *Barry Lyndon*. In my view, *Barry Lyndon* was not Kubrick's "grandest gamble"; that it was not an untimely experiment, a miscalculation, or even a radical departure from his previous films or from American and British films of the period. In fact, I will argue that *Barry Lyndon* was a typical, if not quintessential, 1970s film. The lack of enthusiasm on the part of American audiences, I suggest, was not related to style, genre, or themes: with respect to these elements, *Barry Lyndon* conforms in many ways to what used to be called mainstream, commercial films of that era. The overwhelmingly important difference between *Barry Lyndon* and popular American films of the decade comes down to one issue with multiple resonances: gender.

After exploring the ways that *Barry Lyndon* makes sense as a 1970s film, I conclude by examining the concept of the late style, a problematic associated with the theories of Theodor Adorno (writing on Beethoven) and Edward Said. In its narrowest form, the late style that defines the late career work of an artist is overshadowed by impending death, although death is not necessarily the subject of the work. In "Late: Fictional Time in the Twenty-First Century," Peter Boxall associates a mood and a sense of misgiving with this set of issues. For him, the late style represents "an apprehension of cultural exhaustion or completion" (680). Works of a late style are understood to be disjunctive, dissonant, and resistant, the implication being that an artist may have lingered beyond the point of relevance. Leila Rosenthal argues that lateness "articulates the impossibility of 'going beyond'" (109).

According to the organizational architecture at the Stanley Kubrick Archive at the London College of Communication, *Barry Lyndon* could be understood as a late film. Its precious remains are nestled under the banner of file number 14; Kubrick's final film, *Eyes Wide Shut* (1999), occupies file 17. By the numbers alone, then, *Barry Lyndon* could be considered a representative of Kubrick's late style.

However, the trajectory of the late style can be trumped or superseded by the trope of "the turn." One example of this type of historicizing is R. Barton Palmer's treatment of *Barry Lyndon* as an aberration or digression, a detour from Kubrick's authentic trajectory. For Palmer, the director subsequently made a course correction, which happily resulted in his popular and critical success with *The Shining.* This view overstates the initial response to the latter film, which was nominated for two Razzies—for worst actress and worst director—in the inaugural year of that award. Nevertheless, the retrospective narrative Palmer develops is helpful for examining the historiography of *Barry Lyndon* and may help to clarify what is at stake in thinking about the film's time and its (un)timeliness.

1975: An untimely break?

Aside from the premiere of *Barry Lyndon* in New York on December 18, something of great import seems to have happened in 1975, at least according to film scholars. Dudley Andrew writes that the "soul of cinema" moved beyond first world and second world cinemas in 1975 (215). In the essay, "The Existence of Italy," Fredric Jameson posits 1975 as a moment of rupture. For his part, Elsaesser dates the end of the Golden Age of New Hollywood, inaugurated in 1967, to that year ("American Auteur" 40). The sense of widespread and possibly seismic changes occurring in the industry, and in American culture, during the mid-1970s feeds into the argument that *Barry Lyndon* represents a miscalculation, a retreat into the glory days of the previous two decades' road shows, and prestige releases in the midst of an era rife with revisionism. The project of rewriting Hollywood genres was well underway, nowhere more evident than in the popularity of Francis Ford Coppola's revisionist gangster saga, *The Godfather* (1972), the cycle of disaster films, beginning with *The Poseidon Adventure* (1972) and the rise of another apocalyptic subgenre, the slasher film, beginning with *Texas Chainsaw Massacre* (1974).

In seeking to contextualize *Barry Lyndon* in the 1970s United States, I will use terminology that circulated unproblematically during the 1970s but which no longer enjoys such freedom of movement: the language of film style. Scholars continue to characterize the style of American and British films of the 1970s, although they increasingly recognize the problems with such totalizing gestures. The widespread sense of 1970s cinema in the United States was its break away from classical rules of continuity, with rapid editing, zooms, complex soundtracks, and elliptical editing, but Elsaesser tempers the impression that all 1970s films should be considered in the context of a counterculture. He writes that, while many films of the 1970s were "especially sensitive to the disarticulation of action, the disorientation of perception, and the modulations of affect," they were also replete with "non-classical, romantic, European baroque aesthetics as well as [. . .] antagonistic, critical and countercultural energies" ("American Auteur" 44). All of these elements would seem to recommend *Barry Lyndon* as a quintessential film of the decade. This holds true not just for American film. According to Sue Harper and Justin Smith, "British cinema of the 1970s was predominantly a pictorialist and fantastic cinema, and even those films which deployed realist discourses tended to do so self-consciously" (162).

It's not as though *Barry Lyndon* does not conform to the stylistic techniques for which the 1970s are known, including the use of the zoom lens. Kubrick employs these techniques to different ends, perhaps, repurposing the zoom as a device of still photography rather than using it to simulate and stimulate action. One apt genealogical comparison would be to Coppola's *The Godfather*, partly because that film enacts an internal dialogue regarding the evolution of film language similar to the discourse in *Barry Lyndon* on genres of visual culture. Coppola's opening sequence and the celebrated baptismal montage near the conclusion establish a timeline for film history that mirrors that film's narrative arc from traditional immigrant to modern culture. The opening scene depicting Don Corleone and the undertaker proceeds slowly and sequentially; cinema creates movement from stillness and images out of darkness as the *mise en scène* emerges out of and overwrites a nearly black screen. The penultimate scene externalizing Michael's wrath exposes the temporal and spatial magic of editing.

Although my focus is primarily on American cinema, a second close cousin to Kubrick's *Barry Lyndon* is Derek Jarman's *Jubilee* (1978), a film more often compared to *A Clockwork Orange* than to *Barry Lyndon* because of its punk sensibility (see Upton). Jarman's film treats the spectacle of the British imperial project from a critical perspective inside the empire. Historical revisionism meets time travel in a narrative about anachronism that punctures the pieties and pride of the postcolonial metropolis. To borrow from Roland Greene, writing in a different context, the film "turns a baroque eye on the baroque" (155) in the same way that, in *Barry Lyndon*, Kubrick turns a neoclassical eye on neoclassicism. Both films critique practices of historical representation—for Jarman, Queen Elizabeth II's 1977 Silver Jubilee is deserving of deconstruction— and the aesthetic regime of the British empire. The comparison with *Jubilee* foregrounds the way that Kubrick's film has been given a place in British film history, by virtue of its genre and its arguable conformity to the British heritage cinema tradition (Pidduck 4). In other words, when the film is mentioned, it typically arises in relation to the British costume drama.

Moving from broad generalizations about style to questions of ideology (a term that also marks itself as a product of the 1970s) and revisionism, Robert Kolker writes that *Barry Lyndon* "views the present through its lens" (163). The comment suggests that *Barry Lyndon* could be read as a Vietnam allegory: the film's unwilling soldier protagonist and its release date in 1975, the year of the chaotic US withdrawal from Vietnam, could support this possibility. Following

Elsaesser's logic of the precursor, Kubrick's film would be a harbinger of Michael Cimino's *Deerhunter* (1978) and *Heaven's Gate* (1980), and, less directly, Ashby's *Coming Home* (1978)—films about the irreparable damage, rather than the derring do, associated with war. Evidence certainly exists that Kubrick thought the subject of the Napoleonic wars had contemporary relevance, which may have extended to case of *Barry Lyndon*, given the specific terms in which Kubrick articulated this belief. In the interview with Joseph Gelmis, Kubrick remarks:

> I find that all the issues with which it concerns itself are oddly contemporary— the responsibilities and abuses of power, the dynamics of social revolution, the relationship of the individual to the state, war, militarism, etc.—so this will not be just a dusty historic pageant but a film about the basic questions of our own times, as well as Napoleon's. (45)

Whether or not Kubrick attempted to avoid a dusty pageant, his audience had grown accustomed to a close proximity between his narratives and their own techno-historical reality. *Dr. Strangelove* was released within vivid memory of the 1961 Bay of Pigs fiasco, and the 1968 release of *2001* anticipated the moon landing in 1969. For American audiences in particular, there was a great deal of difference between the revisionist Western, which critically recapitulates Manifest Destiny within the anticolonial sensibility of the anti-Vietnam War movement, turning the former bad guys into good guys, and *Barry Lyndon*, whose diffidence regarding good guys and bad guys makes any political statement—in the polarized framework of the politics of the day—ambiguous. In the early days after the release of the film, reports of the film's subpar box office performance—compared to *A Clockwork Orange* and *The Exorcist*—in Philadelphia were accompanied by an assessment of audience demographics: more than 50 percent were in the 18–24-year-old age group.[1] This was Kubrick's audience, and it was less captivated by this film than his earlier work.

Barry Lyndon may never secure a berth as a "seventies film" in the pantheon of New Hollywood, despite Kubrick's genre experimentation and flirtation with ambivalent antiheroes: both tendencies link *Barry Lyndon* to a range of 1970s films, from revisionist Westerns to urban crime dramas. The experience of a lavish excursion into period filmmaking links Kubrick's film to those of British and European auteurs slumming in Hollywood, including Jack Clayton (*The Great Gatsby* 1973) and Roman Polanski (*Chinatown* 1974).

---

[1] Warner Brothers archives, Correspondence File #1, Burbank, CA.

Having raised the question of genre, I wish to first make the case that the 1970s American film industry, not just British cinema, was a time for the period film. Hollywood was rife with retro-fever and costume extravaganzas, in offerings such as *The Summer of '42* (1971); *The Last Picture Show* (1971); *Cabaret* (1972); *American Graffiti* (1973); *The Way We Were* (1973); *The Sting* (1973); *Paper Moon* (1973); and *Chinatown* (1974). In fact, period costumes from *Bonnie and Clyde*, *The Great Gatsby*, *Chinatown*, and *Cabaret* influenced American fashions—with Bloomingdales creating a clothing line based on the costumes in *The Great Gatsby* (La Ferla)—which gave those films a palpable afterlife in the public imagination. Those retro modern fashions—which included trousers for women as well as provocative flapper dresses—were simpler to translate into mass market ready to wear in the feminist decade of the 1970s than the eighteenth-century designs of Milena Canonero and Ulla-Britt S∅derlund.

The Great Gatsby offers an interesting point of comparison with *Barry Lyndon*, as both films are based on literary novels and turned out to be expensive period productions. *Gatsby* was panned by *Variety* in terms that expressed a barely acknowledged resentment about the rising cost of film productions about wealthy people in the midst of a bad economy: "The fascinating physical beauty of the $6 million-plus film complements the utter shallowness of most principal characters from the F. Scott Fitzgerald novel" (*Variety*). Yet *Gatsby* has been remembered, recuperated, and, finally, remade (Luhrmann 2013), in part because it is understood as an American literary and cultural classic and in part because of the continuing prominence of its high-wattage A-list stars, Robert Redford and Mia Farrow. This observation begins to build a narrative that the uneasy fit between *Barry Lyndon* and American audiences of the 1970s may have had something to do with the film's alien feel, its non-Americanness. R. Barton Palmer's notion that *The Shining* represents a course correction is apt, in that its American location and subtext made it far more accessible than the tale of a Redcoat deserter. That may have been the case as well for *Full Metal Jacket* and *Eyes Wide Shut*, in which red-blooded American male protagonists, not social-climbing Irish wanderers, are subjected to physical and psychological tortures.

Since Kubrick's source material was not American, it was not susceptible to the practices of exploitation that studios were using to market filmed novels such as *Gatsby* and *The Godfather*. These literary adaptations not only offered studios the pre-sold audience but also provided film directors an opportunity to distinguish their work from television. Studios might justify lavish expenditures on costume dramas or historical epics at a time of economic contractions—and the period after the 1973 oil price shocks was certainly that—if attached to a lofty literary tradition. Fitzgerald's *The Great Gatsby* had been adapted for film twice already—in 1926 and 1949—but, more importantly, had attained the status of classic American novel, in part because 150,000 copies were issued in an Armed Services Edition given to American Troops during World War II (Bruccoli 217).

Gatsby was accompanied by a reissue of the source novel; *Barry Lyndon* was not. Apparently, Kubrick's commitment to the British classics did not extend to acquiring prestige by pursuing a promotional tie-in. Correspondence from Fontana books about releasing a paperback version of Thackeray's novel—as they had done with *Dr. Zhivago, Serpico,* and *Murder on the Orient Express*—is contained in the production files at the Kubrick archive at the London College of Communication. The letter from Fontana regarding this proposal is marked with Kubrick's own script: "see their books."[2] The remark implies that simply forging the connection with a literary source would not be enough: for Kubrick to associate his film with that reprint, it needed to be done well. His own reputation was on the line.

The prestige aspect of Kubrick's film represented a double-edged sword in the 1970s, in the midst of the countercultural hangover from the 1960s. Remember that *2001* was on its way to possible obscurity until it was resurrected by a marketing campaign touting the experience to a new generation of smart and possibly stoned film audiences, as "the Ultimate Trip." There was an internal discussion at Warner's as to whether a staid nineteenth-century novel would stimulate more interest in the film than the beautifully illustrated brochure. Prior to the film's release, Warner Brothers representatives expressed concern in interoffice memos that people might encounter difficulty reading the book and even suggested avoiding tie-ins with local bookstores.[3] Seeking the imprimatur of high culture through a novel that was not canonical, though its author might be remembered as such, at a point in time when canonicity was becoming suspect to the youth audience that flocked to Kubrick's work, might be a questionable commercial strategy, as the Warner publicity campaign seems to have recognized.[4]

---

[2] Stanley Kubrick Archive, London College of Communication, SK 14/6/1.
[3] Warner Brothers archive, Correspondence File #3, Burbank, CA.
[4] In a move that indicates not only the flexibility of film and literary linkages but also the continuing importance of serial publication, Christopher Wood, a historical writer best known for his novelization of James Bond films, published *The Further Adventures of Barry Lyndon by Himself* in 1976.

Yet, there was an aspect to the publicity campaign that drew on the literary credentials of Thackeray's novel. In an attempt to burnish the project's educational value, Warner Brothers requested reprints of the *TIME* cover story to distribute to high schools and colleges to help students prepare for classroom discussions of the film. (*TIME* declined the request on the basis that it violated their policy of not allowing the magazine to be used for promotional purposes).[5] A second promotional front involved *Scholastic* magazine. Correspondence in the files at the Warner Brothers archive indicates that 40 school librarians in the Philadelphia area were contacted regarding the potential use of the film in the classroom. One letter mentions the possible publication of excerpts from Trollope's 1879 "Man of Letters" study on Thackeray.[6] These were intended to capitalize on the film's literary and historical merit as well as the upcoming Bicentennial.

The US Bicentennial emerges as an important context for *Barry Lyndon*, and as one potential reason it did not do better at the box office. Joseph Gelmis makes reference to the preparatory activities for the 200-year anniversary of the Declaration of Independence in his review of *Barry Lyndon* in *The Des Moines Register*, entitled "Bicentennial Epic" (7). His linkage between the film and historical commemoration is included in a clippings file at the Stanley Kubrick Archive that collected quotes from American reviewers, in a section labeled "best quotes."[7] Gelmis wrote: "*Barry Lyndon* is as much about the causes of the American Revolution as any film whose characters are Washington, Franklin, and Jefferson" (7). It's reasonable to suggest, however, that US patriotism would be a difficult means by which to draw viewers to a film with an Irish and British context for its Redcoat-clad soldiers.

As a costume drama, it would seem *Barry Lyndon* faced a uphill battle from the outset. Fredric Jameson claims that the costume film fell into "disrepute and infrequency" ("Nostalgia" 283–4) because the wearing of the costumes of the great moments of the past [. . .] is no longer on the cards in an ahistorical period of history" (296). Yet these observations belie the apparent obsession with historical dramas that emerged in the 1970s, particularly in Britain. The television costume dramas that emerged during the 1970s are merely one aspect of a larger engagement with cultural heritage and genealogy, in both Britain and the United States (see Stephanie Rains). Historians and cultural theorists have debated the

---

[5] Warner Brothers archive, Correspondence File #3, Burbank, CA.
[6] Warner Brothers archive, Correspondence File #3, Burbank, CA.
[7] Stanley Kubrick Archive, SK14/7/7.

ideology underlying the heritage industry, with some seeing it as a misguided attempt to preserve outmoded social practices in the face of postmodern variability, particularly in the Reagan and Thatcher 1980s; others defend popular notions of heritage against the elitism of professional historians.

Jameson's pronouncements notwithstanding, the countercultural and postmodern energies of the 1960s, were only slowly making their mark on British film culture. As Sue Harper documents in *Picturing the Past: The Rise and the Fall of the British Costume Film*, during the 1970s one in five British features was a historical film set before World War II, which represented a doubling over films meeting that description in the 1960s (27). She concludes that costume films were popular successes in Britain in the 1970s, especially in the early years of the decade (30). Thus, *Barry Lyndon* does not seem unorthodox in the context of British film culture. Costume films were a popular genre in the first-half of the 1970s, with strongest box office performances coming from "art house auteur films and American financed blockbusters"; in this environment, *Barry Lyndon* "did well" (Harper 30).

Pam Cook probes the reasons the costume drama genre faces obstacles in popular and critical circles alike. She identifies the genre's "perceived femininity," an attribute that is often conflated with inauthenticity (7). Julianne Pidduck concurs, noting the way that these films share "some of the abuse regularly leveled at soap operas and popular romance" (5), and contributes a second ideological dimension, the question of national identity, to the discussion. She asserts that the "challenge facing critics is to distinguish between nostalgic celebration and self conscious critique" (14).

The analysis Cook offers of Andrew Higson's writing on heritage cinema provides some parallels with my thinking on the American audience's response to Kubrick's film, and thus it bears citing at some length. Higson's work, she writes,

> manifests many of the symptoms evident in critical approaches to the historical film: a distrust of decoration and display, which is perceived as obfuscating a more genuinely authentic approach to history; a fear of being "swallowed up" by nostalgia and a concomitant desire for critical distance and irony; a view of history as necessarily offering lessons for the present; and a sense that history should remain uncontaminated by commodification. (69)

In other words, the very dialectic that Kubrick animates (critically) in *Barry Lyndon* between the rational and the sublime, and between an embrace of realist history and the articulation of history as an aesthetic construct, reappears within our expectations regarding, and appraisal of, historical films. Resistance to such works often implies "the distrust of imaginary plenitude believed to characterize history as spectacle, and the recourse to a critical, reasoned view of history" (Cook 70–1).

The costume drama shares this potential problem of spectacularity with another historical genre, the epic, which is also pertinent to *Barry Lyndon*. With the historical epic, as Vivian Sobchak writes, "aesthetic extravagances are seen as essentially in bad taste and its historical depictions as essentially anachronistic" (24). In other words, the plenitude that need not be so vigorously resisted here is the chest-thumping recapitulation of masculinity. Sobchak writes on the matter of the genre's masculinism quite eloquently:

> At first, the purpose of all this hyperformalism seems significant only as a perverse and inflated display of autoerotic spectacle—that is, as cinema tumescent: institutionally full of itself, swollen with its own generative power to mobilize the vast amount of labor and money necessary to diddle its technology to an extended and expanded orgasm of images, sounds, and profits. (25)

For Kristin Thompson, historical epics "celebrate the male body, a figure of physical prowess who must prove his courage and skill" (46). This description might be appropriate for *Spartacus* (1960)—a film Kubrick might have had in mind when he said he wanted to avoid making a dusty historical pageant— whose narrative and whose star, Kirk Douglas, fulfilled these expectations. For Julianne Pidduck, epics are "often associated with masculine auteurist projects and bravura performances by headlining stars"; as such, they stand in contrast with the "more pervasive 'feminine' intimate sphere of literary adaptation, romance and historical biography" (6).

Barry Lyndon straddles the territory between costume drama, literary adaptation, and epic, although its epic ambitions are intentionally undermined from the outset at both narrative and formal levels. I would like to explore the implication of gender, genre, and stardom in the film, asking whether these gender and sexual dynamics might account for the lukewarm embrace of this film by Kubrick's fans and its exclusion from many accounts of American cinema in the 1970s.

First, *Barry Lyndon* participates in what Pam Cook calls the feminization of history achieved by the costume romance film. The film does not foreground the desires of female characters—to the contrary—but it does privilege "intimate and domestic settings and [emphasize] fashion, hairstyles and interior decoration" (77). Thus the film critiques masculinity, but does so in a manner that is as far removed from the hypermasculine display of *The Killing*, *Dr. Strangelove*, and *A Clockwork Orange*—and *Paths of Glory* and *Spartacus* before them—as one could get. In many ways, its depiction of masculinity revives the predatory and manipulative ladies man sensibility of *Lolita*'s Humbert Humbert. To be clear: Kubrick's critique of phallic masculinity is implied in all of these films. The difference is that, in *Barry Lyndon*, the protagonist is granted few opportunities to perform the "hardbody" feats for which 1980s American cinema would become recognized, and for which the antiheroes of 1970s cinema should also be recognized.

Second, in the gendered dynamics of genre, the significance of the casting of Ryan O'Neal as the film's protagonist cannot be overstated. Julianne Pidduck writes of *Barry Lyndon* in the context of a group of costume dramas that "foreground male protagonists through nostalgic prisms of repression and thwarted desire" (45) and emphasizes that these films were marketed on "the strength of male auteurs and period spectacle" (45). In addition, Ryan O'Neal's star persona was a major element in the marketing and discourse of *Barry Lyndon*.

I propose that a major reason American audiences rejected *Barry Lyndon* had to do with star turns rather than the directorial turn. My argument is not meant to assign box office blame, nor is it intended as an assessment of acting quality. Rather, I seek to consider why this film of Kubrick's seems to be a less typical Kubrick film and one less embraced by his American male audience. My primary conclusion is its use of Ryan O'Neal, whose 1970s star persona was that of a "feminist man."

The static qualities of *Barry Lyndon* propose that everything within the frame is on display, theatricalized, and to be looked at, to use Laura Mulvey's potent phrase. The character of Redmond Barry is a womanizer, as discussed in Chapter 3; he is difficult to position fully as a macho, rebellious, masculine role model for identification. As Redmond Barry, he lives as the dependant of a woman, taking her name.

Nowhere is this "problem" of gender more apparent than in casting. Ryan O'Neal's star persona was based on his California pretty boy looks, his career built on playing charming WASPs, from bad boy Rodney Carrington on the television series "Peyton Place" to preppie dreamboat Oliver Barrett III in the unaccountably popular *Love Story* (1970). Before his comic turn playing his daughter Tatum's reluctant father in the retro depression film *Paper Moon*

(1973), O'Neal solidified a persona I am describing as "the feminist man" as the hunky nerd Howard Bannister opposite Barbra Streisand in *What's Up Doc?* (1972). O'Neal built his career on his soft voice and surfer good looks but, more importantly, found his greatest success when he played men bested by, and beset by, smart, bossy women. Despite what would later emerge in his off-screen persona as a violent streak and possible drug addictions—both attributes that in the mid-1970s would have been considered harmless bad boy behavior—O'Neal's stardom rested on roles that inherently undermined macho masculinity: culminating in *Partners* (1982) where he plays John Hurt's gay partner (he is an undercover cop in that role) and *Faithful* (1996) where he is outsmarted by the wife he is trying to murder, Cher. One role that attempted to reverse that trend is *The Driver* (1978), loosely remade as *Drive* (2011), starring Ryan Gosling, a figure whose "Hey Girl" persona represents the latest version of the feminist man.

In short, the counterpart to *Barry Lyndon*'s non-Americanness was its non-manliness. Although Kubrick best-loved films, including *Dr. Strangelove* and *A Clockwork Orange*, were celebrated for undermining masculinity, they did so through gleefully epic displays of said phallic masculinity. The film's too equivocal treatment of masculinity, particularly in the context of a decade whose male role models were Johnny Boy in *Mean Streets*, Michael Corelone in *The Godfather*, and Popeye Doyle in *The French Connection*, estranged the film from both the decade and Kubrick's fans.

Turning point or late style?

In the history of art late works are the catastrophes.

Theodor Adorno

The prerogative of late style is that it has the power to render disenchantment and pleasure without resolving the contradiction between them.

Edward Said

In *The World, the Text, the Critic*, Edward Said describes style as "the recognizable, repeatable, preservable sign of an author who reckons with an audience" (33). In my view, *Barry Lyndon* created unpleasant discontinuities for a particular audience: it sounded a discordant note following on the heels of *Dr. Strangelove*, *2001* and *A Clockwork Orange*, films that offer the pleasures of obvious satire

(*Strangelove*), lethal laddism (*A Clockwork Orange*), and countercultural intellectualism (*2001*). Stanley Kubrick well understood the danger of style, the tension between its bid for uniqueness and its imperative of repetition (Rosenthal 120). His gesture toward a new genre, a new challenge in *Barry Lyndon*, ironically, elucidated the problem all working artists and directors face regarding their adherence to the "original" styles they themselves have created.

Leila Rosenthal closely and astutely reads Edward Said's reading of Adorno's writing on late style, probing the possibility of an aesthetic of both ending and surviving:

> This would be an aesthetic of remaining after the ending; of going beyond without transcendence, of surviving. Refusing closure, and exhibiting a willingness to allow irreconcilable elements to remain, is thus also one way of performing the notion of lateness. (118)

At the risk of over-romanticizing, I would argue for *Barry Lyndon* as evidence of Kubrick's late style, although I am not prepared to submit to the laws of chronology and succession to say that the films that followed it participate in the same ethos. Instead, I adopt Rosenthal's approach to the performance of lateness, one that exhibits a willingness to allow irreconcilable elements to remain. One reason I am comfortable with an ending with irreconcilables is that the film itself ultimately refuses closure, partly through its suggestion that Redmond Barry may survive beyond the ending of his story. He is not in a position to orchestrate a transcendent return, an uplifting redemption. But he endures, somewhere; his temporal survival no longer dependent on the limited technologies of visuality available in the eighteenth, nineteenth, or twentieth centuries.

Bibliography

Adams, Jerold, ed. *The Philosophy of Stanley Kubrick*. Lexington, KY: University Press of Kentucky, 2007.

Adorno, Theodor W. "Late Style in Beethoven." In *Essays in Music*. Selected, with Introduction, Commentary, and Notes by Richard Leppert; New Translations by Susan H. Gillespie. Berkeley, CA: University of California Press, 2002: 564–8.

Agel, Frank. *The Making of Kubrick's 2001*. New York: Signet, 1970.

Ahmed, Sara. *The Cultural Politics of Emotion*. London: Routledge, 2013.

Altman, Robert. *Images* (first draft, number #4059). Lion's Gate Films. Los Angeles, CA: Margaret Herrick Library.

Andrew, Dudley. *Concepts in Film Theory*. Oxford: Oxford University Press, 1984.

—. *Mists of Regret: Culture and Sensibility in Classic French Film*. Princeton, NJ: Princeton University Press, 1995.

—. "The Roots of the Nomadic: Gilles Deleuze and the Cinema of West Africa." In *The Brain is the Screen*, ed. Gregory Flaxman. Minneapolis, MN: University of Minnesota Press, 2000: 215–49.

—. "The Economies of Adaptation." In *True to the Spirit: Film Adaptation and the Question of Fidelity*, ed. Colin McCabe, Kathleen Murray, and Rick Warner. Oxford and New York: Oxford University Press, 2011: 27–39.

Anisman, Martin. *William Makepeace Thackeray's Barry Lyndon: A Scholarly Edition*. New York: New York University Press, 1970.

Ankersmit, Frank. *A New Philosophy of History*. Chicago: University of Chicago Press, 1995.

—. *Sublime Historical Experience*. Palo Alto, CA: Stanford University Press, 2005.

Arnheim, Rudolf. "Caricature: The Rationale of Deformation." In *To the Rescue of Art: Twenty Six Essays*. Berkeley, CA: University of California Press, 1992: 101–14.

Barber, Sian. *The British Film Industry in the 1970s: Capital, Culture and Creativity*. London: Palgrave McMillan, 2013.

Barter, Pavel. *Ballybrando*. Belfast: Hot Shot Films, 2009.

—. "Brando, Depp, The Missing Millions and *Divine Rapture*, the Lost Movie." *The Guardian*. November 26, 2009. www.guardian.co.uk/film/2009/nov/26/brando-depp-divine-rapture.

—. *Castles, Candles, and Kubrick* (Pavel Barter, 2013). "Documentary on *Newstalk*." www.newstalk.ie. Aired October 19, 2013 (accessed December 3, 2013).

Barthes, Roland. "The Death of the Author." In *Image, Music, Text*, trans. Stephen Heath. London: Fontana: 1977: 142–8.

Barton, Ruth. *Irish National Cinema*. London: Routledge, 2004.

Battestin, Martin C. "Adapting Fielding for Film and Television." In *Eighteenth Century Fiction on Screen*, ed. Robert Mayer. Cambridge: Cambridge University Press, 2002: 88–105.

Baudelaire, Charles. *Intimate Journals*, trans. Christopher Isherwood. Mineola, NY: Dover Books, 2006.

Baudrillard, Jean. "History a Retro Scenario." In *Simulacra and Simulation*, trans. Sheila Faria Glaser. Ann Arbor, MI: University of Michigan Press, 1995: 43–8.

Baxter, John. *Stanley Kubrick: A Biography*. New York: Westview Press, 1997.

Bazin, André. *What is Cinema?* Vol. 2, ed. Hugh Gray. Berkeley, CA: University of California Press, 2004.

—. "The Evolution of the Language of Cinema." *What is Cinema?* Vol. 1. Berkeley, CA: University of California Press, 2005: 23–40.

—. "The Ontology of the Photographic Image." *What is Cinema?* Vol. 1. Berkeley, CA: University of California Press, 2005: 9–16.

de Beistegui, Miguel. *Thinking with Heidegger: Displacements*. Bloomington, IN: Indiana University Press, 2003.

Benjamin, Walter. *Reflections: Essays, Aphorisms, Autobiographical Writings*, trans. Edmund Jephcott, ed. Peter Demetz. New York: Harcourt, 1978.

—. *The Arcades Project*, trans. Howard Eiland and Kevin McLaughlin. Cambridge, MA and London: Belknap Press, 1999.

—. "On the Concept of History." Gesammelten Schriften I:2. Suhrkamp Verlag. Frankfurt am Main, 1974, trans. Dennis Redmond, 2005. www.marxists.org/ reference/archive/benjamin/1940/history.htm.

—. *Selected Writings, Volume 4 (1938–40)*. Cambridge, MA: Harvard University Press, 2006.

Bergson, Henri. *Time and Free Will: An Essay on the Immediate Data of Consciousness*, trans. Frank Lubecki Pogson. Mineola, NY: Dover, 2001.

Bermingham, Ann. *Landscape and Ideology: The English Rustic Tradition, 1740–1860*. Berkeley, CA: University of California Press, 1986.

Bloch, Ernst. *Heritage of Our Times*. Berkeley and Los Angeles, CA: University of California Press, 1991.

Bogdanovich, Peter. "What They Say About Stanley Kubrick." *The New York Times*. July 4, 1999. http://www.nytimes.com/1999/07/04/magazine/what-they-say-about-stanley-kubrick.html?pagewanted=all&src=pm.

Bogue, Ronald. *Deleuze on Music, Painting and the Arts*. New York: Routledge, 2014.

Boozer, Jack. "From *Traumnovelle* (1927)—From Script to Screen—to *Eyes Wide Shut* (1999)." In *Authorship in Film Adaptation*, ed. Jack Boozer. Austin, TX: University of Texas Press, 2008: 85–106.

Bordwell, David. "Got Those Death of Film/Movies/Cinema Blues?" *Observations on Film Art*. October 15, 2012. http://www.davidbordwell.net/blog/2012/10/15/got-those-death-of-filmmoviescinema-blues/.

Bordwell, David and Janet Staiger. *Classical Hollywood Cinema: Film Style and Mode of Production to 1960*. New York: Routledge, 1988.

Boxall, Peter. "Late: Fictional Time in the Twenty-First Century." *Contemporary Literature* 53.4 (2012): 681–712.

Brady, Donald. *Film and Film-Making in Waterford: Preliminary Studies*. Waterford: Waterford County Council, 2009. Waterford County Library Website.

Brainard, Ingrid. "The "Sarabande" in Dance and Music." *Dance Chronicle* 23.2 (2000): 193–9.

Brooks, Jodi and Therese Davis. "Untimely Cinema: Cinema Out of Time." *Screening The Past*. Issue 34 (September 2012). http://www.screeningthepast.com/issue-34/.

Brown, Alan. *The Deja Vu Experience*. Hove and New York: Psychology Press, 2004.

Brown, Marshall. *Bulls and Blunders*. Chicago: S.C. Griggs, 1893.

—. *Bulls and Blunders*. Boston, MA: Small, Maynard & Co., 1906.

Buchwald, Emilie. "Gainsborough's Prospect Animated." In *Studies in Criticism and Aesthetics, 1660–1800: Essays in Honor of Samuel Holt Monk*, ed. Howard Anderson and John S. Shea. Minneapolis, MN: University of Minnesota Press, 1967: 358–79.

Cahill, Tim. "The Rolling Stone Interview: Stanley Kubrick in 1987." *Rolling Stone*. August 27, 1987. rollingstone.com/culture/news/the-rolling-stone-interview-stanley-kubrick-in-1987–20110307.

Carlyle, Thomas. *On Heroes, Hero-Worship, and the Heroic in History*. New York, London and Bombay: Longman, Green & Co., 1906.

Chase, David and Steve Inskeep. "David Chase's Must See Movies." Morning Edition. May 2, 2013. wap.npr.org/news/Arts+%26+Life/179812769.

Cheng, Ann Anlin. *The Melancholy of Race: Psychoanalysis, Assimilation, and Hidden Grief*. London and New York: Oxford University Press, 2001.

Chilvers, Simon. "Men's Fashion: Is the Gatsby Look a Coming Trend?" *Guardian*. Friday, May 4, 2012. www.guardian.co.uk.

Chion, Michel. *Audio-Vision: Sound on Screen*. New York: Columbia University Press, 1994.

Ciment, Michel. *Kubrick*, trans. Gilbert Adair. New York: Holt Rinehart & Winston, 1983.

—. *Kubrick: The Definitive Edition*. New York: Faber & Faber, 2001.

—. "The State of Cinema." Address delivered at the San Francisco International Film Festival, 2003. web.archive.org/web/20040325130014. http:/www.sfiff.org/fest03/special/slate.html.

Cinemetrics Database. www.cinemetrics.lv/database/php.

Clark, Jennifer. "Liberating Bicentennial America: Imagining the Nation through TV Superwomen of the Seventies." *Television & New Media* 10.5 (2009): 434–54.

Clarke, Donald. "50 Years, 50 Films: *Barry Lyndon* (1975)." September 17, 2013. *The Irish Times*. www.irishtimes.com/blogs/screenwriter/2013/09/17/50-years-50-films-barry-lyndon-1975/.

Cleary, Joe. "Toward a Materialist-Formalist History of Twentieth-Century Irish Literature." *Boundary* 2 31.1 (2004): 207–41.

Cocks, Geoffrey. *The Wolf at the Door: Stanley Kubrick, History, & the Holocaust*. New York: Peter Lang, 2004.

Cocks, Geoffrey, James Diedrick, and Glenn Perusek. *Depth of Field: Stanley Kubrick and the Uses of History*. Madison, WI: University of Wisconsin Press, 2006.

Colby, Robert A. "*Barry Lyndon* and the Irish Hero." *Nineteenth-Century Fiction* 21.2 (September 1966): 109–30.

Condorcet, Nicolas de. *Sketch for a Historical Picture of the Progress of the Human Mind*. Philadelphia, PA: Lang & Ustick: 1796.

Cook, David A. "Auteur Cinema and the 'Film Generation' in 1970s Hollywood." In *The New American Cinema*, ed. Jon Lewis. Durham, NC: Duke University Press, 1998: 11–36.

Cornfield, Penelope. *Time and the Shape of History*. New Haven, CT: Yale University Press, 2007.

Corrigan, Timothy. "Auteurs and the New Hollywood." In *New American Cinema*, ed. Jon Lewis. Durham, NC: Duke University Press, 1998: 38–63.

Cosgrove, Peter. "The Cinema of Attractions and the Novel in *Barry Lyndon* and *Tom Jones*." In *Eighteenth-Century Fiction on Screen*, ed. Robert Mayer. Cambridge and New York: Cambridge University Press, 2002: 16–34.

Crist, Judith. "Kubrick as Novelist." *The Saturday Review* January 10, 1976: 61–4.

Crocker, Stephen. "Into the Interval: On Deleuze's Reversal of Time and Movement." *Continental Philosophy Review* 34 (2001): 45–67.

Cunliffe, John William and Homer Andrew Watt, eds. "Introduction." In *English Humorists* by William Makepeace Thackeray. Chicago and New York: Scott, Foresman & Co., 1911: 11–30.

Dalle Vache, Angela. *Cinema and Painting: How Art is Used in Film*. London: Athlone Press, 1996.

DeBord, Guy. *The Society of the Spectacle*, 3rd edn [originally published 1967], trans. Donald Nicholson-Smith. New York: Zone Books, 1994.

Dee, Liam. "Metaphysical Remains: Anti-Materialism and Cultural Temporality." *Time & Society* 20.1 (2011): 28–38.

Deleuze, Gilles. *Cinema 2: The Time-Image*, trans. Hugh Tomlinson and Robert Galeta. Minneapolis, MN: University of Minnesota Press, 1989.

Deleuze, Gilles and Melissa McMuhan. "The Brain is the Screen: Interview with Gilles Deleuze on *The Time-Image*." *Discourse* 20.3 (Fall 1998): 47–55.

Deren, Maya. "Cinematography, the Creative Use of Reality." *Dedalus* 9.1 (Winter 1960): 150–67.

D'Lugo, Marvin. "*Barry Lyndon*: Kubrick on the Rules of the Game." In *Explorations in National Cinemas*, Vol. 1, ed. Marc Glasser, Ken Moscowitz, and Hart Wegner. Pleasantville, NY: Redgrave Publishing Company, 1977: 37–45.

Doane, Mary Anne. *The Emergence of Cinematic Time:Modernity, Contingency, the Archive*. Cambridge, MA and London: Harvard University Press, 2002.

Dobbins, Gregory. "Constitutional Laziness and the Novel: Idleness, Irish Modernism, and Flann O'Brien's *At Swim-Two-Birds*." *Novel: A Forum on Fiction* 42.1 (2009): 86–108.

Doherty, Thomas. "Thus Spake Stanley Kubrick." *The Chronicle Review* 53(48) (August 3, 2007): B10.

Duffy, Martha and Richard Schickel. "Kubrick's Grandest Gamble: *Barry Lyndon*." In *Stanley Kubrick Interviews*, ed. Gene D. Phillips. Jackson, MS: University Press of Mississippi, 2001: 159–70. Originally published in *TIME* (December 15, 1975): 32–9.

Dupuy, Jean-Paul. "En mal de père" *Positif* (320) (1987): 59–62.

Ebert, Roger. *Waterloo. Chicago Sun Times*. April 8, 1971. rogerebert.suntimes.com/apps/pbcs.dll/article?AID=/19710408/REVIEWS/104080301/1023.

—. "Great Movie." September 9, 2009. www.rogerebert.com/reviews/barry-lyndon-1975.

—. *Barry Lyndon*, 2009. rogerebert.com/suntimes.com.

Egan, Cos. "*Barry Lyndon*: Kubrick's Irish Odyssey." Press and Publicity Campaign File, SK 14/7/21. Stanley Kubrick Archive, London College of Communication.

Eisenstein, Sergei. *Film Form*, trans. Jay Leyda. New York: Harcourt Brace, 1949.

—. "The Psychology of Composition" [1940], trans. and ed. Alan Upchurch. London: Methuen, 1988.

Elden, Stuart. "Rhythmanalysis: An Introduction." In Henri Lefebvre, *Rhythmanalysis: Space, Time and Everyday Life*, trans. Stuart Elden. London and New York: Continuum, 2004: vii–xv.

Eley, Geoff. "The Past Under Erasure? History, Memory and the Contemporary." *Journal of Contemporary History* 46.3 (2011): 555–73.

Elliott, Kamilla. *Rethinking the Novel/Film Debate*. Cambridge: Cambridge University Press, 2003.

Elsaesser, Thomas. "American Auteur Cinema: The Last—or First—Picture Show." In *The Last Great American Picture Show*, ed. Alexander Horwath Elsaesser and Geoff King. Amsterdam: Amsterdam University Press, 2004: 37–69.

—. "Evolutionary Imagineer: Stanley Kubrick's Authorship." In *Stanley Kubrick. Kinematograph* 20. Frankfurt Am Main: Deutsches Filmmuseum, 2004: 136–47.

—. "Stop/Motion." In *Between Stillness and Movement: Film Photography Algorithms*, ed. Eivind Rossack. Amsterdam: Amsterdam University Press, 2011: 109–22.

—. "Stanley Kubrick's Prototypes." In *The Persistence of Hollywood*. New York: Routledge, 2012: 213–22.

—. "The Museum and the Moving Image: A Marriage Made at the Documentary?" In *Still Moving*, ed. Karen Beckman. Durham, NC: Duke University Press, 2008: 109–22.

Ermarth, Elizabeth Deeds. *Sequel to History: Postmodernism and the Crisis of Representational Time*. Princeton, NJ: Princeton University Press, 1991.

Falsetto, Mario. *Stanley Kubrick: A Narrative and Stylistic Analysis*. New York: Praeger, 2001.

Fischer, Ralf Michael. "Pictures at an Exhibition? Allusions and Illusions in *Barry Lyndon*." In *Stanley Kubrick*, ed. Hans-Peter Reichmann and Ingeborg Flagge. Frankfurt am Mein: Deutsches Filmmuseum, 2004: 168–83.

Fisher, Judith L. "Image versus Text in the Illustrated Novels of William Makepeace Thackeray." In *Victorian Literature and the Victorian Visual Imagination*, ed. Carol T. Christ and John O. Jordan. Berkeley, CA: University of California Press, 1995: 60–86.

Flaherty, Michael G. *A Watched Pot: How We Experience Time*. New York: New York University Press, 2000.

Flaxman, Gregory. *The Brain is the Screen: Deleuze and the Philosophy of Cinema*. Minneapolis, MN: University of Minnesota Press, 2000.

Fletcher, Robert P. "Visual Thinking and the Picture Story in *The History of Henry Esmond*." *PMLA* 113.3 (May 1998): 379–94.

Flynn, Arthur. *The Story of Irish Film*. Dublin: Curragh Press, 2005.

Foucault, Michel. "What is an Author?" In *Language, Counter-Memory, Practice*, trans. Donald F. Bouchard and Sherry Simon, ed. Donald F. Bouchard. Oxford: Blackwell, 1977: 113–38.

Fox, Vicente Molina. "An Interview with Stanley Kubrick." Originally published in *El Pais-Artes* 2.59 (December 20, 1980). *Archivio Kubrick*. archiviokubrick.it/english/words/interviews/1980mystery.html.

Foyster, Elizabeth. "At the Limits of Liberty: Married Women and Confinement in Eighteenth Century England." *Continuity and Change* 17.1 (2002): 39–62.

—. *Marital Violence: An English Family History: 1660–1857*. New York: Cambridge University Press, 2005.

Francois, Jason. "The Vanity of Existence: Form and Content in Stanley Kubrick's *Barry Lyndon*." *The Kubrick Corner*. http://kubrickfilms.tripod.com/id53.html.

Frayling, Christopher. *Ken Adam and the Art of Production Design*. New York: Macmillan, 2005.

French, Philip. "'Proving a Thing Even While You Contradict it': Fictions, Beliefs and Legitimation in *The Memoirs of Barry Lyndon, Esq*." *Studies in the Novel* 27.4 (1995): 493–514.

—. "Not Tonight, Stanley: Philip French Takes Delivery of a 22 lb History of *Napoleon*, Kubrick's 'Film that Never was' and Finds a Fascinating Exploration of Historical Film-Making." *The Observer: Observer Review* (December 13, 2009): 3.

Freud, Sigmund. "Mourning and Melancholia." *The Standard Edition of the Complete Psychological Works of Sigmund Freud*, Vol. XIV (1914–1916). "On the History of the Psycho-Analytic Movement, Papers on Metapsychology and Other Works." 1917: 237–58.

Fried, Michael. *Absorption and Theatricality: Painting and Beholder in the Age of Diderot*. Berkeley, CA: University of California Press, 1980.

Frost, Laura. "Blondes Have More Fun: Anita Loos and the Language of Silent Cinema." *Modernism/Modernity* 17.2 (2010): 291–311.

Galt, Rosalind. *Pretty: Film and the Decorative Image*. New York: Columbia University Press, 2013.

Gaudreault, André and Timothy Barnard. "Titles, Subtitles, and Intertitles: Factors of Autonomy, Factors of Concatenation." *Film History: An International Journal* 25.1–2 (2013): 81–94.

Gelmis, Joseph. "*Bicentennial Epic.*" Des Moines Register. December 27, 1975: 7.

—. "The Film Director as Superstar." In *Stanley Kubrick Interviews*, ed. Gene D. Phillips. Jackson, MS: University Press of Mississippi, 2001: 80–104.

Gengaro, Christine Lee. *Listening to Stanley Kubrick: The Music in His Films*. New York: Rowman & Littlefield, 2013.

Gibbons, Luke. *Transformations in Irish Culture*. Cork: Cork University Press, 1996.

—. *The Quiet Man*. Cork: Cork University Press, 2002.

Gilbert, James. "Auteur with a Capital A." In *Stanley Kubrick's 2001*, ed. Robert Kolker. New York: Oxford University Press, 2001: 29–42.

Gilpin, William. *An Essay on Prints*, 5th edn. London: Caddell & Davies, 1802.

Gilroy, Paul. *Postcolonial Melancholia*. New York: Columbia University Press, 2013.

Goodstein, Liz. *Experience Without Qualities: Boredom and Modernity*. Palo Alto, CA: Stanford University Press, 2005.

Greene, Roland. "Baroque and Neobaroque: Making History." *PMLA* 124.1 (2009): 150–5.

Greenspun, Roger. "A Battle Fought Strictly for the Camera." *The New York Times* April 01, 1971: 50.

Grey, Tobias. "The Cinemascope Spectacular of Books." *New York Magazine* November 29, 2009. nymag.com/arts/books/features/62378/.

Guerlac, Suzanne. *Thinking in Time: An Introduction to Henri Bergson*. Ithaca, CO: Cornell University Press, 2006.

Guest, Haden. "Kubrick's Clockwork." *Criterion Collection*. August 15, 2011. http://www.criterion.com/current/posts/1956-the-killing-kubrick-s-clockwork.

Gunning, Tom. "Literary Appropriation and Translation in Early Cinema." In *True to the Spirit: Film Adaptation and the Question of Fidelity*, ed. Colin McCabe, Kathleen Murray, and Rick Warner. Oxford and New York: Oxford University Press, 2011: 41–57.

Halberstam, Judith. *The Queer Art of Failure*. Durham, NC and London: Duke University Press, 2011.

Hammer, Espen. *Philosophy and Temporality from Kant to Heidegger*. Cambridge: Cambridge University Press, 2011.

Hansen, Miriam Bratu. *Cinema and Experience: Siegfried Kracauer, Walter Benjamin, and Theodor. W Adorno*. Berkeley, CA: University of California Press, 2012.

Harden, Edgar. "Historical Introduction." *The Luck of Barry Lyndon: A Romance of the Last Century* by William Makepeace Thackeray. Ann Arbor, MI: University of Michigan Press, 1999: 229–36.

Harlan, Jan. *Stanley Kubrick: A Life in Pictures*. Warner Brothers, 2001.

Harper, Graeme and Jonathan Rayner. "Introduction: Cinema and Landscape." In *Cinema and Landscape: Film, Nation and Cultural Geography*, ed. Graeme Harper and Jonathan Rayner. London: Intellect Press, 2010: 13–28.

Harper, Sue. "History and Representation: The Case of 1970s British Cinema." In *The New Film History*, ed. James Chapman, Mark Glancy, and Sue Harper. London: Palgrave Macmillan, 2007: 27–40.

Harper, Sue and Justin Smith. "Technology and Visual Style." In *British Film Culture in the 1970s: The Boundaries of Pleasure*, ed. Sue Harper and Justin Smith. Edinburgh: Edinburgh University Press, 2012: 155–72.

Harris, Jonathan Gil. "Untimely Meditations." *Early Modern Culture*, 2007.

Hars-Tschachotin, Boris. "Interview with Ken Adam." In *Stanley Kubrick*. Kinematograph 20/2004. Frankurt am Main: Deutsches Filmmuseum. Howard, James. *Stanley Kubrick Companion*. London: B. T. Batsford, 2000: 88–95.

Hart, Stan and Mort Drucker. "Borey Lyndon." *Mad* (September 1976) (185).

Haslam, Richard. "'A Race Bashed in the Face': Imagining Ireland as a Damaged Child." *Jouvert: A Journal of Postcolonial Studies* 4.1 (1999). english.chass.ncsu.edu/jouvert/v4i1/hasla.htm.

Hayes, Thomas, ed. *The Letters of Thomas Gainsborough*. New Haven, CT: Yale University Press, 2001.

Hediger, Vinzenz. "*Politque des archives*: European Cinema and the Invention of Tradition in the Digital Age." *Rouge* 12 (2008). http://www.rouge.com.au/12/hediger.html.

Herr, Michael. "Kubrick." *Vanity Fair*, Vol. 62 (August 1, 1999). http://www.vanityfair.com/hollywood/classic/features/kubrick-199908.

—. *Kubrick*. New York: Grove Press, 2000.

Hesling, William. "Kubrick, Thackeray and the Memoirs of Barry Lyndon, Esq." *Literature Film Quarterly* (2001): 264–78.

Hitchcock, Peter. *Cultural Memory in the Present: The Long Space: Transnationalism and Postcolonial Form*. Palo Alto, CA: Stanford University Press, 2009.

—. *The Long Space: Transnationalism and Postcolonial Form*. Palo Alto, CA: Stanford University Press, 2010.

Holt, Jason. "Existential Ethics: Where the Paths of Glory Lead." In *The Philosophy of Stanley Kubrick*, ed. Jerold Adams. Lexington, KY: University Press of Kentucky, 2007.

Houston, Penelope. "Kubrick Country," *Saturday Review* (December 25, 1971): 42–4. Reprinted in *Stanley Kubrick Interviews*, ed. Gene D. Phillips. Jackson, MS: University Press of Mississippi, 2001: 108–15.

Howard, James. *Stanley Kubrick Companion*. London: B.T. Batsford, 2000.

Hoy, David Couzens. *The Time of Our Lives: A Critical History of Temporality*. Cambridge: MIT Press, 2009.

Hughes, David. *The Complete Kubrick*. London: Virgin Publishing, 2000.

Hughes, Linda K. and Michael Lund. *The Victorian Serial*. Charlottesville, VA: University of Virginia Press, 1991.

Hunt, Lynn. *Measuring Time, Making History*. Budapest and New York: Central European University Press, 2008.

Hynes, Eric. "Cut Here, Cut There, but It's Still 3 Hours: Thelma Schoonmaker on the Art of Editing Long Movies." *The New York Times* January 17, 2014. nytimes.com.

Ingram, Allan, Clark Lawlor, Stuart Sim, Richard Terry, Leigh Wetherall Dickson, Diane Buie, and Pauline Morris. *18th-Century Blues: Exploring the Melancholy Mind* [Exhibition Guide] 2008. nrl.northumbria.ac.uk/1024/1/beforedepression_ Exhibitionguide.pdf.

Irish Film Board Act. www.irishstatutebook.ie/1980/en/act/pub/0036/print.html#sec4.

Jacobs, Steven. *Framing Pictures: Film and the Visual Arts*. Edinburgh: Edinburgh University Press, 2011.

Jagernauth, Kevin. "Geoffrey Rush Sought to Take Over Lead in Former Marlon Brando & Johnny Depp Project, 'Divine Rapture.'" *IndieWire*. February 22, 2012. http://blogs. indiewire.com/theplaylist/022212/geoffrey-rush-sought-to-take-lead-in-former- marlon-brando-johnny-depp-pic-divine-rapture#

James, Nick. "Passive Aggressive." *Sight and Sound* 20.4 (April 2010): 5.

Jameson, Fredric. "Walter Benjamin, or Nostalgia." *Salmagundi* 10/11 (1969–1970): 52–68.

—. "Nostalgia for the Present." *Postmodernism: The Cultural Logic of Late Capitalism*. Durham, NC: Duke University Press, 1991: 279–96.

—. *Postmodernism, or the Cultural Logic of Late Capitalism*. London and New York: Verso, 1991.

—. "Historicism in *The Shining*." Originally published as "*The Shining*" in *Social Text* 4 (Fall 1981). In *Signatures of the Visible*. New York: Routledge, 1992: 82–98.

—. "Introduction" *Signatures of the Visible*. New York: Routledge, 1992: 1–6.

—. "The Existence of Italy." *Signatures of the Visible*. London: Routledge, 1992: 155–230.

—. "An Unfinished Project." *London Review of Books* 17.15 (August 3, 1995): 8–9.

—. "Postmodernism and Consumer Society." *The Norton Anthology of Theory and Criticism*, ed. Vincent B. Leitch William E. Cain, Laurie A. Finke, Barbara E. Johnson, John McGowan, Tracy Denean Sharpley-Whiting, and Jeffrey J. Williams. New York: Norton, 2001: 1960–74.

—. "The End of Temporality." *Critical Inquiry* 29.4 (Summer 2003): 695–718.

Jaumont, Fabrice. "Stanley Kubrick: The Odysseys." *Universite de Charles de Gaulle—Lille III*, 1995. api.ning.com/files/TheOdysseysofStanleyKubrickbyF.Jaumont.pdf.

Johnson, Samuel. *A Dictionary of the English Language, Vol. 2.* London: A. Knapton, 1785.
matrixfiles.com/JerryKirk/SamuelJohnson-Dictionary/Vol2-1756.pdf

Jordheim, Helge. "Against Periodization: Koselleck's Theory of Multiple Temporalities." *History and Theory* 51.2 (2012): 151–71.

Kael, Pauline. "Kubrick's Gilded Age." *The New Yorker* (December 29, 1975): 49–52.

Kaiser, Matthew. "The World in Play: A Portrait of a Victorian Concept." *New Literary History* 40.1 (Winter 2009): 105–29.

Kennedy, Victor R. "Pictures as Metaphors in Thackeray's Illustrated Novels," *Metaphor and Symbol* 9(2) (1994): 135–47.

Kiberd, Declan. *Inventing Ireland: The Literature of the Modern Nation.* Cambridge: Harvard University Press, 1997.

King, Homay. "The Sadness of the Gaze." In *Stanley Kubrick: Essays on and His Films and Legacy*, ed. Gary Rhodes. Jefferson, NC and London: McFarland, 2008: 123–36.

Klein, Michael. "Introduction" to *English Novel and the Movies*, ed. Michael Klein and Gillian Parker. New York: Frederick Ungar, 1981: 1–13.

—. "Narrative and Discourse in Kubrick's Modern Tragedy." In *English Novel and the Movies*, ed. Michael Klein and Gillian Parker. New York: Frederick Ungar, 1981: 95–120.

Kolker, Robert. *A Cinema of Loneliness*, 4th edn. New York and London: Oxford University Press, 2011.

Koselleck, Reinhart. *Futures Past: On the Semantics of Historical Time*, trans. Keith Tribe. New York: Columbia University Press, 2004.

Krämer, Peter. *A Clockwork Orange.* London: Palgrave Macmillan, 2011.

Kuberski, Philip. "Kubrick's Odyssey: Myth, Technology, Gnosis." *Arizona Quarterly* 64.3 (Autumn 2008): 51–73.

Kubrick, Stanley. Letter to *New York Magazine* dated September 26, 1975. Warner Brothers Archives, *Barry Lyndon* Production File, Burbank, CA.

—. "Words and Movies." *Hollywood Directors: 1941-76*, ed. Richard Kozarski. New York: Oxford University Press, 1977: 306–9.

La Ferla, Ruth. "Film and Fashion: Just Friends." *The New York Times.* March 3, 2010. www.nytimes.com/2010/03/04/fashion/04COSTUME.html?pagewanted=all 6/1/2012.

Lane, Anthony. "The Last Emperor." *The New Yorker* (March 22, 1999): 120–3.

Large, Duncan. "On 'Untimeliness': Temporal Structures in Nietzsche or: 'The Day after Tomorrow Belongs to Me.'" *Journal of Nietzsche Studies* 8 (Autumn 1994): 33–53.

Le Fanu, Mark. "Metaphysics of the Long Take: Some Post-Bazinian Reflections." *P.O.V: A Danish Journal of Film Studies* 4 (1997). http://pov.imv.au.dk/Issue_04/POV_4cnt.html.

Lefebvre, Henri. *Rhythmanalysis: Space, Time and Everyday Life*, trans. Stuart Elden. London and New York: Continuum, 2004.

Lessing, Gotthold. *Laocoön*, trans. Robert Fillmore. London: Routledge, 1874. openlibrary.org.

Lim, Bliss Cua. *Translating Time: Cinema, The Fantastic and Temporal Critique*. Durham, NC: Duke University Press, 2009.

Ljulic, Tatjana. "*Barry Lyndon*, Paintings and the Archive." In *Moving Images, Still Life*. Doctoral thesis, University of Cambridge, 2014.

Lloyd, David. *Irish Times: Temporalities of Modernity*. Dublin: Field Day and Notre Dame Press, 2008.

Lobrutto, Vincent. *Stanley Kubrick: A Biography*. New York: Da Capo Press, 1999.

—. "The Written Word and the Very Visual Stanley Kubrick." In *Depth of Field: Stanley Kubrick. Film and the Uses of History*, ed. Geoffrey Cocks, James Diedrick, and Glen Perusek. Madison, WI: University of Wisconsin Press, 2006: 31–54.

Lyotard, Jean-Francois. *The Inhuman*, trans. Geoffrey Bennington and Rachel Bowlby. Stanford, CA: Polity Press, 1991.

Ma, Jean. "Photography's Absent Times." In *Still Moving: Between Cinema and Photography*, ed. Karen Beckman and Jean Ma. Durham, NC: Duke University Press, 2008: 98–118.

Magel, Eva-Marie. "Everything a Good Story Should Have: Stanley Kubrick and Napoleon." In *Stanley Kubrick's Napoleon: The Greatest Movie Never Made*, ed. Allison Castle. Cologne: Taschen, 2009: 23–8.

Mamber, Stephen. "Simultaneity and Overlap in Stanley Kubrick's *The Killing*." *Postmodern Culture* 8.2 (1998). Project Muse. http://muse.jhu.edu/journals/postmodern_culture/v008/8.2mamber.html.

Marshall, Sarah. "The Grim American History of the 'Bicentennial Minute.'" *The Awl*. March 14, 2013. http://www.theawl.com/2013/03/the-grim-american-history-of-the-bicentennial-minute.

Martin, Theodore. "Thackeray's Works." In *William Thackeray: The Critical Heritage*, ed. Geoffrey Tilloston and Donald Hawes. London: Taylor & Francis, 1995: 169–88. Originally published in *Westminster Review*, new series April 1853, ii, 363–88.

Marx, Karl. *Eighteenth Brumaire of Louis Bonaparte*. Rockville, MD: Wildside Press, 2008.

Mather, Phillip. *Stanley Kubrick at Look Magazine: Authorship and Genre in Photojournalism and Film*. London: Intellect, 2013.

McArthur, Colin. "The Cultural Need for a Poor Celtic Cinema." In *Border Crossing: Film in Ireland, Britain, and Europe*, ed. John Hill, Martin McLoone, and Paul Hainsworth. London and Belfast: British Film Institute and Irish Film Institute, 1994: 112–15.

McAuliffe, John. "Taking the Sing out of the Traveller's Tale: Thackeray's *Irish Sketchbook*." *Irish Studies Review* 9.1 (2001): 25–40.

McDonagh, Martin. *The Cripple of Inishmaan.* London: Vintage International, 1998.

—. *Seven Psychopaths DVD.* Los Angeles: Sony Pictures, 2013.

McGowan, Todd. *The Real Gaze: Film Theory after Lacan.* Albany, NY: SUNY Press, 2007.

McLoone, Martin. *Irish Film: The Emergence of a Contemporary Cinema.* London: BFI Publishing, 2000.

—. *Film, Media and Popular Culture in Ireland: Cityscapes, Landscapes, and Soundscapes.* Dublin: Irish Academic Press, 2008.

McMuhan, Melissa. "The Brain is the Screen: Interview with Gilles Deleuze on *The Time Image. Discourse* 20.3 (Fall 1998): 47–55.

McQuire, Scott. *Visions of Modernity: Representation, Memory, Time and Space in the Age of the Camera.* New York: Sage: 1997.

McQuiston, Katherine. *We'll Meet Again: Musical Design in the Films of Stanley Kubrick.* New York: Oxford University Press, 2013.

McQuiston, Kate. "The Stanley Kubrick Experience: Music, Nuclear Bombs, Disorientation and You." In *Music, Sound and Filmmakers: Sonic Style in Cinema,* ed. James Wierzbicki. New York and London: Routledge, 2012: 138–50.

Meir, Chris. "Kubrick's Narrator and 'the Higher Aesthetic.'" *The Kubrick Corner.* http://kubrickfilms.tripod.com/id57.html.

Michaelson, Annette. "Bodies in Space: Film as Carnal Knowledge." *Artforum* VII(6) (February 1969): 54–63. Reprinted in *The Making of 2001: A Space Odyssey,* ed. Stephanie Schwam. New York: Random House, 2010.

Miller, Mark Crispin. "*Barry Lyndon* Reconsidered." *The Georgia Review* 30.4 (Winter 1976): 827–53.

—. "Kubrick's Anti-Reading of *The Luck of Barry Lyndon.*" In *Perspectives on Stanley Kubrick,* ed. Mario Falsetto. New York: MacMillan, 1996: 226–42.

Mitchell, William John Thomas. "The Politics of Genre: Space and Time in Lessing's *Laocoon.*" *Representations* 6 (Spring 1984): 98–115.

—. *Iconology: Image Text, Ideology.* Chicago: The University of Chicago Press, 2013.

Moore, Wendy. *Wedlock: The True Story of the Disastrous Marriage and Remarkable Divorce of Mary Eleanor Bowes, Countess of Strathmore.* New York: Crown, 2009.

Morris, Robert. "Introduction." *The Memoirs of Barry Lyndon, Esq. Written By Himself* by William Makepeace Thackeray. Lincoln, NE: University of Nebraska Press,1962: vii–xxviii.

Mulvey, Laura. "Max Ophuls's Auteurist Adaptations." In *True to the Spirit: Film Adaptation and the Question of Fidelity,* ed. Colin McCabe, Kathleen Murray, and Rick Warner. Oxford and New York: Oxford University Press, 2011: 75–89.

—. *Death 24x a Second: Stillness and the Moving Image.* London: Reaktion Books, 2006.

Murdoch, Alan. "Ballycotton: The Godfather of All Let Downs." *The Independent.* July 27, 1995. www.independent.co.uk/life-style/ballycotton-the-godfather-of-all-letdowns-1593366.html.

Nanni, Giordano. *The Colonisation of Time*. Manchester: Manchester University Press, 2012.

Naremore, James. *On Kubrick*. London: BFI: 2007.

Nelson, Thomas Allen. *Kubrick: Inside a Film Artist's Maze*, 2nd edn. Bloomington, IN: Indiana University Press, 2000.

"Newsletter," Stanley Kubrick Exhibition. No. 15. March 2005. www.stanleykubrick.de/eng.php?img=img-l-6&kubrick=newsletter15-eng.

Nietzsche, Friedrich. "Letter toward the end of February." In *Friedrich Nietzsche Briefwechsel: Kritische Gesamtausgabe*, ed. Giorgio Colli and Mazzino Montinari. Berlin, Germany: de Gruyter Verlag, 2005: 172.

Nikolajeva, Maria and Carole Scott. "The Dynamics of Picturebook Communication." *Children's Literature in Education* 31.4 (2000): 225–40.

Norden, Eric. "Playboy Interview: Stanley Kubrick." In *Stanley Kubrick Interviews*, ed. Gene D. Phillips. Jackson, MS: University Press of Mississippi, 2001: 47–74.

Notaro, Anna. "Technology in Search of an Artist: Questions of Auteurism/Authorship and the Contemporary Cinematic Experience." *Velvet Light Trap* 57 (Spring 2006): 86–97.

Obalidiston, Nick, ed. *Culture of the Slow: Social Deceleration in an Accelerated World*. New York: Palgrave Macmillan, 2013.

O'Toole, Fintan. *The Lie of the Land, Irish Identities*. London: Verso, 1998.

Palmer, R. Barton. "*The Shining* and Anti-Nostalgia: Postmodern Notions of History." In *The Philosophy of Stanley Kubrick*, ed. Jerold Adams. Lexington, KY: University Press of Kentucky, 2007: 201–20.

Payne, David. *The Reenchantment of Nineteenth-Century Fiction*. London: Palgrave MacMillan, 2005.

Pendreigh, Brian. *On Location: The Film Fan's Guide to Britain and Ireland*. Edinburgh: Mainstream Publishing, 1996.

Perez, Gilberto. "Landscape and Fiction: *A Day in the Country*." In *Film Adaptation*, ed. James Naremore. New Brunsick, NJ: Rutgers University Press, 2000: 129–53.

Pettit, Lance. *Screening Ireland: Film and Television Representation*. Manchester: Manchester University Press, 2000.

Peucker, Brigitte. "Kubrick and Kafka: The Corporeal Uncanny." *Modernism/Modernity* 8.4 (2001): 663–74.

—. *The Material Image: Art and the Real in Film*. Palo Alto, CA: Stanford University Press, 2007.

Pidduck, Julianne. *Contemporary Costume Film*. London: BFI, 2004.

Pilard, Philippe. *Barry Lyndon*. Torino: Lindau, 2007.

Pipolo, Tony. "Stanley Kubrick's History Lessons." *Cineaste* 34.2 (2009): 6–11.

Pisters, Patricia. *The Neuro-Image: A Deleuzian Film-Philosophy of Digital Screen Culture*. Palo Alto, CA: Stanford University Press, 2012.

Porter, James. "Untimely Meditations:Nietzsche's *Zetiatomistik* in Context." *Journal of Nietzsche Studies* 20 (2000): 58–81.

Porter, Roy. *A Social History of Madness*. New York: Plume Press, 1989.

Prawer, Siegbert Salomon. *Breeches and Metaphysics: Thackeray's German Discourse*. Oxford: British Comparative Literature Association and European Humanities Research Centre, 1997.

Radden, Jennifer. "Introduction: From Melancholic States to Clinical Depression." In *The Nature of Melancholy: From Aristotle to Kristeva*, ed. Jennifer Radden. London: Oxford University Press, 2000: 1–40.

Radstone, Susannah. *The Sexual Politics of Time: Confession, Nostalgia, Memory*. New York: Routledge, 2007.

Rains, Stephanie. "Irish Roots: Genealogy and the Performance of Irishness." In *The Irish in Us*, ed. Diane Negra. Durham, NC: Duke University Press, 2006: 130–60.

Raphael, Frederic. *Eyes Wide Open: A Memoir of Stanley Kubrick*. New York: Ballantine Books, 1999.

Ray, Robert B. *A Certain Tendency of Hollywood Cinema*. Princeton, NJ: Princeton University Press, 1985.

—. "How to Teach Cultural Studies." *Studies in the Literary Imagination* 31.1 (Spring 1998): 25–37.

Reichenbach, Hans. *The Direction of Time*. Mineola, NY: Courier-Dover Books, 2012.

Relph, Michael. "Letter from Michael Relph, Chairman, Film Production Association." *Cinema, TV, Today* (December 30, 1972).

Remes, Justin. "Motion(less) Pictures: The Cinema of Stasis." *British Journal of Aesthetics* 52.3 (2012): 257–70.

Rice, Julian. "Kubrick's *Barry Lyndon*: Like Father, Like Son." *Film Criticism* (June 9, 1976): 9–14.

Rich, Frank. "*Barry Lyndon*: A Kubrick Diamond." *The New York Post* (December 19, 1975): 19, 27.

Robey, Tim. "*Barry Lyndon*: Kubrick's neglected masterpiece." *The Telegraph*. February 5, 2009. www.telegraph.com.uk/.

Robinson, Emily. "Authenticity in the Archive: Historical Encounters with 'Pastness.'" In *Desperately Seeking Authenticity: An Interdisciplinary Approach*, ed. Rune Grauland. Copenhagen: Copenhagen Doctoral School in Cultural Studies, 2010: 13–28. www.eurodocsem.net/.

Rockett, Kevin, John Hill, and Luke Gibbons. *Cinema and Ireland*. Syracuse: Syracuse University Press, 1989.

Rodowick, David Norman. *Gilles Deleuze's Time Machine*. Durham, NC: Duke University Press, 1997.

—. *The Virtual Life of Film*. Cambridge: Harvard University Press, 2007.

Romney, Jonathan. "Are You Sitting Comfortably? The Slow, Oblique Existential Film is Making a Comeback." *The Guardian*. October 7, 2000. theguardian.com/film/2000/oct/07/books.guardianreview.

—. "In Search of Lost Time." *Sight & Sound* 20.2 (February 2010): 43–4.

Ronson, Jon. *Stanley Kubrick's Boxes*, 2008. vimeo.com/78314194.

—. "After Stanley Kubrick." *The Guardian*. August 18, 2010. www.guardian.co.uk/ film/2010/aug/18/stanley-kubrick-christiane.

Rose, Charlie. "Stanley Kubrick: A Life in Pictures." PBS. Televised interview with Jan Harlan, Christiane Kubrick, and Martin Scorsese, aired June 15, 2001. http://www. charlierose.com/view/interview/3069.

Rose, Frank. "No Flowers, Send Money: 'Divine Rapture.'" *Los Angeles Times*. December 17, 1995. articles.latimes.com.

Rose, Steve. "*A Clockwork Orange*: The Droog Rides Again." *The Guardian*. May 11, 2011. www.theguardian.com/film/2011/may/11/a-clockwork-orange-cannes.

Rosen, Philip. *Change Mummified: Cinema, Historicity, Theory*. Minneapolis and London: University of Minnesota Press, 2001.

Rosenstone, Robert. "The Historical Film: Looking at the Past in a Postliterate Age." In *The Historical Film: History and Memory in Media*, ed. Marsha Landy. New Brunswick, NJ: Rutgers University Press, 2001: 50–66.

Rosenthal, Leila. "Humanism and Late Style." *Cultural Critique* 67 (Autumn, 2007): 107–40.

Ruchti, Ulrich, Sybil Taylor, and Alexander Walker. *Stanley Kubrick, Director: A Visual Analysis*. New York: W.W. Norton, 2000.

Ruti, Mari. "From Melancholia to Meaning: How to Live the Past in the Present." *Psychoanalytic Dialogues* 15.5 (2005): 637–60.

Said, Edward W. *The World, the Text, and the Critic*. Cambridge: Harvard University Press, 1983.

—. "Thoughts on Late Style." *London Review of Books* 26.15 (August 2004): 3–7.

—. *On Late Style: Music and Literature Against the Grain*. New York: Pantheon Books, 2006.

Sass, Louis A. and Elizabeth Pienkos. "Space, Time and Atmosphere: A Comparative Phenomenology of Melancholia, Mania and Schizophrenia, Part II." *Journal of Consciousness Studies* 20.7/8 (2013): 131–52. Accessed via Academia.edu, pp. 1–25.

Schäfer, Wolf. "Global History and the Present Time." In *Wiring Prometheus: Globalisation, History and Technology*, ed. Peter Lyth and Helmuth Trischler. Aarhus: Aarhus University Press, 2004: 103–25.

Schatz, Thomas. "The New Hollywood." *Film Theory Goes to the Movies*, ed. Jim Collins, Hillary Radner, and Ava Preacher Collins. New York: Routledge, 1993: 8–36.

Schickel, Richard. "All-TIME 100 Films: *Barry Lyndon*." *TIME Entertainment*. January 13, 2010. entertainment.time.com.

Schickel, Richard and Martha Duffy. "Kubrick's Grandest Gamble: *Barry Lyndon*." In *Stanley Kubrick Interviews*, ed. Gene D. Phillips. Jackson, MS: University Press of Mississippi, 2001: 159–70. Originally published in *TIME* (December 15, 1975): 32–9.

Scotsman, The. "TV Review: *Ballybrando*." February 2, 2011. http://www.scotsman.com/ news/tv-review-ballybrando-1-1499491.

Shaviro, Steven. "Slow Cinema versus Fast Films." *The Pinocchio Theory*. May 12, 2010. www.shaviro.com/Blog/?p=891.

Shaw, Daniel. "Nihilism and Freedom in the Films of Stanley Kubrick." In *The Philosophy of Stanley Kubrick*, ed. Jerold Abrams. Lexington, KY: University Press of Kentucky, 2007: 221–34.

Shawe-Taylor, Desmond. *The Conversation Piece: Scenes of Fashionable Life*. London: Royal Collections Enterprises, 2009.

Sklar, Robert. "Stanley Kubrick and the American Film Industry." *Current Research in Film: Audience, Economics, and Law* 4 (1988): 114–24.

Sobchak, Vivian. "'Surge and Splendour': A Phenomenology of the Hollywood Historical Epic." *Representations* 29 (Winter 1990): 24–49.

Soller, Kurt. "The New *Gatsby* Will Be the Most Stylish Movie Ever." *Esquire*: The Style Blog. August 7, 2012. www.Esquire.com.

Sperb, Jason. *The Kubrick Facade: Faces and Voices in the Films of Stanley Kubrick*. New York: Rowman & Littlefield, 2006.

Spiegel, Alan. "Kubrick's *Barry Lyndon*." *Salmagundi* (Fall 1977). Reprinted in *Perspectives on Stanley Kubrick*, ed. Mario Falsetto. New York: GK Hall, 1996: 210–3.

Stam, Robert. *Subversive Pleasures: Bakhtin, Cultural Criticism and Film*. Baltimore, MD: John Hopkins University Press, 1989.

—. "The Dialogics of Adaptation." In *Film Adaptation*, ed. James Naremore. New Brunswick, NJ: Rutgers University Press, 2000: 54–76.

"Stanley Kubrick's *Barry Lyndon*." *Films and Filming* 22(3) (December 1975): 25–8.

Steele, Valerie. "Anti-Fashion: The 1970s." *Fashion Theory: The Journal of Dress, Fashion and Culture*. 1.3 (August 1997): 279–96.

Steensland, Mark. "*The Shining* Adapted." The Terror Trap. n.d. http://www.terrortrap. com/interviews/dianejohnson/.

Steinhardt, Paul and Neil Turok. "A Cyclic Model of the Universe." *Science* 296 (May 22, 2002): 1436–9.

—. *Endless Universe: Beyond the Big Bang*. New York: Doubleday, 2007.

Stephen, James Fitzjames. "*Barry Lyndon*." In *William Thackeray: The Critical Heritage*, ed. Tillotson and Hawes. London: Taylor & Francis, 1995: 26–9. Originally published in *Saturday Review* 27(ii) (December 1856), 783–5.

Subotnik, Rose Rosengard. "Adorno's Diagnosis of Beethoven's Late Style: Early Symptom of a Fatal Condition." *Journal of the American Musicological Society* 29.2 (1976): 242–75.

Sullivan, Erin. "Melancholy, Medicine and the Arts." *The Lancet* 372.9642 (2008): 884–5.

Sunniside Local History Society. "Mary Eleanor Bowes." www. sunnisidelocalhistorysociety.co.uk/eleanor.html 5/30/12.

Sweeney, Ken. "Marlon Brando's Abandoned Irish Comedy." *Belfast Telegraph*, February 22, 2012. belfasttelegraph.co.uk/entertainment/film-tv/news/marlon-brandos-abandoned-irish-comedy-gets-another-chance-17-years-after-fiasco-28717430. html#ixzz1n6PBTOdH.

Thackeray, William Makepeace. *The Second Funeral of Napoleon; in Three Letters to Miss Smith of London*. London: Hugh Cunningham, 1841.

—. *The Irish Sketchbook of 1842*, by Mr. Michael Angelo Titmarsh. London: Chapman & Hall, 1857.

—. *Miscellanies: From Cornhill to Cairo; The Paris Sketch Book; and the Irish Sketch Book*. Cambridge: University Press, Welch, Bigelow & Co., 1871.

—. "A Box of Novels." In *Thackeray's Works in Twenty-Four Volumes*, Vol. XXIII. London: Smith, Elder, & Co., 1886: 44–65.

—. *The Memoirs of Barry Lyndon, Esq., Written by Himself*. Boston, MA: Estes & Laureat, 1888.

—. *Barry Lyndon*, ed. Andrew Sanders. Oxford: Oxford University Press, 1984: 128–9.

—. *The Luck of Barry Lyndon: A Romance of the Last Century*, ed. Edgar F. Harden. Ann Arbor, MI: University of Michigan Press, 1999.

—. "Criticisms and Interpretations" of *The History of Tom Jones, a Foundling*, Vol. I, by Henry Fielding." New York: Bartleby.com, 2000. www.bartleby.com/301/1003.html.

"Thackeray's 'Barry Lyndon.'" *The New York Times*. July 23, 1898. www.nytimes.com/.

Tillotson, Gregory and Donald Hawes. "Introduction." *William Thackeray: The Critical Heritage*. London: Taylor & Francis, 1995: 1–16.

Townsend, James T. and Michael J. Wenger, "The Serial–Parallel Dilemma: A Case Study in a Linkage of Theory and Method." *Psychonomic Bulletin and Review* 11.3 (2004): 391–418.

Trollope, Anthony. *Thackeray*. London: MacMillan & Company, 1879. Project Gutenberg. www.gutenberg.org/files/18645/18645-h/18645-h.htm 5/30/2012.

Truffaut, Francois. "A Certain Tendency of the French Cinema." In *Movies and Methods*, Vol. 1, ed. Bill Nichols. Berkeley, CA: University of California Press, 1976: 224–36.

Tuttle, Harry. "Slow Films, Easy Life." *Unspoken Cinema*. May 12, 2010. unspokencinema.blogspot.ie/2010/05/slow-films-easy-life-sight.html.

Upton, Julian. "Anarchy in the UK." *Bright Lights Film Journal* 30 (2000). brightlightsfilm.com/. http://brightlightsfilm.com/30/jubilee.php#.U-tVwIBdU00.

Vico, Giambattista. *The New Science*. New York: Penguin Classics, 2000.

Walker, Alexander. *Stanley Kubrick: Director*. New York and London: W.W. Norton, 1999.

Warf, Barney and Santa Arias. "Introduction: The Reinsertion of Space in the Humanities and Social Sciences." In *The Spatial Turn*, ed. Barney Warf and Santa Arias. New York: Routledge, 2009: 1–10.

Webster, Patrick. *Love and Death in Kubrick: A Critical Study of the Films from Lolita through Eyes Wide Shut*. Jefferson, NC: McFarland Press, 2010.

White, Hayden. "The Question of Narrative in Contemporary Historical Theory." *History and Theory* 23.1 (1984): 1–33.

Whitrow, Gerald James. *Time in History: Views of Time from Prehistory to the Present Day*. London: Oxford University Press, 1989.

Wickre, Bille. "Pictures, Plurality and Puns: A Visual Approach to Barry Lyndon." In *Depth of Field: Stanley Kubrick and the Uses of History*, ed. Geoffrey Cocks, James

Diedrick, and Glenn Perusek. Madison, WI: University of Wisconsin Press, 2006: 165–84.

"William Thackeray." *Harper's Weekly* VIII(369) (January 23, 1864): 50, 60–1. www.sonofthesouth.net/leefoundation/civil-war/1864/january/william-thackeray. htm (accessed May 30, 2012).

Zygmunt, Lawrence Charles. *Thackeray and the Picaresque World*. Doctoral Dissertation, University of Chicago, ProQuest, UMI Dissertations Publishing, 2010. search.proquest.com.prox.lib.ncsu.edu/docview/610097352?accountid=12725.

Index